America Hijacked

How Deep State actors from LBJ to Obama killed for money and power, and why they hate Trump so much.

Second Edition

S. M. CARLSON

America Hijacked
How Deep State actors from LBJ to Obama killed for money and power,
and why they hate Trump so much.

Second Edition

ISBN: 978-1-7336755-4-3 (paperback)
ISBN: 978-1-7336755-3-6 (hardcover)

By the same author

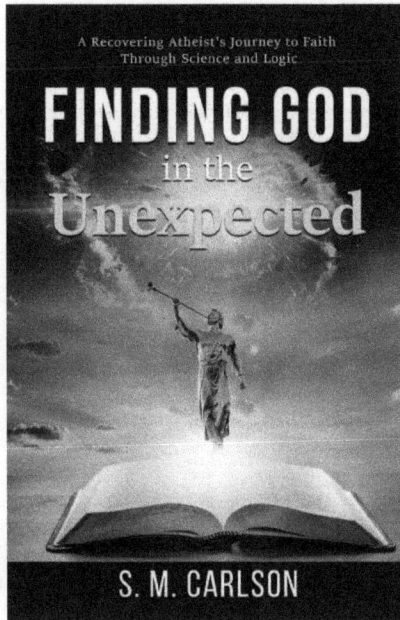

Step into my shoes and experience 'Finding God in the Unexpected.' As a man deeply rooted in scientific understanding, I once believed the realms of faith and reason were worlds apart.

Yet, as I navigated life's complexities, I began to see their intricate dance, revealing a harmonious union where both can coexist. This isn't merely a chronicle of my spiritual awakening but an intimate reflection on how tangible evidence and deep-seated faith can meld into a beautifully coherent worldview. Whether you resonate more with skepticism or belief, my personal odyssey promises not only to challenge but to resonate deeply, evoking a sense of wonder.

Embark on this journey with me, and together, let's explore a universe where science and faith illuminate the profound tapestry of existence.

www.SMCarlson.com

Table of Contents

Prologue

Growing up in sunny Florida during the1980s, I viewed America as the world's shining beacon: the unparalleled land of the free and the home of the brave. My father's tales of valor, as a Deputy Sheriff who had served honorably as a United States Navy Corpsman during the Vietnam War, instilled in me a deep-seated sense of patriotism.

As a child, my memories of the first Gulf War remain hazy. As an eight-year-old, school teachers simplified the intricate geopolitical landscape for us, portraying a clear narrative of American heroes confronting a "*bad guy*". Shielded by our innocence, we couldn't grasp the deep intricacies of war. Instead, we felt an overwhelming pride for our servicemen and women, manifesting in heartfelt handmade thank-you cards and gift baskets my school sent to the troops.

Spending my formative years during the 90s was an experience quite distinct from what previous or subsequent generations have faced. This was during a decade characterized by optimism and relative tranquility, especially in the United States. The Cold War had drawn to a close, and the all-encompassing tension it had brought began to dissipate. Technological advancements were rapidly changing our world, and pop culture — from music to television — was in a golden era of creativity.

For many of us, childhood during this time was a sheltered existence. The threats and tragedies that did arise on the international scene, such as the Battle of Mogadishu, were often relegated to brief segments on the evening news. They seemed distant and disconnected from our daily lives. We were more engrossed in the adventures of Saturday morning cartoons or the latest PC video game than in the complexities of global politics. The somber realities of war and conflict felt like chapters from a history book rather than pressing news stories. This protective bubble, an almost idyllic phase of American adolescence, allowed many of us to enjoy a childhood that, in retrospect, seems all too fleeting in the face of today's hyper-connected and tumultuous world.

The blissful shield of childhood innocence, the reality of the world's complexities and evil, was profoundly shattered on a singularly tragic day: September 11, 2001. Orchestrated by 19 terrorists, these horrifying attacks became the first major assault on American soil in many generations, permeating the national consciousness with a previously unfamiliar terror and vulnerability. Suddenly, the insulated world of my childhood, punctuated by distant events like the Battle of Mogadishu, was forcefully breached by an unmistakable reminder of global strife and malice.

This catastrophic event not only marked a poignant shift in national and global paradigms but also dramatically altered my journey. My father's legacy, which was intertwined with a deep-seated commitment to our nation, beckoned me toward service in the aftermath of such an unparalleled national tragedy. I found myself stepping into the robust, disciplined world of the U.S. Navy, pledging my service during Operations Enduring Freedom and Iraqi Freedom.

My tenure in service, though limited to just under a year due to a preexisting medical condition, was nonetheless a transformative chapter in my life's narrative. Despite its brevity, my time in the Navy indelibly impacted my transition from youth's innocence to adulthood's responsibilities and realities. Every drill, operation, and moment of camaraderie amongst my fellow Ship Mates instilled within me an unshakeable and profound patriotism.

The experiences accumulated during that pivotal year created a lens through which I would come to view the world, developing a nuanced understanding of power, service, and sacrifice. This crucial juncture underpinned my subsequent endeavors and perspectives and underscored the precious fragility of peace and security, ideals I had taken for granted in my more youthful days. As I traversed into adulthood and beyond, these insights would become instrumental in navigating the multifaceted tapestry of American politics and global dynamics in the ensuing years.

However, my return to civilian life introduced me to a world of contrasting narratives. I encountered the so-called "*9/11 Truthseekers,*" individuals who believed that our government might have played a part in that devastating day. Their claims seemed absurd, but out of curiosity and at a friend's insistence, I delved into their documentaries.

To my surprise, some conspiracy theories, while initially far-fetched, presented information that demanded attention. The deeper

I dug into America's recent history, the more I realized that powerful interests manipulated the course of events, not always for the broader good.

In this book, I aim to navigate the intricate web of conspiracy theories, focusing on facts and offering a balanced analysis. Join me as we unearth the pivotal events and hidden narratives that have sculpted our nation's journey.

-- Steven

Introduction

From the very inception of recorded history, the corridors of power have echoed with whispers of political figures leveraging their influence for personal gains. Though universally acknowledged, this sentiment often remains in the shadows, seemingly accepted by the masses. Is it a deep-seated flaw embedded within humanity's psyche or a resigned acceptance of a troubling reality?

In the first edition of this book, I embarked on a journey to shed light on these murkier recesses of political power. The response was overwhelming, and your feedback was invaluable. This second edition comes after much reflection and countless hours of further research. Addressing grammar and stylistic issues was only the tip of the iceberg. As more details about various subjects surfaced, I felt compelled to revisit certain topics, adding depth, nuance, and further context. Moreover, as we approached 2024, additional chapters found their way into this volume, ensuring a comprehensive view of our current landscape.

I want to emphasize a foundational concept that anchors this narrative: my goal in highlighting instances where politicians might have reaped undue advantages from their positions isn't to universally vilify them. The landscape of politics and power is riddled with shades of gray, and these nuances warrant our attention. Let's imagine a scenario: Acme Widget Co. and Some Other Great Widget Co. both present equivalent products to the government for consideration. Suppose Acme secures a subtle edge, not because its product is superior, but due to a strategic political 'donation.' At first glance, this arrangement might seem questionable. However, if the end product provided to the taxpayers remains consistent in quality and value, then we must question where the true harm lies. The central concern should be whether such transactions detract from or compromise the well-being of the citizens. If the answer is 'no' and the only fallout is a missed business opportunity for the competitor, then the ethical dilemma surrounding the donation, while undeniably present, might not carry the weight of detriment we initially assign to it when considering the broader public benefit.

My paramount concern delves deeper than mere transactional politics between corporations and government entities. When influential corporations or entire industries employ their considerable lobbying prowess to sway governmental decisions towards massive expenditures—be it on products, services, campaigns, or, most distressingly, wars—the genuine harm to our citizenry becomes palpable. When our government, under the influence of such lobbying, funnels billions into propping up third-world dictators with financial aid and military equipment, the consequences often reverberate in ways we fail to foresee. The immediate fiscal cost that U.S. taxpayers bear is just the tip of the iceberg. All too often, these interventions set the stage for future military entanglements, dragging the U.S. Armed Forces into complex quagmires. These actions result in a massive drain of resources and, tragically, in the irreplaceable loss of American lives. This intertwining of lobbying, foreign intervention, and subsequent conflict represents the most sinister side of the power-play, overshadowing any isolated incident of political favoritism or individual indiscretion.

Sadly, we're far from a utopian existence devoid of corruption. However, if our moral compass pivots on the Latin principle *'primum non nocere'* — *"first, do no harm"* — then perhaps we can cultivate a more balanced view of these events. Of course, disparities will exist, but as long as these deviations don't culminate in harm, can we perceive them in a slightly different light?

Yet, while minor infractions may occasionally slide under the radar, the media's propensity to dwell on them, often to the detriment of more egregious transgressions, is concerning. Issues of seismic importance, like covert wars, clandestine assassinations, suppressed assaults, and environmental depredations for profit, often fade amidst a barrage of sensationalist headlines.

Is this orchestrated obscurity a mere coincidence? Or might there be insidious threads connecting media moguls and the enigmatic *"deep state"* elites? The ones are reaping vast rewards from this orchestrated chaos. As a society, are we merely pawns in a grand game of distraction?

This book cannot possibly encapsulate every dark corner of conspiracy and controversy. I aim to distill the essence of the most pressing issues, drawing from a vast reservoir of research and external resources for a holistic perspective. I've sometimes even played the devil's advocate, offering counterpoints to enable a well-rounded understanding.

Before diving in, I would like to reiterate that this is not disparaging the noble U.S. Armed Forces and Law Enforcement communities. Their valor remains untainted, even when caught up in power plays orchestrated by a select few. This book transcends partisan divides. It's an unmasking of a deeply rooted corruption, a malignant force undermining the very foundation of our great nation.

The issue at stake here is not a battle of "left" vs " right", it is the deep state's corruption that has undermined the safety, security, and future of this great country.

Part I: Background

To understand how the deep state has usurped power and hijacked this country, we must look back over the past half-century of American history and international policy.

VIETNAM

In stark contrast to many Cold War administrations that preceded and followed it, the Kennedy Administration was notably reluctant to escalate tensions with North Vietnam. This reluctance was rooted in Kennedy's broader vision for peaceful coexistence and his apprehension about the potential pitfalls of direct military engagement in Asia.[1] This nuanced approach was jeopardized after his tragic assassination in 1963, as the new leadership under President Lyndon B. Johnson harbored markedly different views.

Johnson faced a delicate balancing act: how to transition towards a more aggressive stance on Vietnam without appearing to undermine or contradict Kennedy's legacy, especially given the nation's palpable grief and nostalgia for JFK. Moreover, Johnson's urgency to demonstrate leadership and determination further intensified this political conundrum.[2]

One alleged tactic was to manipulate intelligence documents from the Kennedy era, revising them to insinuate that Kennedy had privately acknowledged the inevitability of war with North Vietnam. This manipulation aimed to create an illusion that Johnson's aggressive policy was not a sharp deviation but a continuation of Kennedy's vision.[3]

Among the most contentious pieces of evidence pointing to this manipulation is the Report of a Honolulu Conference on November 20,

---

[1] Dallek, Robert. "JFK's Second Term." The Atlantic, June 2003
[2] Beschloss, Michael R. "Taking Charge: The Johnson White House Tapes, 1963-1964." Simon & Schuster, 1997.
[3] Newman, John M. "JFK and Vietnam: Deception, Intrigue, and the Struggle for Power." Warner Books, 1992

1963, a pivotal meeting discussing Vietnam's ongoing conflict[4]. Moreover, National Security Action Memorandum 273 (NSAM-273), drafted shortly after Johnson's inauguration, further fueled suspicions. This memorandum, resulting from Johnson's meetings with United States Secretary of Defense Robert S. McNamara and other top brass, included provisions that seemed to pave the way for escalated military action in Vietnam:

> *"7. Planning should include different levels of possible increased activity, and in each instance there should be estimates of such factors as:*
>> *A. Resulting damage to North Vietnam;*
>> *B. The plausibility of denial;*
>> *C. Possible North Vietnamese retaliation;*
>> *D. Other international reaction.*
> *Plans should be submitted promptly for approval by higher authority."*[5]

Such rapid policy adjustments, coming mere days after Johnson assumed the presidency, prompted many to question the authenticity and integrity of the information guiding these decisions. Some argue that manipulating intelligence reports and studies was a calculated endeavor to engineer consensus for an impending war under the guise of continuity between the Kennedy and Johnson administrations.[6]

---

[4] "Report of a Honolulu Conference on Vietnam," National Archives, November 20, 1963.
[5] National Security Action Memorandum 273," The John F. Kennedy Presidential Library and Museum, November 26, 1963.
[6] Scott, Peter Dale. "The War Conspiracy: JFK, 9/11, and the Deep Politics of War." Skyhorse, 2013.

The Gulf of Tonkin

The Gulf of Tonkin Incident eventually provided a significant public psychological justification for American military involvement in Vietnam, consisting of two separate naval confrontations between the USS Maddox and North Vietnamese naval forces. While both events have been collectively addressed as the Gulf of Tonkin Incident, the exact nature and veracity of these events, especially the second one, have been subjects of intense scrutiny and debate.

The first of these confrontations occurred on August 2, 1964. That day, the USS Maddox, a destroyer in the U.S. Navy, was on a signals intelligence mission as part of OPLAN 34A,[7] a covert operation to gather information and carry out espionage against North Vietnam. During its patrol, it was confronted by torpedo boats from North Vietnam's 135th Torpedo Squadron. The initial reports claimed that the North Vietnamese initiated the confrontation, attacking the Maddox with torpedoes and machine-gun fire. In the ensuing melee, the Maddox responded vigorously, firing over 280 3-inch (75 mm) and 5-inch (130 mm) shells. As the smoke cleared, one American aircraft was reported damaged, and while there were no U.S. casualties, the North Vietnamese suffered four fatalities and six injuries.[8]

However, the controversy reached its zenith with the purported second incident two days later on August 4. According to initial reports by the U.S. National Security Agency (NSA), a second maritime engagement took place, seemingly corroborating the aggressive stance of the North Vietnamese. This incident would become pivotal in President

---

[7] Moïse, Edwin E. "Tonkin Gulf and the Escalation of the Vietnam War." The University of North Carolina Press, 1996.
[8] Logevall, Fredrik. "Choosing War: The Lost Chance for Peace and the Escalation of War in Vietnam." University of California Press, 2001.

Johnson's argument for escalating U.S. involvement in Vietnam. Yet, evidence began to emerge that contradicted the official narrative. Analysts and researchers pointed out that the alleged confrontation might have resulted from "*Tonkin ghosts,*" which were false radar images and not actual North Vietnamese torpedo boats.[9]

These phantom radar blips were believed to be a result of a combination of factors, including turbulent weather conditions, technical glitches, and perhaps most damningly, overeager sonar operators and radar technicians. In the heightened tension of the situation, it's conceivable that personnel aboard the U.S. vessels misinterpreted these radar anomalies as hostile North Vietnamese boats. Subsequent investigations and declassified information have further muddied the waters. Prominent officials and NSA historians have since acknowledged that the Maddox, one of the U.S. destroyers involved, was engaged in covert intelligence operations, which might have contributed to the confusion. The very idea that a decision as monumental as the escalation of war could be based on such tenuous and possibly mistaken interpretations is both haunting and a stark reminder of the heavy consequences that can stem from the interplay of technology, human interpretation, and geopolitical maneuvering.

This incident and its subsequent resolution passed by the U.S. Congress fundamentally shifted the dynamics of the Vietnam War, giving the U.S. President authorization to use conventional military force in Vietnam. However, with time and the benefit of subsequent investigations, many historians and analysts now believe that the events

---

[9] Hanyok, Robert J. "Skunks, Bogies, Silent Hounds, and the Flying Fish: The Gulf of Tonkin Mystery, 2-4 August 1964." Cryptologic Quarterly, Winter 2000/Spring 2001.

were either misrepresented or exaggerated to justify a preordained military escalation.[10]

Evidence that North Vietnam had attacked the Maddox was still being sought on the night of August 4 when President Johnson addressed the public:

> *"The initial attack on the destroyer Maddox, on August 2, was repeated today by a number of hostile vessels attacking two U.S. destroyers with torpedoes. The destroyers and supporting aircraft acted at once on the orders I gave after the initial act of aggression. We believe at least two of the attacking boats were sunk. There were no U.S. losses."*

Messages recorded that day indicate that both President Johnson and Secretary McNamara had serious concerns as to the validity of the reports;[11] however, they continued with their plans to inform the American people that these attacks on the U.S. posed a grave and immediate danger and required an immediate military response.

The distorted facts of the Gulf of Tonkin Incident were used as a pretext to escalate the U.S. Armed Forces involvement in the ongoing tensions, with many people calling for full out war with North Vietnam. On May 4, 1964, William Bundy, Assistant Secretary of State for East Asian and Pacific affairs called for the U.S. to *"drive the communists out of South Vietnam,"* even if that meant attacking both North Vietnam and communist China.

---

[10] McNamara, Robert S., and Brian VanDeMark. "In Retrospect: The Tragedy and Lessons of Vietnam." Times Books, 1995.
[11] Wise, David (1973). *The Politics of Lying: government deception, secrecy, and power.* New York: Vintage Books. ISBN 0-394-47932-7.

One perspective that has been extensively debated was put forward by the renowned Vietnam People's Army General, Võ Nguyên Giáp. With years of military experience and a profound understanding of the geopolitical scenario, Giáp speculated that the USS Maddox's presence in the Gulf of Tonkin was not a mere coincidence. Instead, he believed it was a deliberate maneuver by U.S. strategists to provoke a reaction from North Vietnam, thereby giving the U.S. a rationale to escalate the situation into a full-fledged conflict.[12]

Giáp was not alone in his suspicions. Various American government officials, privy to the intricate details of the military and political strategy of the time, echoed similar sentiments.[13] Some of them expressed concerns, albeit in private conversations and memos, that the Maddox's mission was less about routine patrolling and more about eliciting a reaction that could be used as a pretext for war.[14]

Furthermore, the sailors aboard the USS Maddox, those who were at the forefront of the incident, shared analogous doubts. While many initially believed they were operating as part of a routine mission, the subsequent events and the urgency with which the incident was reported and acted upon led some to reconsider.[15] Whispered conversations among the crew and later testimonies by a few veterans of the incident hinted at the possibility that their mission might have had ulterior motives.[16]

---

[12] Giáp, Võ Nguyên. "How We Won the War." Translated by Van Dao Hoang and M. Oanh Nguyen. Philadelphia: Recon Publications, 1976.

[13] Logevall, Fredrik. "Choosing War: The Lost Chance for Peace and the Escalation of War in Vietnam." University of California Press, 2001.

[14] Moïse, Edwin E. "Tonkin Gulf and the Escalation of the Vietnam War." UNC Press Books, 1996.

[15] McNaughton, John T. "The Pentagon's Role in the Gulf of Tonkin Events: Memory and the Lessons of the Vietnam War." In Behind the Vietnam War, edited by David L. Anderson, 145-168. Texas A&M University Press, 2002.

[16] Veterans for Peace. "Revisiting the Gulf of Tonkin Incident: Personal Narratives and Official Records." Symposium Proceedings, 1994.

The doubts about the Maddox's purpose in the Gulf weren't baseless. In the larger context of the Cold War, Vietnam had become a crucial battleground for influence between the United States and the Soviet bloc.[17] The U.S., eager to halt the spread of communism, sought opportunities to bolster its position and commitment in Southeast Asia.[18] Such an aggressive posture in the Gulf of Tonkin could have been an attempt to justify an escalated involvement in Vietnam based on defending American and, by extension, Western interests in the region.[19]

As with many events that unfold in the shadowy world of geopolitical strategy, the full truth about the Maddox's mission might never be entirely clear. Yet, the multiple voices of skepticism — from both the Vietnamese and American sides — indicate that the Gulf of Tonkin Incident wasn't just a simple naval confrontation but a significant turning point in the history of the Vietnam War and Cold War geopolitics.[20]

> According to Raymond McGovern, a retired CIA officer stated:
> "[the CIA,] *President Lyndon Johnson, Defense Secretary Robert McNamara and National Security Advisor McGeorge Bundy all knew full well that the evidence of any armed attack on the evening of August 4, 1964, the so-called "second" Tonkin Gulf incident, was highly dubious. [...] During the summer of 1964, President Johnson and the Joint Chiefs of Staff were eager to widen the war in Vietnam.*

---

[17] Gaddis, John Lewis. "The Cold War: A New History." Penguin, 2005.
[18] Karnow, Stanley. "Vietnam: A History." Penguin Books, 1997.
[19] McMaster, H. R. "Dereliction of Duty: Johnson, McNamara, the Joint Chiefs of Staff, and the Lies That Led to Vietnam." Harper Perennial, 1998.
[20] Herring, George C. "America's Longest War: The United States and Vietnam, 1950-1975." McGraw-Hill, 2002.

They stepped up sabotage and hit-and-run attacks on the coast of North Vietnam."[21]

This plan was carried out by sending the Maddox, equipped with the latest in electronic spying gear, to the Gulf of Tonkin to collect signals intelligence from the North Vietnamese coast. These coastal approaches were seen as a helpful way to get the North Vietnamese to turn on their coastal radars. Once that was accomplished, knowing full well they were visible on radar, it was authorized to approach the coast as close as 8 miles (13 kilometers) to provoke an attack from North Vietnam.

"*The President expects that all senior officers of the government will move energetically to insure full unity of support for establishing U.S. policy in South Vietnam.*"[22] Which, in effect, served as presidential-sanctioned extortion, secretly changing Kennedy's plans for withdrawal from Vietnam and ordering all senior officers in the administration to fall in line with the new directive. While simultaneously making it appear to the American people that Johnson was following in the footsteps of the beloved Kennedy.

In recorded audio, Johnson said to former treasury secretary and longtime friend Robert Anderson:

"O.K. Here's what we did: We [were] within their 12-mile [territorial waters] limit, and that's a matter that hasn't been settled. But there have been some covert operations in that area that we have been carrying on-blowing up some bridges and things of that kind, roads and so forth. So I imagine they wanted to put a stop to it. So they come out there and fire

---

[21] Robert Parry. "Consortiumnews.com".
(http://www.consortiumnews.com/2008/011108a.html)

[22] U.S.G ed., IV.C.1, pp. 1-3; Gravel ed., III:17-18.

and we respond immediately with five-inch guns from the destroyer [Maddox] and with planes overhead. And we cripple them up-knock one of them out and circle the other two. And then we go right back where we were with that destroyer and with another one and plus plenty of planes standing by. And that's where we are now.[23]

James Bamford, retired United States Navy intelligence analysis writes in his book, *Body of Secrets*, that the primary purpose of the *Maddox*:

"was to act as a seagoing provocateur—to poke its sharp gray bow and the American flag as close to the belly of North Vietnam as possible, in effect shoving its five-inch cannons up the nose of the communist navy... The Maddox' mission was made even more provocative by being timed to coincide with commando raids, creating the impression that the Maddox was directing those missions..."

Thus, the North Vietnamese had every reason to believe that *Maddox* was involved in these actions.[24]

In 1995, McNamara met with former Vietnam People's Army General Võ Nguyên Giáp to ask what happened on August 4, 1964, in the second Gulf of Tonkin Incident. *"Absolutely nothing,"* Giáp replied. Giáp claimed that the attack had been imaginary[25].

---

[23] President Johnson and Robert Anderson, 9:46 AM, Aug, 3 1964, Tape WH6408.03, Citation #4632, LBJ Recordings

[24] Bamford, James in *Body of Secrets*, Anchor, Reprint edition (April 30, 2002), ISBN 978-0385499088

[25] Robert J. Hanyok, "*Skunks, Bogies, Silent Hounds, and the Flying Fish: The Gulf of Tonkin Mystery*, 2–4 August 1964" *Cryptologic Quarterly*, Winter 2000/Spring 2001 Edition, Vol. 19, No. 4 / Vol. 20, No. 1. (https://web.archive.org/web/20160131235457/http://www.nsa.gov/public_info/_files/gul

In the documentary "*The Fog of War: Eleven Lessons from the Life of Robert S. McNamara*," released in 2003, former U.S. Secretary of Defense Robert S. McNamara took a candid look back at his time during the Kennedy and Johnson administrations. Directed by the acclaimed filmmaker Errol Morris, the film serves as a reflective confession and introspective analysis of the pivotal moments and decisions made during McNamara's tenure.

A significant revelation from the documentary was McNamara's admission regarding the Gulf of Tonkin incident. McNamara stated unequivocally that the attack on the USS Maddox, cited as the reason for the U.S. escalation in Vietnam, never occurred. He elaborated, explaining that the confusion, high tension, and unreliable intelligence led to a belief that an attack had occurred. In his own words, the circumstances were clouded by the "*fog of war.*"

This admission was startling for several reasons. Firstly, the Gulf of Tonkin Resolution, passed by the U.S. Congress in the aftermath of the purported attack, authorized President Lyndon B. Johnson to increase U.S. military presence in Vietnam, leading to a full-scale war. The fact that a central premise for this escalation was based on an event that didn't transpire underscores the dangers of acting on unverified or misinterpreted intelligence.

Furthermore, McNamara's acknowledgment also sheds light on the bureaucratic processes of the U.S. government. It raised questions about the speed and nature of decision-making during crises and highlighted the immense responsibility and power vested in crucial government officials.

---

f_of_tonkin/articles/rel1_skunks_bogies.pdf)

The implications of their decisions, as demonstrated by the Vietnam War, had far-reaching consequences for the American and Vietnamese people.

While McNamara's revelation did not change the historical facts of the Vietnam War, it did serve as a moment of reckoning. His candidness in "*The Fog of War*" provided a unique perspective, emphasizing the need for thorough fact-checking, open dialogue, and caution when making decisions that could lead nations into conflict.[26]

Through the testimony of some of those involved and the declassification of official government reports, the truth of the fabrications of the Gulf of Tonkin Incident used to justify the war has now come to light. Even though the attacks that happened were not directly provoked, they were a direct result of the OPLAN 34A raids, which was, in essence, an American operation.

It's evident that the President and his administration were aware of the questionable nature of the attacks in the Gulf of Tonkin. Despite this, the narrative presented to the American people emphasized the need to counteract the supposedly unprovoked aggression by North Vietnam.

As the author, I have delved deep into this era, and I grapple with understanding the motivations of the key players of the time. Were they motivated by war profiteering to instigate a conflict that would ultimately benefit them financially, politically, and personally? Or were they staunch idealists who believed their objectives were so vital that they could bend the truth to achieve them? Their conscious decision to manipulate facts to bolster public support for the war is evident.

---

[26] Morris, Errol, director. "The Fog of War: Eleven Lessons from the Life of Robert S. McNamara." Sony Pictures Classics, 2003.

Yet, I wonder if a more forthright approach would have been more effective. Why not present the unvarnished truth to the American populace, laying out why they believed war was necessary to curb communism's influence in Vietnam? Was there an underlying fear that their arguments, when stripped of embellishments, wouldn't be persuasive enough to garner public support? If they doubted their ability to convince the public, what made them so resolute in their own convictions?

Such questions beckon deeper introspection, not just about this specific incident but about the very nature of political decision-making and the dynamics between leadership and the populace in times of potential conflict.[27]

Additional Reading:
"The Kennedy Assassination and the Vietnam War" by Pete Dale Scott: https://history-matters.com/essays/vietnam/KennedyVietnam1971/KennedyVietnam1971.htm

---

[27] Herring, George C. "America's Longest War: The United States and Vietnam, 1950–1975." McGraw-Hill, 2013.

Iran-Contra and Iraq

The Iran-Contra affair was more than just a straightforward scandal; it was a watershed moment in the annals of U.S. foreign policy. Transcending the confines of a typical political controversy, its tentacles reached into multiple geopolitical arenas. With interconnected actions spanning Central America to the Middle East, it wove a tapestry of diplomatic, covert, and strategic complexities. Not only did it challenge the very limits of international law and governance, but it also exposed the vulnerability of checks and balances within the U.S. governmental system. This affair showcased the lengths to which certain factions within an administration might go, operating in the shadows to further their agendas, even when they diverged from official policy or domestic law.

Mohammad Reza Pahlavi, the last Shah of Iran, was overthrown by the Iranian Revolution on February 11, 1979. The United States supported the Shah and was the largest supplier of arms to his country to help him maintain power. After his ousting, the Islamic Republic of Iran inherited most U.S.-provided weapons and required a constant supply of spare parts from the U.S. to keep them operational. This steady supply stopped when Iranian students stormed the American embassy in Tehran in November 1979 and took 52 Americans hostage; U.S. President Jimmy Carter saw Iran's support for terrorism and imposed an arms embargo on Iran.[28]

In September 1980, the Middle East's geopolitical landscape was jolted as Iraq, led by Saddam Hussein, launched a brazen invasion into Iran. This military aggression thrust Iran into a dire position,

---

[28] Kornbluh, Peter & Byrne, Malcolm The Iran-Contra Scandal: A Declassified History, New York: New Press, 1993 page 213.

urgently needing both weaponry and essential spare parts to reinforce its defensive capabilities against the Iraqi onslaught. For the U.S., the unfolding situation was intricate. Both Iran and Iraq had been designated by the U.S. as state sponsors of terrorism, heightening the U.S.'s reservations about strengthening either nation's regional influence.[29] The warfare not only amplified immediate concerns but also highlighted the broader challenge of ensuring a regional equilibrium, preventing either nation from becoming an overwhelmingly dominant force.[30]

In light of these dynamics, the U.S. adopted what was informally termed the "*dual containment*" strategy.[31] This involved a nuanced approach of indirectly engaging with both sides to ensure that neither Iraq nor Iran could attain a clear-cut victory, thereby preserving the Middle East's precarious balance of power.[32]

Under President Carter's administration and subsequent incoming President Ronald Reagan, the United States navigated a diplomatic tightrope. Both presidents maintained a consistent stance of restricting arms sales to Iran. This decision aimed to prevent further escalating the conflict and signal a particular stance in a volatile Middle Eastern political landscape.

A group of senior Reagan administration officials in the Senior Interdepartmental Group concluded in a secret security briefing

---

[29] U.S. Department of State. Patterns of Global Terrorism. Washington, D.C.: U.S. Government Printing Office, 1980.
[30] Gause, F. Gregory III. "The Illogic of Dual Containment." Foreign Affairs, vol. 73, no. 2, 1994, pp. 56-66.
[31] Convay, Barbara. "America's Misguided Policy of Dual Containment in the Persian Gulf." Cato Foreign Policy Briefing No. 33. Cato Institute, November 10, 1994.
[32] Brzezinski, Zbigniew. "The U.S. and the Middle East." The Grand Chessboard: American Primacy and Its Geostrategic Imperatives. Basic Books, 1997, pp. 124-138.

report on July 21, 1981, that the arms embargo was mainly ineffective because Iran could always buy arms and spare parts from other countries, such as the Soviet Union. The conclusion was that the United States should start covertly selling Iran weapons to keep Iran from falling into the Soviet sphere of influence while maintaining plausible deniability for the United States.

In the beginning, publicly, the U.S. remained officially neutral after Iraq invaded Iran. However, as the war progressed, with growing concern, Iran would get support from the Soviet Union, allowing them a more substantial presence in the area. While at the same time, the U.S. also provided resources, political support, and some "*non-military*" aircraft to Iraq[33] and Iran. To prevent either side from striking a clear victory and keeping them each in a tie.

By February 1982, the U.S. was in a precarious position. Initially, the American strategy aimed to maintain a balance of power in the region, and the limited assistance provided to Iran was seen as a necessary counterweight to Iraq's aggressive maneuvers. However, this calculated support appeared to tilt the scales more than anticipated. As Iranian forces began gaining momentum and made considerable advancements on the battlefield, there were growing apprehensions within U.S. foreign policy circles that Iran might secure a decisive victory. Such an outcome was not in line with U.S. objectives; an overwhelmingly dominant Iran could further destabilize the region and challenge U.S. interests. The balance Washington sought was now in jeopardy, as its nuanced approach threatened to embolden one side over the other inadvertently.

---

[33] Stork, Joe; Lesch, Ann M. "*Background to the Crisis: Why War?*". *Middle East Report*. Middle East Research and Information Project (MERIP) (167, November–December 1990): 11–18. JSTOR 3012998. (https://www.jstor.org/stable/3012998)

"[in] a nightmare scenario [...] Iranians invade Iraq, they defeat Iraq, and then head straight for Israel, which is distracted and debilitated by its ongoing adventure in Lebanon", Nick Veliotes, Assistant Secretary of State for Near Eastern and South Asian Affairs[34]

As a result, the U.S. gradually abandoned its policy of neutrality. The U.S. State Department first removed Iraq from the list of State Sponsors of Terrorism to ease the transfer of dual-use technology.

In March 1982, Iran began a successful counteroffensive against Iraq (Operation Undeniable Victory), and this forced the U.S. to increase its support for Iraq to prevent Iran from forcing a surrender of Iraq. President Reagan signed National Security Study Memorandum (NSSM) 4-82 *"review of U.S. policy toward the Middle East"* and then in June, Reagan signed a National Security Decision Directive (NSDD) co-written by NSC official Howard Teicher, which determined: *"The United States could not afford to allow Iraq to lose the war to Iran."*[35]

While Iraq was the initial aggressor, the scales of conflict began to tilt due to the initial support provided by the U.S. to Iran. As Iran gained the upper hand, alarm bells rang across global political corridors. There were rising concerns that if Iran's power surge went unchecked, it could wield overwhelming influence in the Middle

---

[34] Blight, James G.; et al. (2012). *Becoming Enemies: U.S.-Iran Relations and the Iran-Iraq War, 1979-1988.* Rowman & Littlefield Publishers. pp. 20–21, 97,

[35] Yaphe, Judith (2013). *"Changing American Perspectives on the Iran-Iraq war"*. *The Iran-Iraq War: New International Perspectives.* Routledge. ISBN 9780415685245.

East, a scenario many nations, especially Western powers, found deeply unsettling.

The U.S. substantially increased its backing for Iraq to counterbalance Iran's advances and maintain a regional equilibrium. The nature of this support was both vast and varied: it ranged from billions in economic aid, invaluable military intelligence, dual-use technology meant for both civil and military applications,[36] and weaponry from third countries to the transfer of elite special operations training. This strategic aid was instrumental in bolstering the Iraqi military capabilities, ensuring they could stall Iran's momentum and maintain a semblance of balance on the battlefield.

However, as geopolitics often demands uncomfortable compromises, a dark underside emerged in this alliance. Reports and evidence began surfacing of Iraq using chemical weapons against Iranian forces, a blatant transgression of international norms and treaties.[37] Yet, driven by the larger objective of curbing Iran's influence, agencies like the CIA often looked the other way, ignoring these violations. Such compromises underscored the complexity of international politics, where moral lines sometimes blur in the face of broader strategic objectives.

The implications of the U.S. government's actions during the Iran-Iraq War go beyond mere geopolitical maneuvering. A troubling and less discussed aspect of the conflict is the direct provision of dangerous materials, which included biological weapons, to Iraq.

---

[36] Friedman, Alan. *Spider's Web: The Secret History of How the White House Illegally Armed Iraq*, Bantam Books, 1993.

[37] Harris, Shane; Aid, Matthew M. (2013-08-26). "*Exclusive: CIA Files Prove America Helped Saddam as He Gassed Iran*". *Foreign Policy*. Retrieved 2017-05-07.

Such actions starkly contrast the non-proliferation principles and containment that the U.S. espoused on the world stage.

In 1994, a report that cast light on this dark corner of U.S. foreign policy was released. Commonly referred to as the Riegle Report, after Senator Donald Riegle, who chaired the Senate Banking Committee that produced it, the document is a chilling record of U.S. complicity in arming Saddam Hussein's regime with materials that had the potential for use in biological warfare.

On February 9, 1994, the report detailed:
> *"pathogenic, toxigenic, and other biological research materials were exported to Iraq pursuant to application and licensing by the U.S. Department of Commerce. ... These exported biological materials were not attenuated or weakened and were capable of reproduction."*[38]

The specificity of the report's details paints a picture that is hard to dismiss. It itemized 70 distinct shipments from the United States to various Iraqi government agencies spanning three years. These weren't just benign substances either. The list of materials included the causative agent of anthrax, Bacillus anthracis, a deadly bacterium with a history of being weaponized.

> *"It was later learned that these microorganisms exported by the United States were identical to those the UN*

---

[38] U.S. Senate Banking Committee. Second Staff Report on U.S. CBW-Related Dual-Use Exports to Iraq, May 25, 1994. (http://www.gulfwarvets.com/arison/banking.htm)

inspectors found and recovered from the Iraqi biological warfare program. "[39]

The report's conclusion, though it doesn't justify the actions, gives a perspective on the complicated geo-political strategy of the time. It's a stark reminder of how cold calculations during power struggles can often overshadow moral implications. And while the immediate intention might not have been for Iraq to weaponize these materials, the U.S. unquestionably provided the means.

The revelation begs several moral and ethical questions. What level of responsibility does a country bear when it provides another nation with the tools for mass destruction, even if not the explicit intention to use them as such? How does one reconcile the overt policy of non-proliferation with such clandestine actions? The Riegle Report serves as a grim testament to the often shadowy and complex dealings of international politics, where short-term strategic gains can sometimes overshadow long-term ethical considerations.

The oscillations of power in the Iran-Iraq war presented a dynamic theater of geopolitical intrigue. As the years progressed, the U.S. was entangled in a meticulous dance, navigating the treacherous waters of covert support, shifting allegiances from one side to the other. This was more than a mere quest for regional stability but a deliberate strategy to ensure that neither nation could establish a clear and unassailable dominance. Throughout the conflict's duration, the U.S. persisted in supplying an arsenal of sophisticated weaponry,

---

[39] Riegle, Jr., Donald W. U.S. Chemical and Biological Warfare-Related Dual Use Exports to Iraq and their Possible Impact on the Health Consequences of the Gulf War, Committee on Banking, Housing and Urban Affairs, May 25, 1994. (http://www.gulfweb.org/bigdoc/report/riegle1.html)

further stoking the flames of a war that seemed interminable. While the overt objective was to hinder the ascendancy of either nation, underlying this was a dual agenda: cementing U.S. influence in the region and facilitating significant profits for the military-industrial complex. In this strategic play, the line between friend and foe was perpetually blurred, and the true costs extended far beyond the immediate theater of conflict.

Weapons for Hostages

Even with the Iran-Iraq War battling, the U.S. had complex regional concerns. In early July 1985, under a veil of secrecy, Michael Ledeen, a consultant of National Security Adviser Robert McFarlane, requested assistance from Israeli Prime Minister Shimon Peres for help in the sale of arms to Iran.[40] After meeting with an Israeli diplomat named David Kicmche, Leeden and McFarlane confirmed rumors the Iranians were prepared to have Hezbollah release American hostages in Lebanon in exchange for weapons.[41]

The plan was for Israel to ship weapons through an intermediary (identified as Manucher Ghorbanifar) to the Islamic Republic. These weapons would be used to support the supposedly moderate and politically influential Ayatollah Khomeini. At the time, it was believed he was seeking a rapprochement with the United States; after the transaction, the United States would reimburse Israel with the same weapons while receiving the monetary benefits from the sale.[42] Under this plan, the U.S. was able to obtain the release of the hostages

---

[40] The American-Israeli Cooperative Enterprise. Retrieved 7 June 2008. (https://www.jewishvirtuallibrary.org/jsource/U.S.-Israel/Iran_Contra_Affair.html)
[41] Kornbluh, Peter & Byrne, Malcolm *The Iran-Contra Scandal: A Declassified History*, New York: New Press, 1993 page 214.
[42] Reagan, Ronald (1990), p. 504

and also profit from the sale of weapons while at the same time maintaining plausible deniability about the entire affair.

McFarlane in a memo to Shultz and Weinberger wrote:
"The short term dimension concerns the seven hostages; the long term dimension involves the establishment of a private dialogue with Iranian officials on the broader relations ... They sought specifically the delivery from Israel of 100 TOW missiles ..." [43]

Shultz warned Reagan, *"we were just falling into the arms-for-hostages business and we shouldn't do it."* [44]

On August 20, 1985, amidst the backdrop of the Iran-Iraq war and the evolving geopolitical dynamics, Israel, a close U.S. ally, initiated a transaction that would set off a chain of events with far-reaching consequences. The Jewish state sent 96 American-made TOW missiles to Iran, a move facilitated by the enigmatic and controversial arms dealer Manucher Ghorbanifar.[45] A few weeks later, on September 14, 1985, the arsenal was expanded further by delivering an additional 408 TOW missiles, showcasing the increasing depth and intricacy of these covert arms exchanges.[46]

Notably, the day after the second delivery, on September 15, 1985, a significant development occurred: Reverend Benjamin Weir,

---

[43] Kornbluh, Peter & Byrne, Malcolm *The Iran-Contra Scandal: A Declassified History*, New York: New Press, 1993 page 214.

[44] Kornbluh, Peter & Byrne, Malcolm *The Iran-Contra Scandal: A Declassified History*, New York: New Press, 1993 page 214.

[45] Draper, Theodore. "The Road to Iran-Contra." The New York Review of Books. April 9, 1987.

[46] Walsh, Lawrence E. "Final Report of the Independent Counsel for Iran/Contra Matters." U.S. Court of Appeals for the District of Columbia. August 4, 1993.

who had been held captive by the radical Shia group, the Islamic Jihad Organization, was released. This raised questions about a possible quid pro quo, hinting at the intricacies and under-the-table deals that might have been at play behind the scenes.[47]

The arms transfers didn't cease there. On November 24, 1985, a third consignment arrived in Iran. This time, it was 18 Hawk anti-aircraft missiles, a potent defensive weapon system that could bolster Iran's aerial defense capabilities significantly.[48]

These transactions weren't merely about weapons; they were emblematic of the multifaceted and often clandestine relationships between nations, proxies, and non-state actors during one of the Middle East's most turbulent periods.

On July 26, 1986, in a move that brought relief yet also raised eyebrows, Hezbollah — the Shiite militant group backed by Iran — released Father Lawrence Jenco, an American hostage who had served as the head of Catholic Relief Services in Lebanon.[49] Jenco's captivity, like that of other Western hostages in Lebanon, had become a significant point of concern for the U.S., and his release was seen as a significant breakthrough.

Following this event, William Casey, the formidable and often enigmatic head of the Central Intelligence Agency (CIA), made a rather unexpected move. Recognizing the opportunity to build goodwill and facilitate further negotiations or releases, Casey

---

[47] Sick, Gary. "October Surprise: America's Hostages in Iran and the Election of Ronald Reagan." The New York Times. October 15, 1991.

[48] Waas, Murray, and Craig Unger. "In the Loop: Bush's Secret Mission." The New Yorker. November 2, 1992.

[49] Wright, Robin. "Sacred Rage: The Wrath of Militant Islam." Simon & Schuster. 2001.

proposed a unique expression of gratitude. He urged the U.S. administration to authorize the shipment of small missile parts to the Iranian military forces.[50] The idea, seemingly paradoxical given the ongoing hostilities between the U.S. and Iran, was a testament to the complex, multifaceted nature of international diplomacy and covert operations during this period.

The proposal and subsequent events opened up debates and discussions on the ethics, strategies, and long-term implications of such quid pro quo arrangements and whether they truly served the interests of the United States or were merely short-term solutions to deeply ingrained geopolitical challenges.[51]

This clandestine support to Iran stood in stark contrast to the U.S.'s overt backing of Iraq. Unlike the shadowy deals with Iran, the U.S. government's endorsements for Iraq were conspicuous and frequently debated in the public domain. The halls of Congress were often abuzz with discussions and debates surrounding America's stance on the Iran-Iraq War. While covert operations remained hidden, the overt support for Iraq was undeniable and even openly acknowledged by top government officials.[52]

A particularly revealing moment came in 1992 when veteran journalist Ted Koppel, on ABC's Nightline, laid bare the extent of U.S. involvement. Koppel reported that during the Reagan and Bush

---

[50] Woodward, Bob. "Veil: The Secret Wars of the CIA, 1981-1987." Simon & Schuster. 1987.
[51] Byrne, Malcolm. "Iran-Contra: Reagan's Scandal and the Unchecked Abuse of Presidential Power." University Press of Kansas. 2014.
[52] U.S. Congress. House. "U.S. Chemical and Biological Warfare-Related Dual-Use Exports to Iraq and Their Possible Impact on the Health Consequences of the Gulf War." 103rd Cong., 2nd sess., 1994. House Report 103-900.

administrations, there was not just a passive acknowledgment but active encouragement for various forms of support to Iraq. This included financial aid, technology transfers, chemicals, and even weaponry. The dual strategy, Koppel suggested, was evidence of a broader U.S. policy of maintaining a strategic balance in the Middle East, even if it meant playing both sides of the conflict.[53]

Public Disclosure of the events in Iran

Iranian forces that opposed support from the U.S. became aware of the weapon trade. Mehdi Hashemi, a senior official in the Islamic Revolutionary Guard Corp, leaked to the Lebanese magazine *Ash-Shiraa*, exposing the arrangement on November 3, 1986.[54]

The Iranian government confirmed the *Ash-Shiraa* story; then ten days later, on November 13, President Reagan appeared on television from the Oval Office to address these concerns:

> *"My purpose was ... to send a signal that the United States was prepared to replace the animosity between [the U.S. and Iran] with a new relationship ... At the same time we undertook this initiative, we made clear that Iran must oppose all forms of international terrorism as a condition of progress in our relationship. The most significant step which Iran could take, we indicated,*

---

[53] Nightline: Arming Iraq – A Special Report." ABC News. June 9, 1992.
[54] Cave, George. "*Why Secret 1986 U.S.-Iran 'Arms for Hostages' Negotiations Failed*".
Washington Report on Middle Eastern Affairs. Retrieved 9 January 2007.
http://www.wrmea.com/backissues/0994/9409008.htm

would be to use its influence in Lebanon to secure the
release of all hostages held there."[55]

Nicaragua

Amidst the complex geopolitical web in the Middle East, a parallel covert operation was unraveling thousands of miles away in Central America. At the nexus of this operation was U.S. Marine Corps Lieutenant Colonel Oliver North, a high-ranking member of the National Security Council. North's role was not just confined to the orchestration of arms deals with Iran; he was instrumental in diverting funds procured from these sales to support another critical U.S. foreign policy objective: countering communist expansion in the Americas.[56]

In Nicaragua, the Sandinista National Liberation Front, or the Sandinistas, had taken power. With their leftist, communist-leaning ideology and their overtly anti-American stance, they were perceived by the U.S. administration as a potential domino that could trigger further communist expansion in the region. In response, the U.S. covertly supported the Contras, a group of anti-Sandinista paramilitary fighters. Their objective was clear: wage a guerrilla war against the Sandinistas and halt the march of communism in Central America.[57]

---

[55] Reagan, Ronald (November 13, 1986). "*Address to the Nation on the Iran Arms and Contra Aid Controversy*". Ronald Reagan Presidential Foundation. Retrieved 7 June 2008. http://www.reagan.utexas.edu/archives/speeches/1986/111386c.htm

[56] Draper, Theodore. "The Iran-Contra Affair." The New York Review of Books, November 5, 1987.

[57] Dickey, Christopher. "Contras: A 'Counterrevolutionary' Band." The Washington Post, March 11, 1985.

However, the U.S.'s support for the Contras was not without its controversies. In fact, the U.S. Congress had explicitly banned aid to the Contras due to human rights concerns. This legislative embargo made North's operations both secretive and critical. By funneling proceeds from arms sales to Iran, North effectively bypassed Congressional restrictions, ensuring that the Contras received the necessary funding to continue their operations against the Sandinista government.[58]

This dual theater of war—simultaneously playing out in the Middle East and Central America—revealed the intricate lengths to which the U.S. was willing to go to safeguard its interests during the Cold War era, even if it meant operating in the gray zones of legality and morality.

Any support by the U.S. of the Contras was a direct violation of the Boland Amendment, where Congress expressly prohibited the U.S. from funding or supporting the Contras:

> *"None of the funds provided in this Act may be used by the Central Intelligence Agency or the Department of Defense to furnish military equipment, military training or advice, or other support for military activities, to any group or individual . . . for the purpose of overthrowing the government of Nicaragua."*

The Contras were heavily involved in cocaine trafficking. This was confirmed by multiple intelligence sources on the ground, including one of the Contra leaders, in 1985:

---

[58] Walsh, Lawrence E. "Final Report of the Independent Counsel for Iran/Contra Matters." U.S. Court of Appeal for the District of Columbia, August 4, 1993.

> *"told U.S. authorities that his group was being paid $50,000 by Colombian traffickers for help with a 100-kilo cocaine shipment and that the money would go 'for the cause' of fighting the Nicaraguan government."*

According to the report, the U.S. State Department paid over $806,000 to *"four companies owned and operated by narcotics traffickers"* to carry humanitarian assistance to the Contras.[59]

> *"I quickly discovered that the Contra pilots were, indeed, smuggling narcotics back into the United States, using the same pilots, planes, and hangers that the Central Intelligence Agency and the National Security Council, under the direction of Lt. Col. Oliver North, used to maintain their covert supply operation to the Contras."*[60]

For a considerable period, the operations had remained shrouded in secrecy, with only a select few in the higher echelons of the U.S. government privy to the true extent of the activities.

However, secrets in the world of espionage and covert operations have the nasty habit of unraveling in the most unexpected ways. This was made starkly evident on October 5, 1986, when a plane operated by Corporate Air Services HPF821, a U.S. government front company managed by the CIA,[61] was downed over Nicaraguan skies

---

[59] Subcommittee on Terrorism, Narcotics, and International Communications and International Economic Policy, Trade, Oceans, and Environment of the Committee on Foreign Relations, United States Senate (1989). *Drugs, law enforcement, and foreign policy : A report.* Washington: GPO.
(https://babel.hathitrust.org/cgi/pt?id=pst.000014976124)
[60] Greg Szymanski. "Former DEA Agent Wants George H. Bush, Negroponte and Other Higher-Ups Held Accountable for Illegal Drug Smuggling", March 5, 2006
[61] "Hasenfus: Nothing But the Fact." Envío, No. 65, November 1986.

by a surface-to-air missile. The plane's cargo was a veritable arsenal, replete with *"60 collapsible AK-47 rifles, 50,000 AK-47 rifle cartridges, several dozen RPG-7 grenade launchers, and 150 pairs of jungle boots."*[62]

The implications were seismic. The downing of the plane risked exposing a covert operation, which the U.S. administration had painstakingly tried to keep out of the public domain. The revelation threatened to become a major political scandal, with potential ramifications for U.S. foreign policy and the reputations of those involved.

In a frantic effort to contain the fallout and shield the broader contours of the operation, Oliver North, a key player in the Iran-Contra operation, took drastic measures. Over five days, from November 21 to November 25, 1986, North embarked on a frantic mission to eliminate the paper trail that could incriminate him and several others in the U.S. administration. Documents were shredded, files were hidden, and evidence that could provide insights into the full scope of the operation in Nicaragua was obliterated.[63]

North's actions can be seen as a desperate attempt at damage control, a last-ditch effort to prevent a geopolitical scandal of immense proportions. Nevertheless, as history would have it, the affair eventually came to light, becoming one of the most significant scandals in U.S. political history.

The Iran-Contra affair was more than just a political scandal; it provided a rare window into the U.S. intelligence apparatus's

---

[62] Woodward, Bob. "The Secret Wars of the CIA." The Washington Post, June 13, 1987.
[63] Walsh, Lawrence E. "Final Report of the Independent Counsel for Iran/Contra Matters." U.S. Court of Appeal for the District of Columbia, August 4, 1993.

intricate, often shadowy workings. As details of the covert operations began to surface, many involved found themselves entangled in legal complications.

In 1989, as North stood trial, one of the most compelling testimonies came from his secretary, Fawn Hall. Ms. Hall, an individual who worked closely with North during the height of the operations, provided a detailed account of the frantic actions taken to conceal evidence. With unwavering composure, she testified about assisting North in altering official United States National Security Council (NSC) documents. Their modus operandi involved shredding crucial papers that could incriminate many involved and removing others from the White House altogether.[64]

North, for his part, attempted to provide a rationale for the destruction of these documents. He argued that his actions were not driven by a desire to shield himself or the administration from potential legal repercussions but rather by a sense of duty to protect the lives of the individuals involved in the covert operations. These operations had numerous domestic and international participants, and any exposure could have put them at risk.[65]

Nevertheless, North's explanations did little to exonerate him in the eyes of the law. The trial concluded with North being convicted on three counts: accepting an illegal gratuity, obstructing a congressional inquiry, and destroying documents. However, in a twist that further exemplified the complex legal nature of the case, North's convictions were later overturned on appeal. The grounds for

---

[64] "North's Secretary Says She Helped Alter Memos." The New York Times, May 11, 1989.
[65] "Oliver North's Explanation." Los Angeles Times, July 8, 1987.

this decision rested on a technicality: North had previously been granted immunity for his testimony before Congress, and this protected testimony was improperly used against him in his criminal trial.[66]

The Iran-Contra affair and the subsequent trial highlighted the tension between the need for state secrecy in the realm of national security and the principles of transparency and accountability in a democratic system.

During his presidential election campaign in 1988, Vice President George Bush tried to keep his distance from the Iran-Contra affair and completely denied any knowledge by saying he was "*out of the loop.*" Though his diaries included a passage, "[he was] *one of the few people that know fully the details.*"[67]

Israeli journalist Ronen Bergman claims that Bush not only knew about the weapons sales and drug shipments but he was personally briefed by Amiram Nir, a counterterrorism adviser to the then Israeli Prime Minister, during a visit to Israel:

> "*Nir could have incriminated the incoming President. The fact that Nir was killed in a mysterious chartered airplane crash in Mexico in December 1988 has given rise to numerous conspiracy theories,*" writes Bergman.[68]

[66] Johnston, David. "Appeals Court Voids North's Iran-Contra Convictions; Prosecutor Plans to Seek Review by Full Court." The New York Times, July 21, 1990.
[67] "*The Iran-Contra Affair 20 Years On*". Gwu.edu. Retrieved 2014-08-18. (http://www.gwu.edu/~nsarchiv/NSAEBB/NSAEBB210/index.htm)
[68] Bergman, Ronen. The Secret War with Iran: The 30-Year Clandestine Struggle Against the World.

As the Iran-Contra scandal receded into the annals of history, one action brought it back into the forefront of public discourse. On December 24, 1992, President George H. W. Bush exercised his presidential authority to pardon six government officials who had been implicated and found guilty in connection to the affair, they were Elliott Abrams, Duane R. Clarridge, Alan Fiers, Clair George, Robert C. McFarlane, and Caspar W. Weinberger.[69]

Given the magnitude of the Iran-Contra scandal and its implications, Bush's decision to grant these pardons sparked widespread speculation and debate. The timing and nature of the pardons led many to posit that Bush was not simply showing leniency but might have been ensuring the loyalty and silence of those who could potentially implicate him further. To some observers, there may have been an underlying quid pro quo: in exchange for their silence, these officials received the ultimate reprieve from the highest office in the land.[70] However, this could never be independently verified, only speculated.

As we delve deeper into the intricacies of this multifaceted geopolitical drama, it's essential to note that the Iran-Contra affair spanned multiple presidencies and had implications that rippled across both domestic and international terrains. While this chapter has explored the dynamics between Iran and Iraq, subsequent chapters will unravel the Contra side of the equation, shedding light on how this scandal's tentacles reached the Bush and Clinton families' political legacies.

---

[69] Walsh, Lawrence E. "Final Report of the Independent Counsel for Iran/Contra Matters." U.S. Department of Justice, August 4, 1993.
[70] Brinkley, Douglas. "Pardoning the Iran-Contra Affair: George H. W. Bush's Bad Precedent." The Atlantic, April 15, 2018.

IRAQ IN THE 80S & 90S

As the tension between the United States and Iraq heightened, leading to the Gulf War, the U.S. administration under President George H. W. Bush made a series of allegations against Iraq to muster international support. One of the claims was that Saddam Hussein's forces were massing on the border of Saudi Arabia, posing a direct threat to the oil-rich kingdom.

With the Iran-Iraq War officially over, in October 1989, President Bush signed National Security Directives 26, which begins:
> *"Access to Persian Gulf oil and the security of key friendly states in the area are vital to U.S. national security." With respect to Iraq, the directive stated, "Normal relations between the United States and Iraq would serve our longer term interests and promote stability in both the Persian Gulf and the Middle East."*[71]

War with the U.S. Begins

In just a few short months, on August 2, 1990, directly against the goals of NSD 26, the Persian Gulf War would officially start. The U.S., with a coalition of 35 nations, established a defensive position to protect Saudi Arabia from Iraq. President George H. W. Bush said, *"I took this action to assist the Saudi Arabian Government in the defense of its homeland,"* asking the American people for their *"support in a decision I've made to stand up for what's right and condemn what's wrong, all in the cause of peace."*

---

[71] "National Security Directive 26" (PDF). The White House. 1989-10-02. Retrieved 2006-10-12. (http://www.fas.org/irp/offdocs/nsd/nsd26.pdf)

As Scott Peterson reported for *The Christian Science Monitor* in 2002, a crucial part of the first Bush administration's case *"was that an Iraqi juggernaut was threatening to roll into Saudi Arabia. Citing top-secret satellite images, Pentagon officials estimated in mid-September [of 1990] that up to 250,000 Iraqi troops and 1,500 tanks stood on the border, threatening the key U.S. oil supplier."*[72]

In January 1991, Jean Heller, a journalist from the St. Petersburg Times (now the Tampa Bay Times), challenged the U.S. government's narrative. Heller secured two sets of satellite images of the Saudi-Kuwaiti border area, taken by the commercial satellite company Sovinformsputnik, which were analyzed by experts from Boston's Commercial Satellite Imagery division of Litton Industries, a major defense contractor.[73]

When analyzed, the photographs from the *Sovinformsputnik* satellite showed a vast expanse of the desert but no signs of a massive Iraqi military presence as the U.S. government had claimed. The barren landscape in the satellite images seemed to contradict the U.S. narrative of an imminent Iraqi invasion of Saudi Arabia.[74]

The implications of Heller's investigation were substantial. It raised questions about the accuracy and reliability of intelligence presented by the U.S. administration to garner support for the war. Furthermore, it prompted debates among policymakers, defense

---

[72] *In war, some facts less factual*, Scott Peterson, The Christian Science Monitor, September 6, 2002 http://www.csmonitor.com/2002/0906/p01s02-wosc.html
[73] Heller, Jean. "Photos Don't Show Buildup U.S. Described." St. Petersburg Times, January 6, 1991.
[74] Stauber, John, and Sheldon Rampton. "Toxic Sludge is Good For You: Lies, Damn Lies, and the Public Relations Industry." Common Courage Press, 1995.

analysts, and journalists about whether the U.S. had exaggerated or even fabricated intelligence to justify its actions in the Gulf.[75]

For clarification, she contacted the office Secretary of Defense Dick Cheney *"for evidence refuting the Times photos or analysis, offering to hold the story if proven wrong."* Their official response, per Heller, was *"Trust us."*[76]

Heller later told Peterson (The Christian Science Monitor) that the Iraqi buildup on the border between Kuwait and Saudi Arabia *"the whole justification for Bush sending troops in there, and it just didn't exist."*

However, the U.S. government dismissed the significance of the commercial satellite photos and stood by its assessment of the threat posed by Iraq. As the war unfolded, this episode became one of several instances where the integrity and interpretation of intelligence data came under scrutiny.

While the presence of the Iraqi military on the Saudi-Arabian border was not proven, In the early hours of August 2, 1990, Iraqi forces, under the command of President Saddam Hussein, swiftly invaded and subsequently annexed Kuwait. The brazen act was precipitated by a series of economic and territorial disputes, notably the contention that Kuwait was overproducing oil and thereby depressing its price, gravely impacting Iraq's war-ravaged economy.[77]

---

[75] MacArthur, John R. "Second Front: Censorship and Propaganda in the Gulf War." University of California Press, 1992.
[76] Heller, Jean (1991-01-06). *"Photos don't show buildup"*. St. Petersburg Times.
[77] Simons, Geoff. "Iraq: From Sumer to Saddam." Macmillan Press Ltd., 1994.

Moreover, Iraq alleged that Kuwait was slant-drilling into its Rumaila oil field, further deepening the rift between the two nations.[78]

Internationally, the invasion was met with almost immediate condemnation. The United Nations Security Council (UNSC) swiftly passed Resolution 660, which demanded the unconditional withdrawal of Iraqi forces from Kuwait. Additionally, the resolution called the invasion a *"breach of international peace and security."*[79]

While the UNSC was unanimous in its condemnation, the sentiment within the United States and its Western allies was more divided about the direct military involvement. Though the invasion was seen as blatant aggression, it was initially unclear whether this Middle Eastern conflict warranted a large-scale U.S. military intervention. The American public, still harboring memories of the long and contentious Vietnam War, was wary of another potential quagmire.[80]

The administration of President George H. W. Bush understood the need to galvanize public and international support if they were to commit ground forces. To this end, a concerted effort was made to paint Saddam Hussein as a threat not just to Kuwait but to the entire Middle Eastern region and, by extension, to the global energy supply. Emphasis was placed on Iraq's alleged military buildup on the Saudi border and the potential threat to the kingdom's vast oil reserves.[81]

---

[78] "Iraq Accuses Kuwait of Oil Overproduction." The New York Times, July 18, 1990.

[79] United Nations Security Council. "Resolution 660 (1990)." Adopted by the Security Council at its 2932nd meeting, August 2, 1990.

[80] Halliday, Fred. "The Gulf War and its Aftermath: First Reflections." International Affairs 67, no. 2 (1991): 223-234.

[81] Bacevich, Andrew J. "American Empire: The Realities and Consequences of U.S. Diplomacy." Harvard University Press, 2002.

To help with public sentiment, a 15-year-old woman named Nayirah testified to the Congressional Human Rights Caucus in October 1990. She stated that while volunteering at Kuwait's al-Adan hospital, Iraqi troops removed babies from their incubators, leaving them *"to die on the cold floor."*[82]

Her first-hand account was so moving there was an immediate outcry across the country to send American forces to Kuwait to rid the country of the Iraqi military[83]. Portions of her testimony were aired that evening on ABC's Nightline and NBC's Nightly News. Representative John Porter commented that never before had he heard such *"brutality and inhumanity and sadism."*[84] Seven U.S. senators cited her testimony in speeches[85] urging Americans to support the war, and President Bush repeated the story on at least ten separate occasions in the following weeks. With the rush of public support, the Bush Administration had the political capital to mobilize ground forces into Kuwait.

The initial conflict aimed at evicting Iraqi troops from Kuwait commenced with an aerial and naval bombardment on January 17, 1991, and persisted for five weeks. The ground assault began on February 24. The coalition forces achieved a decisive victory, swiftly liberating Kuwait and making inroads into Iraqi territory with

---

[82] CSPAN Video Recording (https://www.youtube.com/watch?v=LmfVs3WaE9Y)
[83] Krauss, Clifford (January 12, 1992). *"Congressman Says Girl Was Credible"*. *The New York Times*. (https://www.nytimes.com/1992/01/12/world/congressman-says-girl-was-credible.html)

[84] Brosnan, James W. (October 11, 1990). *"Witnesses describe atrocities by Iraqis"*. *The Commercial Appeal.*
[85] http://www.dougwalton.ca/papers%20in%20pdf/95Pity.pdf

minimal resistance. A mere 100 hours after launching the ground campaign, the coalition halted its advance and declared a ceasefire.

The aftermath of the Gulf War

On March 15, 1991, shortly after Kuwait was liberated, John Martin, an ABC reporter, reported:

> *"patients, including premature babies, did die, when many of Kuwait's nurses and doctors stopped working or fled the country"*[86] and discovered that Iraqi troops *"almost certainly had not stolen hospital incubators and left hundreds of Kuwaiti babies to die."*[87]

In 1992, investigative journalism cast a long shadow on the veracity of 15-year-old Nayirah's claims in her testimony. In an article in The New York Times, John MacArthur revealed that Nayirah was no ordinary Kuwaiti citizen but the daughter of Saud Nasir al-Sabah, Kuwait's ambassador to the United States.[88]

Furthermore, it was revealed that her appearance before Congress was not a spontaneous act of conscience but had been orchestrated by the public relations firm Hill & Knowlton on behalf of a group called Citizens for a Free Kuwait. While Citizens for a Free Kuwait presented itself as a grassroots organization, it was later revealed to be a front for the Kuwaiti government, which had poured millions into

---

[86] Arthur, John (January 6, 1992). *"Remember Nayirah, Witness for Kuwait?"*. The New York Times.

[87] Cohen, Mitchel (December 28, 2002). *"How George Bush, Sr. Sold the 1991 Bombing of Iraq to America"*. CounterPunch.
(https://web.archive.org/web/20110429012920/http://www.counterpunch.org/cohen1228.html)

[88] MacArthur, John R. "Remember Nayirah, Witness for Kuwait?" The New York Times, January 6, 1992.

an extensive PR campaign to galvanize U.S. support against Iraq.[89] Hill & Knowlton, which was the largest PR firm in the world at the time, had been hired by Citizens for a Free Kuwait to craft a compelling narrative that would catalyze American intervention.

In the aftermath of these revelations, there was considerable debate about the role of public relations in shaping foreign policy and the lengths to which governments might go to manipulate public sentiment. The Nayirah incident serves as a cautionary tale about the power of emotion-laden stories in swaying public opinion and the importance of corroborating such accounts with rigorous fact-checking.

Subsequent investigations by Amnesty International, Human Rights Watch/Middle East Watch, and independent journalists would show that testimony by Nayirah was entirely bogus[90] and was nothing more than war propaganda designed to increase support for the Persian Gulf War.

Andrew Whitley, Director of Middle East Watch, stated:
"While it is true that the Iraqis targeted hospitals, there is no truth to the charge which was central to the war propaganda effort that they stole incubators and callously removed babies allowing them to die on the floor. The stories were manufactured from germs of truth by people outside the country who should have known better."

---

[89] Stauber, John and Rampton, Sheldon. "Toxic Sludge Is Good For You: Lies, Damn Lies and the Public Relations Industry." Common Courage Press, 1995.
[90] http://www.counterpunch.org/cohen1228.html

The Kuwaiti government hired Kroll Associates to investigate the statements of Nayirah. During their nine-week investigation, they conducted over 250 interviews, and the findings were published in The Kroll Report. In her interviews with Kroll, Nayirah said that she had only personally witnessed a single baby outside its incubator for "no more than a moment," and that she had *only stopped by [the hospital] for a few minutes.* The fact is she was never a volunteer there.[91]

History has a way of repeating itself, particularly regarding the means employed to justify wars. The manipulation of information and the strategic use of propaganda by the U.S. government and senior officials appear to be recurring themes when analyzing the lead-up to military interventions. The public, whose sons and daughters are called to fight these wars, is owed the unvarnished truth, yet, as seen in the case of the Gulf War and previously in Vietnam, they are too often provided with carefully curated narratives instead.

It raises the pressing question: Why the deception? If a war is necessary, shouldn't the facts alone suffice in rallying the public behind the cause? Why resort to embellished tales or, worse, outright deception? Does the reliance on such tactics indicate an underlying uncertainty about the war's righteousness or strategic importance?

As the author, I am reminded of my earlier reflections in the Vietnam chapter of this book. We are faced with instances where the

---

[91] Ted Rowse, "*Kuwaitgate - killing of Kuwaiti babies by Iraqi soldiers exaggerated,*" *Washington Monthly* (September 1992).
(http://findarticles.com/p/articles/mi_m1316/is_n9_v24/ai_12529902/)

truth appears to be malleable in the hands of those with the power to shape public opinion. The trust citizens place in their elected officials and institutions is sacred and should be treated with the utmost respect. To manipulate or distort truths, especially concerning matters as grave as war, is a betrayal of this trust and a grave disservice to the nation's principles.

The necessity of war is a profound decision that carries with it the weight of lives lost and futures altered. If such a decision is to be made, it must rest on the solid foundation of truth. Anything less is a profound disservice to the soldiers who fight and the citizens who support them. If the genuine reasons cannot withstand public scrutiny, one must ask: Is the war justifiable, or are other undisclosed motives at play?

THE SEPTEMBER 11 ATTACKS (9/11)

The Day of the Attacks

On the clear morning of September 11, 2001, a series of unprecedented and devastating terrorist attacks struck the heart of the United States. Landmarks like the towering World Trade Center in New York City, the symbol of America's military might—the Pentagon in Washington, D.C., and a quiet field in Pennsylvania became the unexpected battlegrounds. By the end of that harrowing day, 2,996 innocent souls had perished, with over 6,000 more bearing physical injuries and countless others emotionally scarred.

I recall that day with startling clarity. It was a time when I was teetering on the cusp of adulthood, having just received my high school diploma. The day started like any other, with the familiar backdrop of a local Tampa, Florida, radio station's morning show, the Bubba the Love Sponge Show on '98 Rock. However, the show's usual humor was replaced by an uncharacteristically somber tone.

As the initial reports of a plane crash into the North Tower of the World Trade Center emerged, many—including myself—were gripped by a mix of shock and disbelief. The idea of an airliner mistakenly hitting such a prominent landmark seemed implausible, yet the horrifying truth suggested otherwise. Many hoped, perhaps naively, that this was nothing more than a tragic accident—a grave miscalculation by a pilot or a technical malfunction. In those initial moments, that assumption, tragic as it was, brought a certain level of solace; it was a tragic mishap, not a malevolent act.

In 2001, the era of round-the-clock news coverage was still in its infancy, but a few 24-hour news stations had begun to make their mark. Fox News was among them. As I tuned in, the nature of the day's events had taken an undeniably darker turn. The second plane, Flight 175, had already sliced into the South Tower of the World Trade Center. The fireball that erupted and the chilling imagery of the impact left no room for ambiguity—this was no accident. This was a deliberate act of terror on an unprecedented scale. The message conveyed to the audience was surreal: *America was under attack*.

I remember being gripped by disbelief and horror as the images played out before our eyes were hauntingly unforgettable. Towering skyscrapers, once symbols of American ambition and achievement, were now cloaked in plumes of smoke. And as the events of the day unfolded, the gravity of the situation became all the more clear.

Television news anchors, trained to remain composed despite the most unsettling events, struggled to make sense of the unfolding tragedy. Their voices, tinged with horror and disbelief, attempted to navigate the situation. The newsroom buzzed with activity, with producers hurriedly patching in experts over the phone to provide some context or insight. The word "*terrorists*" began to permeate the conversation, echoing the sentiments of millions of viewers coming to the same grim conclusion.

At 9:04 a.m., mere minutes after the second plane's impact, Fox News anchor Jon Scott ventured a name that would soon become synonymous with the atrocities of that day: Osama bin Laden. While other groups and motives were discussed, bin Laden quickly emerged as a prime suspect with his history of anti-American sentiment and connections to previous attacks against U.S. interests. As the hours ticked by and more details came into focus, the world would realize the magnitude of the threat posed by extremist ideologies.

In that fateful moment, my understanding of global politics and the complexities of international conflicts was very basic. Like many young adults my age, I was more preoccupied with navigating my transition from adolescence to adulthood, figuring out my plans, and managing life's everyday challenges. The mention of "terrorists" and names like "*Osama bin Laden*" were foreign to me, not just in the literal sense but in my comprehension of the larger global picture.

I recall the overwhelming confusion mixed with a sudden and intense curiosity. Who were these people, and why would they commit such horrendous acts? My knowledge was primarily limited to what I'd learned in school, which hadn't touched on contemporary geopolitics or extremist ideologies in any depth.

For me and countless others, that day was not just a horrifying wake-up call to the immediate tragedy unfolding before our eyes; it was a jarring introduction to a much larger, more interconnected, and more complex world than we'd previously realized. It felt like a curtain had been abruptly pulled back, revealing a stage of players and plots I had been unaware of. The sudden rush of names, groups, and geopolitical dynamics was disorienting, and I scrambled to catch up to understand what had led us to this terrifying moment.

By the time the clock struck 9:15 am, NBC was airing unverified reports from United Airlines that one of their planes had been hijacked before its devastating impact on the South Tower of the World Trade Center. The realization was sinking in: this wasn't just an isolated incident or tragic accident. The United States was under a meticulously planned terrorist attack, and in its wake, the very fabric of American life seemed destined to change forever.

While I was glued to the television, absorbing every detail I could, the familiar sound of my local radio station provided a backdrop to the chilling visuals. I was drawn to the voice of Bubba, the show's host, who had shifted gears from his usual programming to address the unprecedented events unfolding. He was fielding calls from local Tampa Bay residents, trying to piece together any local connections to the national nightmare. Some shared sightings of Air Force One soaring in the skies nearby. Given its proximity to where President George W. Bush was when the tragic news first reached him, these observations didn't seem far-fetched.

Yet, as the minutes turned into hours, other accounts emerged— stories that seemed more complicated to reconcile with reality. Some callers spoke of acquaintances or family members at MacDill Air Force Base, whispering of a close call where Air Force One almost landed. They claimed the aircraft was turned away due to a sudden high alert at the base, given concerns of a direct threat to CENTCOM, especially after the Pentagon was targeted.

The situation was fluid, and the atmosphere was thick with fear, uncertainty, and speculation. As is often the case in moments of crisis, rumors spread quicker than facts, and the line between the two became increasingly blurred. In pre-social media, word of mouth and radio were powerful conduits of information, both confirmed and unverified. The raw emotions of the day, combined with the desire to make sense of the senselessness, led to a flurry of claims, suppositions, and assumptions. Some were rooted in reality, while others were products of anxious minds trying to grapple with an event of such monumental scale and horror.

>**Side bar note**<
Some readers may not be familiar with the Tampa Bay area and may not know that it is also the home of the United States Central Command (CENTCOM) at MacDill Air Force Base and has the primary command responsibility for the Middle East.

I have read conspiracy theories that, while not explicitly mentioning the same radio station I was listening to, they have claimed that crisis actors called in phone calls such as this to disseminate disinformation. These theorists have put forward no compelling evidence, so I do not have a lot of confidence in this analysis. It is more reasonable to believe there was no *"vast conspiracy"* that could account for the phone calls to the radio station. The risks of having additional persons knowing of the disinformation campaign would outweigh any benefit to any conspirators.

The more likely story is that these callers were ordinary people; some may have been on the fringe of sanity, but most were probably ordinary people. They were scared, had bits of information presented to them second or third-hand, and the absence of the entire story allowed their imaginations to fill in the missing pieces into a storyline that made sense to them. Similar to the telephone game you probably played as a child, once the story made it to the end of the line of kids, it was a completely different narrative than initially spoken in the first person.

The remainder of that day, like millions of other Americans, I found myself transfixed by the television screen. The endless stream of expert interviews, the heartbreaking testimonials, the chilling replays, and the gripping live footage seemed impossible to tear away from. As I sat there, absorbing each revelation and every ounce of speculation, I felt a profound mix of shock, grief, and anger. The magnitude of the tragedy was beyond comprehension, and the whys and hows clouded my mind incessantly.

In the immediate aftermath, clarity was hard to come by. The scope of what had transpired was so vast, so unprecedented, that the path to understanding seemed nearly insurmountable. Every new piece of information, every eyewitness account, and every expert analysis only deepened the layers of this intricate and painful narrative. And though the years that followed would shed light on many facets of the events of 9/11, the full scope and depth of the truth remained, in many ways, elusive. Even now, over twenty years later, with countless inquiries, investigations, and testimonies, we've only begun to scratch the surface, with many questions left unanswered.

Driven by a deep-seated sense of duty and patriotism, and like many of my peers, I felt a call to action in the wake of the tragedy. The horrifying events of that September morning stirred something primal within me—a determination to stand up, to serve, and to fight for our country. It was with this spirit, compelled by the events of 9/11 and a desire to defend our nation's values and freedoms, that I made the life-altering decision to enlist in the United States Navy. It was a commitment to serve, to safeguard, and to ensure that the sacrifices of that fateful day would never be forgotten.

Planning and Preparations

The planning and preparations for the 9/11 attacks were intricate and spanned over several years. Khalid Sheikh Mohammed, often referred to as the "*architect*" of the 9/11 attacks, presented the idea to Osama bin Laden as early as 1996, although the plan's roots could have existed earlier.[92] Bin Laden, the head of the militant Islamist organization al-Qaeda, immediately showed interest, and from that point, the wheels were set in motion.

During the next few years, multiple potential targets were deliberated upon. Initially, the planners considered attacking nuclear facilities but decided against it, fearing such an attack could "*get out of hand.*"[93] The ultimate list focused on symbolic targets—sites representing the financial, military, and political power of the U.S. The World Trade Center, an icon of American economic might; the Pentagon, the nerve center of the U.S. military; and a prominent political symbol, the White House or the U.S. Capitol Building, were decided upon.

However, pinning down the final intended target of the plane that crashed in Pennsylvania remains challenging. Flight 93, headed toward Washington, D.C., went down in a field in Shanksville, Pennsylvania, after passengers attempted to retake control of the plane from the hijackers. The exact target—whether the White House or the U.S. Capitol—has been a point of contention. While some evidence, such as the testimony of captured al-Qaeda members, suggests the White House was the intended target, other information

---

[92] National Commission on Terrorist Attacks Upon the United States. "The 9/11 Commission Report." 2004.
[93] National Commission on Terrorist Attacks Upon the United States. "The 9/11 Commission Report." 2004.

points toward the Capitol. For instance, Khalid Sheikh Mohammed initially envisioned attacking the White House and then the Capitol.[94] Given that the passengers on Flight 93 acted before the plane reached D.C., the true destination of the aircraft remains one of the many lingering questions about that day.

Beyond the target selection, meticulous care went into other planning aspects, including choosing the operatives to execute the plan. The 19 hijackers were carefully selected and underwent extensive ideological and practical training in preparation for their mission.[95] This involved not just flight training but also learning to acclimate and blend into American society, understanding how to navigate the U.S. air travel system, and undergoing rigorous physical and mental preparations.

In essence, the 9/11 attacks were not the result of hasty planning but a culmination of years of careful strategy, preparation, and execution. The attacks' scale, precision, and devastation were a stark reflection of this extensive planning.

Financial Support

The official report by the 9/11 Commission stated:
"[the] 9/11 plotters eventually spent somewhere between $400,000 and $500,000 to plan and conduct their attack". They also reported the "origin of the funds remains unknown." and "we have seen no evidence that

---

[94] National Commission on Terrorist Attacks Upon the United States. "The 9/11 Commission Report." 2004.
[95] National Commission on Terrorist Attacks Upon the United States. "The 9/11 Commission Report." 2004.

any foreign government-or foreign government official-
supplied any funding. [96]

The intricate web of finances that funded the operations of extremist networks like al-Qaeda has always been of significant interest, especially in the aftermath of the September 11 attacks. Money is the lifeblood of any major operation, and this was no different for the terror activities coordinated by Osama bin Laden and his associates. In light of this, the efforts to track and unravel these financial networks became a primary objective for U.S. intelligence and law enforcement agencies.

Yassin al-Qadi emerged as a particularly striking figure in this endeavor. Hailing from one of the wealthiest Saudi Arabian families, al-Qadi had already made a name for himself in international business circles, particularly with significant investments in the United States, especially in Chicago. But his alleged connections to extremist networks and Osama bin Laden, in particular, brought him to the forefront of U.S. intelligence concerns post-9/11. The U.S. Department of the Treasury designated him as a Specially Designated Global Terrorist (SDGT) because of these purported links.

It's worth noting that the narrative around al-Qadi was multifaceted. On the one hand, there were allegations of his financing extremist activities. On the other, there were testimonies from various business associates that painted him in a more innocuous light. One such account came from an associate who spoke with *Computerworld*

[96] "National Commission on Terrorist Attacks Upon the United States". 9-11commission.gov. Retrieved 2011-09-11. (http://www.9-11commission.gov/report/911Report_Ch5.htm)

Magazine, a former business associate described his relationship with Yassin al-Qadi:

> *"I met him a few times and talked to him a few times on the telephone. He never talked to me about violence. Instead, he talked very highly of his relationship with [former President] Jimmy Carter and [Vice President] Dick Cheney."*[97]

This individual's interactions with al-Qadi were far removed from the image of a radical financier. Instead, they emphasized al-Qadi's pride in his high-profile connections in the U.S., including mentions of former President Jimmy Carter and Vice President Dick Cheney.[98] Such associations, whether close or distant, raised even more questions about al-Qadi's true involvement and the extent of his ties to both legitimate and illicit entities. The Muwafaq Foundation, which American authorities have confirmed was an arm of bin Laden's terror organization, was headed by Yassin al-Qadi.[99]

However, the complexities surrounding al-Qadi continued. Over time, legal battles would ensue, with al-Qadi vehemently denying any involvement with terrorist organizations and seeking to clear his name on various fronts. This individual's multi-dimensional nature and his story become emblematic of the broader challenges faced in the fight against global terrorism. How does one differentiate between legitimate business dealings and covert financial support for

---

[97] Computerworld Magazine September 3, 2006
(https://web.archive.org/web/20060903074522/http://www.computerworld.com/securityt opics/security/story/0,10801,77682,00.html)
[98] Computerworld Magazine September 3, 2006
[99] "*Wahhabis in the Old Dominion*". Theweeklystandard.com. 2002-04-08.
R(http://www.theweeklystandard.com/Content/Public/Articles/000/000/001/072kqska.as p)

extremist causes? The case of Yassin al-Qadi underscores the magnitude of this dilemma, reflecting the intricate, shadowy nature of global finance and its potential intersections with terror networks.

One of al-Qadi's business holdings was a company named Ptech which supplied high-tech computer systems to the FBI, the Internal Revenue Service, the United States Congress, the United States Army, the Navy, the Air Force, the North Atlantic Treaty Organization, the Federal Aviation Administration (FAA), and the White House. However, he wasn't the only one of interest to investigators at Ptech, multiple other individuals with suspected radical ideologies, including Yacub Mirza and Hussein Ibrahim. The latter served as the Vice President and Chief Scientist of Ptech and was also the vice chairman of a now-defunct investment group called BMI, which the FBI has named as a conduit used by al-Qadi to launder money to Hamas militants.[100]

Former FBI agent Robert Wright Jr. told ABC's, Brian Ross:
> *"September 11th is a direct result of the incompetence of the FBI's International Terrorism Unit", specifically referring to the Bureau's hindering of his investigation into Yasin al-Qadi.[101]*

According to Senator Bob Graham, Chairman of the Senate Intelligence Committee:

---

[100] October 3, 2003, at the Wayback Machine.
(https://web.archive.org/web/20031003130110/http://wbz4.com/iteam/local_story_3431
45212.html)
[101] "*Primetime Investigation FBI Terrorist Cover Up*". Billstclair.com. 2002-12-19. Archived from the original on 2006-02-13. Retrieved 2011-09-1
(https://web.archive.org/web/20060213211232/http://billstclair.com/911timeline/2002/a
bcnews121902b.html)

"Two of the Sept. 11, 2001, hijackers had a support network in the United States that included agents of the Saudi government, and the Bush administration and FBI blocked a congressional investigation into that relationship … a direct line between the terrorists and the government of Saudi Arabia, and an attempted coverup by the Bush administration."[102]

In Graham's book Intelligence Matters, he makes clear that some details of that financial support from Saudi Arabia were part of a block of 27 pages in the 9/11 Commission's final report that were blocked from public release by the administration, despite the pleas of leaders of both parties on the House and Senate intelligence committees.[103]

Mujahideen and the Soviet-Afghan War

To understand the intricate web of events that led to the September 11th attacks, one must delve into the chronicles of the Mujahideen and their role in the Soviet-Afghan War. Moreover, this era marked the inception of Osama bin Laden's journey to infamy.

The Mujahideen, meaning *"those who engage in Jihad,"* were the Afghan rebel groups that banded together to fight the Soviet intervention in Afghanistan. Their resistance was characterized by guerilla warfare tactics, using the mountainous terrain to their

---

[102] Boston Globe, Frank Davies, September 5, 2004
(http://archive.boston.com/news/nation/articles/2004/09/05/911_hijackers_tied_to_saudi
_government_graham_says_in_book/)
[103] *"National Commission on Terrorist Attacks Upon the United States"*. 9-
11commission.gov. (http://www.9-11commission.gov/report/911Report_Ch5.htm)

advantage and capitalizing on local knowledge to wage a war of attrition against the better-equipped Soviet forces.[104]

Spanning just over nine tumultuous years, the Soviet-Afghan War commenced in December 1979 and culminated in February 1989. Fought primarily in Afghanistan's rugged terrains and lofty mountains, the objective was clear: to repulse the Soviet Army and regain Afghan sovereignty.

However, there's more to this conflict than meets the eye. Rooted deeply in the proxy battles of the Cold War, the Afghans weren't left to their own devices against the military might of the Soviet Union. They received substantial backing from an unlikely coalition of the United States, Saudi Arabia, and Pakistan. This support wasn't just moral or verbal; it was tangible and potent, manifesting in state-of-the-art weaponry, vital intelligence, and considerable financial aid.

One of the young Arab men fighting in the Mujahideen was a young Saudi named Osama bin Laden, the son of a wealthy Saudi family that owned multiple successful businesses in the construction and oil industries. While not a supporter of the Western World, he was indifferent to them.

Bin Laden emerged during this period as a significant financier and supporter of the Mujahideen, rallying Arab fighters to join the cause and channeling funds and resources from the wealthy elite of Saudi Arabia. Though not as involved in the actual combat as often portrayed, bin Laden's role in establishing and funding training camps and fostering connections between various militant groups

---

[104] Coll, Steve. "Ghost Wars: The Secret History of the CIA, Afghanistan, and Bin Laden, from the Soviet Invasion to September 10, 2001." Penguin Books, 2005.

cannot be understated. His experience and networking in Afghanistan provided a foundation for his future endeavors, most notably the formation of al-Qaeda.

In essence, the Soviet-Afghan War wasn't merely a regional skirmish. It was emblematic of the larger ideological struggle of the era. The Soviets, representing the Communist bloc, squared off against the Mujahideen, who, bolstered by Western and Islamic allies, became symbols of resistance against communist expansion. The irony lies in the fact that the weapons and training provided by the U.S. to the Mujahideen would later be used against American troops and interests in the subsequent War on Terror.[105]

By the end of the 1980s, the war had drained the Soviets both financially and militarily, culminating in their eventual withdrawal from Afghanistan. Though the Mujahideen celebrated victory, the power vacuum left behind set the stage for years of civil strife and the rise of extremist factions, including the Taliban and al-Qaeda.

It was not until the buildup to the first Iraq War (The Persian Gulf War/Iraq War I) that bin Laden and his fighters went to the Saudis and told them Arabs should protect their lands, not the godless infidels of the West as he thought of the U.S. and their Allies. When the Saudis instead asked for assistance from the U.S., bin Laden saw this as an insult and vowed revenge. Under his leadership, bin Laden formed al-Qaeda.

---

[105] Rashid, Ahmed. "Taliban: Militant Islam, Oil, and Fundamentalism in Central Asia." Yale University Press, 2001.

Prior Intelligence of 9/11 Attacks

The late 1990s and early 2000s were rife with intelligence indicating a looming al-Qaeda threat, yet several pieces of this jigsaw puzzle went unnoticed or unheeded.

One critical interception took place in late 1999. The National Security Agency (NSA), the U.S. premier signals intelligence body, picked up a phone call hinting at an impending meeting. The call participants mentioned a rendezvous between Walid bin Attash, known as "*Khallad*," and Khalid al-Mihdhar. This meeting was set for Kuala Lumpur, Malaysia, and was to include other al-Qaeda affiliates, Nawaf al-Hazmi and Abu Bara al-Yemeni.

While the NSA quickly discerned that "*something nefarious might be afoot*,"[106] strangely, the dots were not connected. The agency should have escalated or acted decisively, even with this tangible lead pointing towards potential malevolent intent.

Parallelly, the Central Intelligence Agency (CIA) was in possession of its own set of crucial data. Saudi intelligence had flagged Mihdhar and Hazmi as bona fide al-Qaeda operatives to the CIA. This warning should have, under regular circumstances, set off alarm bells. Moreover, in a covert operation, a CIA team had infiltrated Mihdhar's hotel room in Dubai. What they unearthed was startling: Mihdhar was equipped with a U.S. visa. This discovery meant that he had legal clearance to enter American soil.

---

[106] Wright, Lawrence (2006), *The Looming Tower: Al-Qaeda and the Road to 9/11*, Knopf, ISBN 978-0-375-41486-2

Fast forward to the fateful day of September 11, 2001, two of these very names — al-Mihdhar and al-Hazmi — would be indelibly etched into the annals of infamy. They were among the group that hijacked American Airlines Flight 77, ruthlessly guiding it to its doom at the Pentagon. As for Abu Bara al Yemeni, he too was slated to play a direct role in this dreadful scheme. However, his inability to secure a U.S. visa was an inadvertent barrier, saving countless lives.

This backdrop of missed opportunities, fragmented intelligence, and bureaucratic stagnation set the stage for the events of 9/11. The tragedy emphasizes the critical need for fluid intelligence sharing, both on an international scale and between various departments.[107]

In another glaring oversight, Malaysian intelligence had diligently tracked the conspiratorial meeting between these men. Recognizing the potential implications, they relayed their findings — including the critical information that the al-Qaeda associates were en route to Bangkok — to the CIA. Yet, this intelligence, vital in retrospect, became ensnared in a web of inter-agency politics and compartmentalization.

An FBI liaison stationed at Alec, the CIA's dedicated unit for tracking Osama bin Laden and al-Qaeda, sensed the magnitude of the situation. This individual, appreciating the gravity of the intercepted information, sought to bridge the communication gap by informing the FBI. However, this effort was met with rebuff and bureaucracy. The liaison was curtly informed, "*This is not a matter for*

---

[107] National Commission on Terrorist Attacks Upon the United States. "The 9/11 Commission Report." W. W. Norton & Company, 2004.

the FBI."[108] Such decisions to withhold intelligence, coupled with a series of missed opportunities, contributed to the tragic failure to preempt the horrors of 9/11.

By late June, senior counter-terrorism official Richard Clarke and CIA director George Tenet were *"convinced that a major series of attacks was about to come,"* although the CIA believed that the attacks would likely occur in Saudi Arabia or Israel.[109] Clarke would later write that:

> *"Somewhere in CIA there was information that two known al-Qaeda terrorists had come into the United States... in [the] FBI there was information that strange things had been going on at flight schools in the United States... They had specific information about individual terrorists... None of that information got to me or the White House.*"[110]

In late 1999 SOCOM (Special Operations Command) began a highly classified data-mining operation named Able Danger. By January 2000, the team had identified an al-Qaeda terrorist cell in Brooklyn and identified a man named Atta as a member.[111] On at least three separate occasions in mid-2000, Captain Phillpot asked his superiors for permission to read the FBI into the investigation. Military lawyers denied each request due to claims the data they were

---

[108] Wright, Lawrence (2006), *The Looming Tower: Al-Qaeda and the Road to 9/11*, Knopf, ISBN 978-0-375-41486-2 pp. 310–312.

[109] Wright, Lawrence (2006), *The Looming Tower: Al-Qaeda and the Road to 9/11*, Knopf, ISBN 978-0-375-41486-2 pp. 235–236

[110] Wright, Lawrence (2006), *The Looming Tower: Al-Qaeda and the Road to 9/11*, Knopf, ISBN 978-0-375-41486-2 pp. 242–243

[111] Lt. Col. Shaffer's Written Testimony: *Able Danger and the 9/11 Attacks*, Armed Services Committee, US House of Representatives, February 15, 2006

harvesting may not be legal to disclose. This left the FBI unaware of the cell in Brooklyn.[112]

Just when this information was about to gain a public platform during a 2005 Senate hearing, a gag order was imposed on critical members of the Able Danger team. This order, issued by Secretary of Defense Donald Rumsfeld, effectively muzzled these individuals from revealing potentially game-changing intelligence.[113] Thomas Kean and Lee Hamilton, co-chairs of the 9/11 Commission both stated that *Able Danger* was not "*historically significant.*"[114]

Erik Kleinsmith, who held a significant position as the Chief of Intelligence of the Land Information Warfare Activity, shed some light on the ambiguity of the situation. His testimony was revealing, albeit limited. Kleinsmith detailed how he was instructed to destroy a staggering 2.5 terabytes of data related to Able Danger in either May or June of 2000.[115] This order came just over a year before the devastating 9/11 attacks.

The decision to erase such a vast amount of data naturally raises suspicions. Was this deletion a deliberate attempt to conceal knowledge of an imminent attack? Did certain echelons of power have foreknowledge they wished to suppress? Alternatively, was this a routine data purge, an unfortunate coincidence devoid of malevolent intent?

---

[112] Lt. Col. Shaffer's Written Testimony: *Able Danger and the 9/11 Attacks*, Armed Services Committee, US House of Representatives, February 15, 2006
[113] Senator Joe Biden's comment during September 21, 2005, Senate Hearing
[114] Kean-Hamilton Statement on Able Danger, August 12 2005
[115] Able Danger and Intelligence Information Sharing, Hearing before the Committee on the Judiciary, United States Senate, September 21, 2005.
(https://www.gpo.gov/fdsys/pkg/CHRG-109shrg25409/html/CHRG-109shrg25409.htm)

Given the strategic importance of the information — potentially pointing to a significant terrorist threat on U.S. soil — the decision to destroy it is perplexing, to say the least. It's challenging to rationalize why SOCOM, or any branch of U.S. intelligence, would dismiss and delete data that could avert a national catastrophe, regardless of their confidence level in its veracity[116].

Such actions and official attempts to stifle discourse only amplify doubts and foster speculation. These lingering questions must be addressed in the quest for transparency and understanding.

In June 2001, a "*high-placed member of a U.S. intelligence agency*" told BBC reporter Greg Palast that "*after the [2000] elections, the agencies were told to 'back off' investigating the bin Laden family and Saudi royals.*"[117]

In July, a Phoenix-based FBI agent, Kenneth Williams, sent a message to FBI headquarters, Alec Station, and to FBI agents in New York, alerting them to "*the possibility of a coordinated effort by Osama bin Laden to send students to the United States to attend civil aviation universities and colleges.*"[118]

On July 10, Richard Blee, head of CIA's al Qaeda unit, requested an emergency meeting with national security advisor Condoleezza Rice and informed her:

---

[116] Thompson, Mark. "The Rise and Fall of Able Danger: A Familiar Defense Department Refrain." Time Magazine, August 17, 2005.
[117] "Greg Palast report transcript - 6/11/01". *BBC News*. November 8, 2001. Retrieved May 22, 2010. (http://news.bbc.co.uk/1/hi/events/newsnight/1645527.stm)
[118] Wright, Lawrence (2006), *The Looming Tower: Al-Qaeda and the Road to 9/11*, Knopf, ISBN 978-0-375-41486-2 pp. 350

"There will be significant terrorist attacks against the United States in the coming weeks or months. The attacks will be spectacular. They may be multiple."[119]

Blee recommended to Rice:
"Getting into the Afghan sanctuary, launching a paramilitary operation, creating a bridge with Uzbekistan."[120]

On August 6, the CIA's Presidential Daily Brief, designated "For the President Only", was entitled *"Bin Ladin [Laden] Determined to Strike in U.S."* The memo noted that *"The FBI information ... indicates patterns of suspicious activity in this country consistent with preparations for hijackings or other types of attacks."*[121]

The saga of Zacarias Moussaoui is a clear example of intelligence oversight and the challenges agencies face in preventing terror attacks. It underscores the importance of proactive intelligence sharing and the potentially devastating consequences of missed signals.

In the weeks leading up to 9/11, an astute Minnesota flight school became alarmed by Moussaoui's behavior, particularly his inclination to ask questions that were deemed *"out of the ordinary."* Such inquiries raised red flags for the school's administrators, prompting them to alert the FBI promptly.[122] On investigation, the

---

[119] Snippet from the film *The Spymasters: CIA in the Crosshairs*
[120] Chris Whipple, *The Attacks Will be Spectacular*, Politico, November 12, 2015
[121] "THE OSAMA BIN LADEN FILE: National Security Archive Electronic Briefing Book No. 343". *The National Security Archive*. The National Security Archive. Retrieved March 14, 2016.
(http://nsarchive.gwu.edu/NSAEBB/NSAEBB343/)
[122] Eggen, Dan. "FBI Knew Terror Suspect's Flight School Plans." The Washington Post, May 18, 2002.

FBI discovered Moussaoui's radical ties and his recent trips to Pakistan, adding layers of suspicion.

Despite these warning signs, bureaucratic hurdles impeded deeper investigations. The INS apprehended Moussaoui for overstaying his visa; however, the FBI was hamstrung by legal constraints. The decision by the FBI headquarters to decline a request to search Moussaoui's laptop, citing a lack of probable cause, was a fateful one.[123] It's possible that the laptop contained crucial evidence or leads about the looming attacks.

Although Moussaoui was in custody on an immigration violation when the attacks occurred, his eventual indictment post-9/11 was substantial. He was charged on multiple counts, including conspiring to commit acts of terrorism and to use weapons of mass destruction; his indictment painted a portrait of a man deeply entrenched in the plot against the U.S.[124]

The Moussaoui episode, in retrospect, serves as a case study of the importance of swift intelligence action, the need to lower bureaucratic impediments in the face of credible threats, and the imperative of inter-agency communication.

The weeks and months leading up to the 9/11 attacks exposed an intricate web of missed signals, ignored leads, and institutional roadblocks within and between U.S. intelligence and law enforcement agencies. In this period, it wasn't necessarily the absence

---

[123] Lichtblau, Eric. "Before 9/11, Unshared Clues and Unshaped Policy." The New York Times, June 4, 2002.

[124] United States vs. Zacarias Moussaoui, Criminal No. 01-455-A. Indictment. U.S. District Court for the Eastern District of Virginia, 2001.

of information that led to the catastrophe but rather the inability of these agencies to piece together the jigsaw of intelligence into a coherent and actionable picture.

Multiple reports have highlighted how international intelligence communities had flagged Osama bin Laden's intentions of orchestrating a significant attack, possibly within the U.S. For instance, certain memos discussed al-Qaeda operatives' plans to utilize airplanes as missiles, targeting prominent landmarks. Moreover, there were noticeable red flags, like al-Qaeda members registering in U.S. flight schools.[125]

Yet, one of the most profound obstacles in this pre-9/11 intelligence landscape was the *"wall"* that separated criminal investigations from intelligence operations. This division often acted as an impediment, hindering the free flow of critical information between agencies, such as the CIA and the FBI.[126]

Though conspiracy theories surrounding 9/11 are myriad and persistent, the evidence does not suggest a grand scheme within the U.S. government to permit the attack knowingly. However, certain individuals may need to pay more attention to critical information rather than focus on their pursuit of personal or departmental ambitions. It's a reflection, perhaps, of bureaucratic self-interest overriding national security imperatives. But predominantly, the underlying malaise was the institutional culture of rivalry and possession, where departments were protective of their 'turfs' and

---

[125] Shenon, Philip. "The Commission: The Uncensored History of the 9/11 Investigation." Twelve, 2008.
[126] Zegart, Amy B. "Spying Blind: The CIA, the FBI, and the Origins of 9/11." Princeton University Press, 2009.

hesitant to share information. More than any other factor, this insular mindset may have inadvertently paved the way for one of the darkest days in American history.[127]

The lessons from 9/11 underscore the imperatives of inter-agency collaboration, trust, and the prioritization of national security over departmental politics.

WTC Tower Collapse

I will not spend much time covering the World Trade Center towers collapse in this book. You might be wondering why. The answer to this question is both simple and complex at the same time. Allow me to explain.

The collapse of the Twin Towers is one of the most scrutinized events in modern history. Multiple theories, investigations, and analyses have attempted to explain the precise causes and mechanics behind the collapse.

Among the many firsthand accounts from that tragic day, the statements and experiences of those directly at Ground Zero, particularly members of the FDNY and other first responders, provide invaluable insights into the unfolding catastrophe.

Father John Delendick, a chaplain for the FDNY, was on the scene that fateful day and witnessed the horrific events firsthand. According to some accounts, after observing the explosion at the top of the South Tower, Father Delendick sought clarity on the nature

---

[127] Gellman, Barton. "Breakdown: How America's Intelligence Failures Led to September 11." Penguin, 2002.

of the explosion. In his quest for answers, he spoke with FDNY Chief Ray Downey, an esteemed department figure renowned for his expertise in building collapses.

Downey's response to Delendick's query was indeed thought-provoking. He mentioned that the explosion seemed too symmetrical to be solely the result of burning jet fuel and suggested the possibility of bombs being present in the building.[128] Such a statement from an expert like Downey was bound to be taken seriously.

However, it's crucial to note that the initial chaos and shock of the situation might have led many to try to make sense of the unimaginable scene unfolding before them, possibly leading to speculative explanations in the immediate aftermath.

The 9/11 Commission Report used the term *"pancake collapse"* to describe the failure of the floor systems surrounding the towers' central core of the towers.[129] This term suggests that the floors fell one on top of the other successively. It's essential, however, to contextualize this statement. The use of *"pancake collapse"* simplifies the dynamics of the collapse. In reality, the process was more multifaceted.

The core of the Twin Towers consisted of 47 interconnected steel columns, providing crucial vertical support. While the 9/11 Commission Report noted the hollow nature of this core, it did not explicitly deny the existence of these core columns. Instead, it appears

---

[128] "Ground Zero 360." National September 11 Memorial & Museum.
[129] "The 9/11 Commission Report: Final Report of the National Commission on Terrorist Attacks Upon the United States." Official Government Edition, 2004.

to have overlooked their significance in the overall structural integrity of the buildings.

The National Institute of Standards and Technology (NIST) conducted a comprehensive study, separate from the 9/11 Commission Report, to explain the towers' collapse. According to NIST, the towers' design was a significant factor in their vulnerability. When the planes struck, they dislodged the fireproofing, exposing the steel to extreme heat. This caused the trusses to fail, pulling the perimeter columns inward and eventually collapse.[130]

While the term *"pancake collapse"* might be an oversimplification, it's just one perspective of the events that transpired. Various experts and institutions have provided a plethora of research into the collapse, attempting to piece together the most accurate account. Still, the debate around the specifics of the towers' collapse remains controversial and is a testament to the lingering emotions and questions surrounding the tragic events of that day.

The official investigation concluded that the buildings collapsed due to the impacts of the planes and the fires that resulted from them.[131] I strongly disagree with the narrative and explanation by NIST; however, I concede that I am not a structural engineer and cannot speak intelligently on this subject. NIST states, in part, that the unique construction of the Twin Towers deviated from standard

---

[130] National Institute of Standards and Technology (NIST). "Final Report on the Collapse of the World Trade Center Towers." 2005.
[131] Lipton, Eric (August 22, 2008). *"Fire, Not Explosives, Felled 3rd Tower on 9/11, Report Says"*. *The New York Times*. Archived from the original on March 9, 2011. (https://web.archive.org/web/20110309235941/http://www.nytimes.com/2008/08/22/nyregion/22wtccnd.html)

construction practices at the time by bringing the structural support that would typically be found throughout a specific floor and relocating them to the center and the outside walls.

A prominent group that has consistently voiced skepticism about the official explanation for the towers' collapse is "Architects & Engineers for 9/11 Truth." Founded by Richard Gage, a seasoned architect from the San Francisco Bay Area, this non-profit organization has become a rallying point for professionals in the architecture and engineering fields who question the mainstream narrative surrounding the 9/11 attacks.

Gage, supported by his coalition of professionals, raises serious doubts about the conventional understanding that the towers' collapse was solely due to the planes' impact and the subsequent fires.[132] Instead, *Architects & Engineers for 9/11 Truth* posits that substantial evidence indicates the possibility of a controlled demolition being involved in the collapse of the World Trade Center buildings.[133]

Gage has repeatedly mentioned that a significant amount of evidence points toward explosive demolition. He cites the collapse's symmetrical nature, molten steel's presence, and the discovery of what some claim to be thermite residues in the debris, among other factors, as indicative of a controlled demolition.[134]

---

[132] Beam, Christopher (April 8, 2009). "*Heated Controversy*". *Slate*.
(https://web.archive.org/web/20090518074848/http://www.slate.com/id/2215703)
[133] Beyond Misinformation: What Science Says About the Destruction of World Trade Center Buildings 1, 2, and 7." Architects & Engineers for 9/11 Truth. 2015.
[134] Gage, Richard. "Blueprint for Truth – The Architecture of Destruction." Architects & Engineers for 9/11 Truth. 2008.

It is worth noting, however, that while Gage and his organization have garnered support from some professionals and a segment of the public, the broader scientific and engineering community has primarily upheld the conclusions drawn by NIST. Still, groups like "*Architects & Engineers for 9/11 Truth*" highlight the ongoing debates and complexities surrounding the understanding of the tragic events of 9/11.

Gage criticized NIST for not having investigated the complete sequence of the collapse of the World Trade Center towers,[135] and claims that "*the official explanation of the total destruction of the World Trade Center skyscrapers has explicitly failed to address the massive evidence for explosive demolition.*"[136]

He further argues that the buildings of the World Trade Center could not have collapsed at the speed that has been observed without first tearing apart several columns of their structures with the help of explosives.[137]

He maintains that the "*sudden and spontaneous*" collapse of the towers would have been impossible without a controlled demolition and that pools of molten iron found in the debris of the buildings were evidence of the existence of the explosive thermite.[138]

---

[135] Potocki, P. Joseph (August 27, 2008). "*Down the 9-11 Rabbit Hole*". *Bohemian*. (https://web.archive.org/web/20090604091229/http://www.bohemian.com/bohemian/08.27.08/cover-911.truth-0835.html)

[136] Beam, Alex (Jan 14, 2008). "*The truth is out there . . . Isn't it?*". *The Boston Globe*. (https://web.archive.org/web/20090603232630/http://www.boston.com/ae/tv/articles/2008/01/14/the_truth_is_out_there____isnt_it)

[137] Lachapelle, Judith (May 1, 2010). "*Le "mystère" de la Tour 7*". *La Presse*. (https://web.archive.org/web/20100503003859/http://www.cyberpresse.ca/international/en-vedette/201005/01/01-4276172-le-mystere-de-la-tour-7.php)

[138] "*Un arquitecto estadounidense presenta en Madrid su versión alternativa al 11-S*". Telecinco. November 8, 2008. El ingeniero estructural del complejo WTC, advierte Gage,

Additional experts conclude similar findings, including physicist Steven Jones: *"evidence points overwhelmingly to the conclusion that all three buildings were destroyed by controlled demolition."*[139]

As an outsider to the fields of structural engineering and controlled demolition, it's challenging to fully grasp the intricate details and nuances of the arguments surrounding the collapse of the World Trade Center towers. However, from a layperson's perspective, the explanations presented by groups such as *"Architects & Engineers for 9/11 Truth"* can sometimes seem more straightforward and plausible. When presented cohesively, their arguments and evidence challenge the conventional understanding of the events that transpired on that fateful day.

However, the human factor is a significant challenge to the controlled demolition theory. For such an operation requiring the covert placement of explosives throughout the towers without detection, the number of individuals needed to be involved would be considerable. This isn't just about the people placing the explosives, but those involved in the planning, acquisition of materials, timing, and execution of such a massive covert operation. The logistics behind such an enormous undertaking would be immense.

---

llama la atención sobre la piscina de magma que ardió durante semanas tras el atentado. Una evidencia que demuestra la existencia del agente incendiario 'Thermite', empleado para "fundir y cortar columnas y vigas de acero.
(http://www.telecinco.es/informativos/internacional/noticia/51928/Un+arquitecto+estado unidense+presenta+su+version+alternativa+al+11S+en+Madrid)
[139] Steven Jones, Robert Korol, Anthony Szamboti, and Ted Walter, *15 Years Later: On the Physics of High-rise Building Collapses,* Europhysics News, July-August 2016: 22-26

Moreover, in the decades since the attacks, there hasn't been any substantial whistleblowing or leaks from individuals associated with such an alleged operation. It's hard to imagine that in a conspiracy of this magnitude, no one involved would come forward with concrete evidence or undergo a crisis of conscience. The sheer number of individuals who would have to keep such a monumental secret presents a significant barrier to the controlled demolition theory's credibility.

To many, including myself, while the technical arguments for controlled demolition may seem convincing on the surface, this human element and the near-impossible requirement for universal secrecy raise doubts about its validity. The convergence of human behavior, ethics, and the potential for information leaks makes it a challenging narrative to embrace fully.

WTC Building 7 Collapse

While the Twin Towers collapse was undeniably tragic, another aspect of 9/11 that intrigues me deeply on a purely academic level is the fall of WTC Building 7. Unlike the towers, this building wasn't struck by a plane, and it endured less damage than several other structures in the WTC complex when the towers crumbled – yet those other buildings remained standing. According to NIST, uncontrolled fires throughout the day were the primary cause of Building 7's collapse. They emphasized that stored diesel fuel wasn't a significant factor, and neither was the structural impact from the falling Twin Towers.[140]

---

[140] *"Questions and Answers about the NIST WTC 7 Investigation"*. NIST. (https://www.nist.gov/public_affairs/factsheet/wtc_qa_082108.cfm)

Throughout modern history, only three steel-framed structures have collapsed primarily due to fires,[141] and all three were part of the World Trade Center complex on 9/11. Unlike the Towers, Building 7 had a standard steel frame construction without any unusual structural designs that might explain its collapse. While one might argue — however improbable — that the unique design of the Twin Towers contributed to their fall, such an argument cannot be made for Building 7. It remains an anomaly that such a conventionally designed building collapsed in this manner.

To support its position, Architects & Engineers for 9/11 Truth points to the "*free fall*" acceleration of Building 7 during part of the collapse,[142] to "*lateral ejection of steel,*" and to "*mid-air pulverization of concrete.*"[143]

> *"Among the most egregious examples is the explanation for the collapse of WTC 7 as an elaborate sequence of unlikely events culminating the almost symmetrical total collapse of a steel frame building into its own footprint at free-fall acceleration."[144]*

[141] "*Questions and Answers about the NIST WTC 7 Investigation*". NIST. (https://www.nist.gov/public_affairs/factsheet/wtc_qa_082108.cfm)
[142] Gage, Richard; Roberts, Gregg; Chandler, David. "*Conspiracy theory or hidden truth? The 9/11 enigmas.*" *World Architecture News.* (http://www.worldarchitecturenews.com/index.php?fuseaction=wanappln.commentview& comment_id=158)
[143] Beam, Christopher (April 8, 2009). "*Heated Controversy*". *Slate.* (https://web.archive.org/web/20090518074848/http://www.slate.com/id/2215703)
[144] *A Nation Challenged: The Site, Engineers Half a Culprit in the Strange Collapse of 7 World Trade Center: Diesel Fuel*, New York Times, November 29, 2001.

NIST claims no one, including bystanders, media, NYPD, or NYFD, reported hearing or seeing explosions before, during, or after the attacks on the towers.[145] This is a blatant lie as over 100 NYFD firefighters reported hearing sounds of explosions,[146] as did countless members of the media, NYPD, and WTC employees.[147]

NIST claims the towers fell directly from the damage sustained by the impact of the jet aircraft and the subsequent fires that burned and that no explosives were needed nor used.[148] The problem with this assessment by NIST is the towers were specifically engineered to handle impacts from aircraft of similar size[149] due to the proximity to nearby Newark Liberty International Airport and LaGuardia Airport. This also ignores the fact that jet fuel, nor office fires that only reached 1,800 degrees Fahrenheit at the maximum, can generate enough heat to melt steel, which requires temperatures greater than 2,700 degrees Fahrenheit.[150]

NSIT initially claimed WTC 7 collapsed due to a raging inferno fed by massive storage tanks filled with diesel fuel.[151] However, after some deeper investigation, even NSIT realized this claim's absurdity

[145] NIST, *Answers to Frequently Asked Questions*, August 30, 2006, Question #2
[146] Graeme MacQueen, *118 Witnesses: The Firefighters' Testimony to Explosions in the Twin Towers*, the Journal of 9/11 Studies, Vol 2, August 2006, pg 47-106.
[147] David Ray Griffin, *Explosive Testimony: Revelations about the Twin Towers in the 9/11 Oral Histories*, 911Truth.org, January 18, 2006.
[148] NIST NCSTAR 1, Final Report on the Collapse of the World Trade Center Towers, September 2005: xxxviii
[149] Federal Emergency Management Agency (2002), *World Trade Center Building Performance Study: Data Collection, Preliminary Observations, and Recommendations.*
[150] *Twin Tower Fires Not Hot Enough to Melt or Weaken Steel!*, YouTube: 9/11 Truth Videos.
[151] FEMA, *World Trade Center Building Performance Study*, Chapter 5, Section 6.2, "Probable Collapse Sequence".

and removed the diesel fuel claim, stating nothing more than "*the first known instance of the total collapse of a tall building primarily due to fires.*"[152] This is about as close to a direct admission that their claims are total BS, saying that they cannot find any other steel frame structure in history to ever fail in this way.

In Summary

After all of my research, it is clear there is more to the WTC attack and collapse than the official story is able to explain. It is highly likely that explosives were used within the Twin Towers and Building 7. The questions to ask now are: how did the explosives get in the building, and why were they placed there? Who benefited from all three buildings collapsing?

We were told that Osama bin Laden and Al-Qaeda are to blame for the attacks[153], yet the FBI did not list 9/11 as one of his wanted crimes.[154] When pressed, the FBI stated they had "*no hard evidence*" that connected bin Laden to the attacks.[155] Of course, this could be due to the fact that most of the evidence was classified and could not be declassified for a criminal conviction, which would preclude the FBI from including those charges.

Putting the FBI aside for the moment, if we accept that he was responsible for planning the attack, how did they get explosives into

---

[152] NIST NCSTAR 1A, *Final Report on the Collapse of World Trade Center Building 7,* November 2008

[153] *The 9/11 Commission Report, p 302*

[154] Federal Bureau of Investigations, *Most Wanted Terrorists,* (http://web.archive.org/web/2010101161759/http://www.fbi.gov/wanted/topten/usama-bin-laden)

[155] Ed Haas, *FBI says: ' No Hard Evidence Connecting Bin Laden to 9/11',* (http://web.archive.org/web/20090207113442/www.teamliberty.net/id267.html)

the buildings? If they planned on using explosives to destroy the buildings, why waste time with the planes? Why not just rig the explosives and blow up the buildings? Why all the theatrics with crashing planes? Did they want the collapses on live TV to have a larger emotional impact? While interesting to postulate, these later questions are of less importance than the first question I proposed. How did they get these explosives into the buildings?

A few conspiracy theories state that President Bush's brother, Marvin Bush,[156] was the owner/principal of the company Securacom, which provided security for WTC, United Airlines, and Dulles International Airport. While an interesting theory, I could not find any concrete evidence of these claims short of conspiracy theory websites quoting each other. The rest of the information I found refused these claims as misleading or completely false.[157]

Larry Silverstein's acquisition of the World Trade Center lease not long before the 9/11 attacks certainly raised eyebrows among conspiracy theorists. In July 2001, just weeks before the terrorist attacks, Silverstein Properties, in partnership with Westfield America, secured a 99-year lease for the Twin Towers and other parts of the complex, paying a total of $3.2 billion.[158] While the upfront payment was significantly less, the lease committed them to regular rent payments to the Port Authority of New York and New Jersey.

[156] 9/11 Conspiracy Theories." RationalWiki.
https://rationalwiki.org/wiki/9/11_conspiracy_theories.
[157] "The Debunker's Guide to 9/11 Conspiracy Theories." Popular Mechanics, 7 Feb. 2005. https://www.popularmechanics.com/military/a6384/debunking-911-myths-world-trade-center/
[158] Rebuilding The World Trade Center: A Timeline." CNN Money. 2013. http://money.cnn.com/interactive/news/economy/rebuilding-world-trade-center/.

The fact that Silverstein took out an insurance policy that specifically covered acts of terrorism only fueled the conspiracy theories.[159] After the attacks, Silverstein sought compensation for the loss of the buildings, arguing that the two plane crashes should be considered separate events, which would entitle him to double the policy limits. After a drawn-out legal battle, he was awarded $4.55 billion, less than the $7 billion he had initially sought but still a significant amount.[160]

Another element that theorists have pointed out is Silverstein's comment in a PBS documentary where he recalls discussing Building 7 and states they decided to *"pull it,"* a term some claim refers to controlled demolition.[161] However, supporters of Silverstein and many experts interpret his statement to mean evacuating firefighters and first responders from the area, not demolishing the building.

Then there's the asbestos issue. The Twin Towers were constructed at a time when asbestos was commonly used as a fire retardant. It has been estimated that removing the asbestos from the towers would have been a costly venture, potentially upwards of $1 billion. Theorists argue that the towers' destruction conveniently saved Silverstein this immense cost, further insinuating a potential motive for foul play.

---

[159] Gravois, John. "Debunking The 9/11 Myths: Special Report." Popular Mechanics. 2005. https://www.popularmechanics.com/military/a6384/debunking-911-myths-world-trade-center/.
[160] Bagli, Charles V. "Trade Center's Owner Settles With Its Insurers." The New York Times. 2007. https://www.nytimes.com/2007/05/24/nyregion/24insure.html.
[161] America Rebuilds II: Return to Ground Zero." PBS. 2003. https://www.pbs.org/americarebuilds2/timeline/timeline.html.

However, these conspiracy theories are widely debunked by experts and have been challenged on many fronts. For one, orchestrating such a plot would require the collusion of an inconceivably vast number of people. Additionally, there's no direct evidence linking Silverstein or any of his associates to the attacks. Critics of the conspiracy theory suggest it's a simplistic and speculative way of looking at a deeply tragic and complex event.

The intrigue doesn't end with Silverstein and the financial dimensions of the attacks. In the wake of the tragedy, testimonies from individuals working in the World Trade Center added another layer to the conspiratorial claims. These statements focused on alleged unusual activities in the towers leading up to September 11.

For instance, there were reports of "*power downs*" and upgrades to the fire and security systems[162] of the buildings in the weeks preceding the attacks. According to some theories, such activities could have allowed explosives or other sabotage equipment to be covertly installed in the towers. Skeptics of these claims, however, argue that regular maintenance and updates are standard procedure for buildings of this size and importance and should not be considered suspicious.

One testimony that gained particular traction in the conspiracy theory community came from Daria Coard, a guard at the North Tower. She reported that there was heightened security two weeks before the attacks, with bomb-sniffing dogs working extended 12-hour shifts due to increased phone threats targeting the World Trade

---

[162] Curtis Taylor, Newsday, September 12, 2001
(http://web.archive.org/web/20050127000302/http:/www.nynewsday.com/news/local/ma nhattan/wtc/ny-nyaler122362178sep12,0,6794009.story)

Center. What struck many as odd was Coard's claim that on September 6, 2001, just five days before the attacks, the bomb-sniffing dogs were suddenly withdrawn.[163]

These testimonies, while intriguing, are often used selectively by conspiracy theorists to craft a narrative that may not consider the full context. It's essential to approach these claims critically, ensuring they are not isolated from other evidence or events. Nevertheless, combining these reports with previous suspicions creates a mosaic of doubt for some, even if mainstream narratives and expert analyses have largely debunked them.

Once again if we are able to take these theories on their face value, it would be very suspicious and would provide some avenue for how the explosives entered the building. Unfortunately, we may be unable to verify exactly how and by whom the explosives were placed. All we know for sure is: they were placed there and detonated by someone.

I postulate that it is possible senior members of U.S. intelligence agencies up to and including the Bush administration wanted to allow this attack to take place, and they either turned a blind eye to the evidence or actively participated in guaranteeing a successful outcome for this terrorist operation. Who personally or what country would benefit most from a war in the Middle East? Or is it possible a third-party country such as Saudi Arabia or Israel, also wanting the U.S. to enter into a prolonged Middle Eastern war, covertly rigged the buildings with explosives and allowed the al-Qaeda plot to take place in hopes of using bin Laden as a scapegoat for the blame?

---

[163] WTC Workers Recall Bomb Sniffing Dogs' Removal, Unusual Activities Before 9/11." The Guardian. 2001.
https://www.theguardian.com/world/2001/sep/25/september11.usa2.

We know from the *Prior Intelligence* section above that individuals privy to the entire 9/11 Commission Report claim there was ample evidence to blame Saudi Arabia for their financial support; however, for international diplomacy, it was classified and not presented in the report's public release.

To keep this manuscript concise and to the point of my overarching thesis on the corruption that has hijacked America, I will keep the analysis of WTC short. I invite readers to read the documents on www.ae911truth.org for more details.

Additional Reading:

- An excellent timeline of events can be found at https://en.wikipedia.org/wiki/Timeline_for_the_day_of_the_September_11_attacks
- Architects & Engineers for 9/11 Truth: www.ae911truth.org
- Video Summary of Building 7 collapse: https://www.ae911truth.org/evidence/videos/video/2-architects-and-engineers-solving-the-mystery-of-building-7
- Pilots for 9/11 Truth: www.pilotsfor911truth.org

OPERATIONS ENDURING FREEDOM AND IRAQI FREEDOM

In the wake of the Soviet withdrawal from Afghanistan, the country was thrust into a turbulent power vacuum.[164] Various factions vied for control, and amidst this chaos, the nation's political landscape began to reshape. A significant player during this period was the Northern Alliance, a conglomerate of various ethnic and regional groups. Its leader, Abdur Rab Rasool Sayyaf, believed that in the strategic game of power politics, hosting Osama bin Laden—already a well-known figure for his anti-Western sentiments and activities[165]—might provide some leverage against the rising Taliban forces.

Sayyaf's hopes, however, backfired. Rather than helping to contain the Taliban, bin Laden's arrival facilitated a formidable alliance between his al-Qaeda network and the Taliban under the leadership of Mullah Omar.[166] This alliance not only expedited the Taliban's rise to power but also integrated al-Qaeda's extremist ideologies with the Taliban's own stringent interpretation of Sharia law.[167] The result was a regime that implemented a puritanical version of Islamic governance. Cultural activities that were once part and parcel of Afghan life, like music, television, and sports, were vehemently prohibited. Punishments for perceived transgressions

---

[164] Coll, Steve. Ghost Wars: The Secret History of the CIA, Afghanistan, and bin Laden, from the Soviet Invasion to September 10, 2001. New York: Penguin Press, 2004.

[165] Bergen, Peter. The Osama bin Laden I Know: An Oral History of al Qaeda's Leader. New York: Free Press, 2006.

[166] Rashid, Ahmed. Taliban: Militant Islam, Oil and Fundamentalism in Central Asia. New Haven: Yale University Press, 2000.

[167] Ibid

were severe, often involving public executions or amputations.[168] Women's rights were curtailed drastically, with their public presence and activities heavily restricted.[169]

The world, particularly the West, watched with increasing concern.[170] But it was the horrifying events of September 11, 2001, that dramatically changed the trajectory of Afghanistan's history. With clear links traced back to bin Laden and al-Qaeda, the U.S. found both a reason and an international mandate to intervene.[171]

On October 7, 2001, barely a month after the 9/11 attacks, President George W. Bush announced the launch of Operation Enduring Freedom.[172] This campaign began with targeted airstrikes against Taliban and al-Qaeda positions in Afghanistan.[173] Supported by an international coalition and in conjunction with the Northern Alliance on the ground, the U.S. aimed to dismantle the al-Qaeda network and oust the Taliban from power.[174] The military operation later expanded and evolved into what is now known as the War on Terror, leading the U.S. into multiple theaters of war, most notably Iraq, under the banner of Operation Iraqi Freedom in 2003.[175]

[168] Jones, Seth G. In the Graveyard of Empires: America's War in Afghanistan. New York: W. W. Norton & Company, 2009.

[169] Skaine, Rosemarie. The Women of Afghanistan under the Taliban. Jefferson, NC: McFarland & Company, 2002.

[170] Coll, Steve. Ghost Wars: The Secret History of the CIA, Afghanistan, and bin Laden, from the Soviet Invasion to September 10, 2001. New York: Penguin Press, 2004.

[171] National Commission on Terrorist Attacks Upon the United States. The 9/11 Commission Report. New York: W. W. Norton & Company, 2004.

[172] Bush, George W. Decision Points. New York: Crown Publishers, 2010.

[173] Woodward, Bob. Bush at War. New York: Simon & Schuster, 2002.

[174] National Commission on Terrorist Attacks Upon the United States. The 9/11 Commission Report. New York: W. W. Norton & Company, 2004.

[175] Ricks, Thomas E. Fiasco: The American Military Adventure in Iraq. New York: Penguin Press, 2006.

Opium

Afghanistan's history with opium is a telling example of how global geopolitics and local dynamics can converge to create an unexpected outcome. In the 1980s, before the Soviet invasion and the subsequent war, Afghanistan was a minor player in the world opium market, contributing to less than 1% of the global supply.[176] However, the situation dramatically shifted during the Mujahideen's resistance against the Soviet occupation.

The CIA's involvement in supporting the Mujahideen is well documented. As part of its Cold War strategy, the U.S. saw the Mujahideen as a defensive wall against the spread of communism in the region.[177] The agency funneled arms and money to various Mujahideen factions through Pakistan's Inter-Services Intelligence (ISI).[178] At the same time, the socio-economic fabric of Afghanistan deteriorated rapidly due to the ongoing war. With traditional agricultural systems disrupted, many farmers turned to opium cultivation as a reliable source of income.[179] The region's opium production skyrocketed, and by the end of the decade, Afghanistan accounted for almost 40% of the global opium supply.[180]

The rise of the Taliban in the 1990s, marked by their strict interpretation of Islamic law, had an initially contradictory effect on

---

[176] McCoy, Alfred W. The Politics of Heroin: CIA Complicity in the Global Drug Trade. Chicago: Lawrence Hill Books, 2003.
[177] Coll, Steve. Ghost Wars: The Secret History of the CIA, Afghanistan, and Bin Laden, from the Soviet Invasion to September 10, 2001. New York: Penguin Press, 2004.
[178] Ibid
[179] Chouvy, Pierre-Arnaud. Opium: Uncovering the Politics of the Poppy. London: I.B. Tauris, 2010.
[180] United Nations Office on Drugs and Crime. World Drug Report 2001. Vienna: UNODC, 2001.

opium production. Despite the drug trade financing many of the Mujahideen factions from which the Taliban had emerged, once in power, the Taliban leadership decreed a ban on opium cultivation in 2000,[181] enforcing it with their typical sternness. This dramatically dropped production – from 3,200 tons in 1999 to a meager 185 tons a year later.

However, the post-9/11 scenario, marked by the U.S.-led coalition's intervention and the subsequent ousting of the Taliban, saw another shift in opium cultivation. With the central authority weakened and local warlords regaining prominence in many regions, opium once again became the crop of choice for many Afghan farmers.[182] By 2007, Afghanistan produced over 92% of the world's heroin, a grim reflection of the nation's unstable socio-political landscape.[183]

Taking the Battle to Iraq

The decision to wage war on Iraq after the Afghanistan intervention was controversial and remains the subject of much debate. After the 9/11 attacks, there was a nearly unanimous consensus in the U.S. for a military response against the perpetrators, leading to the invasion of Afghanistan.[184] However, the subsequent focus on Iraq was perplexing for many, as the Saddam Hussein regime had no apparent ties to the 9/11 attacks or al-Qaeda.

---

[181] Rashid, Ahmed. Taliban: Militant Islam, Oil, and Fundamentalism in Central Asia. New Haven: Yale University Press, 2000.

[182] Mansfield, David. "The Economic Superiority of Illicit Drug Production: Myth and Reality—Opium Poppy Cultivation in Afghanistan." Third World Quarterly 28, no. 3 (2007): 555-577.

[183] United Nations Office on Drugs and Crime. World Drug Report 2008. Vienna: UNODC, 2008.

[184] Woodward, Bob. Bush at War. New York: Simon & Schuster, 2002.

President Bush and key figures in his administration made the case for the invasion of Iraq based on several grounds, with the primary justification being Iraq's alleged possession of weapons of mass destruction (WMDs) and the potential for these weapons to fall into the hands of terrorists.[185] But as the world would come to realize post-invasion, no such WMDs were found, leading many to question the true motivations behind the war.[186]

The atmosphere post-9/11 was fraught with fear and anxiety. Intelligence failures, inadequacies in national security infrastructure, and the overwhelming tragedy of the terrorist attacks posed many uncomfortable questions. For some critics, the shift in focus to Iraq appeared strategic, a means to divert attention from these pressing questions and reshape the narrative.[187]

The fact that 15 of the 19 hijackers were Saudi nationals did raise eyebrows, especially given the close relationship between the Saudi royal family and the Bush family. The rapid evacuation of members of the Saudi royal family and the bin Laden family from the U.S. immediately post-9/11, despite an FAA ban on all non-military flights, added to the suspicions.[188] Many felt these actions raised valid concerns about the U.S. 's priorities and relationships with foreign entities.

---

[185] Pillar, Paul R. "Intelligence, Policy, and the War in Iraq." Foreign Affairs 85, no. 2 (2006): 15-27.
[186] Duelfer, Charles. Comprehensive Report of the Special Advisor to the DCI on Iraq's WMD. Washington, D.C.: Central Intelligence Agency, 2004.
[187] Clarke, Richard A. Against All Enemies: Inside America's War on Terror. New York: Free Press, 2004.
[188] Unger, Craig. House of Bush, House of Saud: The Secret Relationship Between the World's Two Most Powerful Dynasties. New York: Scribner, 2004.

The Iraq War's initiation and subsequent developments prompted significant debate about the Bush administration's motivations, priorities, and the complexities of U.S. foreign policy. The war overshadowed many pressing questions arising from the 9/11 attacks, creating a new narrative that the world grappled with for years to come.

In the months leading up to the invasion of Iraq, President Bush and members of his administration indicated they possessed information that demonstrated a link between Saddam Hussein and al-Qaeda. Stating:

> *"Iraq could decide on any given day to provide a biological or chemical weapon to a terrorist group or individual terrorists. Alliance with terrorists could allow the Iraqi regime to attack America without leaving any fingerprints."*[189]

Newsweek magazine published a story about Saddam Hussein and al-Qaeda joining forces to attack U.S. interests in the Gulf Region. ABC News broadcast a story of this link soon after.[190]

Vice President Dick Cheney told *Meet the Press* on December 9, 2001, that Iraq was harboring Abdul Rahman Yasin, a suspect in the

---

[189] President Bush Outlines Iraqi Threat". *White House news release* (Press release). The White House. 2002-10-07. (https://georgewbush-whitehouse.archives.gov/news/releases/2002/10/print/20021007-8.html)
[190] Link between Saddam and al-Qaeda - ABC News video report (http://www.mediaresearch.org/rm/cyber/2004/binladen061704/segment1.ram)

1993 World Trade Center bombing,[191] and repeated the statement in another appearance on September 14, 2003, saying:

> *"We learned more and more that there was a relationship between Iraq and al-Qaida that stretched back through most of the decade of the '90s, that it involved training, for example, on BW and CW, that al-Qaida sent personnel to Baghdad to get trained on the systems that are involved. The Iraqis providing bomb-making expertise and advice to the al-Qaeda organization. We know, for example, in connection with the original World Trade Center bombing in '93 that one of the bombers was Iraqi, returned to Iraq after the attack of '93. And we've learned subsequent to that, since we went into Baghdad and got into the intelligence files, that this individual probably also received financing from the Iraqi government as well as safe haven."[192]*

In an interview with National Public Radio in January 2004, Cheney stated that there had been *"overwhelming evidence"* of a relationship between Saddam and al-Qaeda based on evidence including Iraq's purported harboring of Yasin.[193]

Notwithstanding the official stance of the Bush Administration, in hindsight the consensus of intelligence experts has been that

---

[191] *"The Vice President Appears on NBC's Meet the Press"*. *White House news release* (Press release). The White House. 2001-12-09. (https://georgewbush-whitehouse.archives.gov/vicepresident/news-speeches/speeches/print/vp20011209.html)
[192] Transcript for Sept. 14 - *Meet the Press"*, MSNBC. (http://msnbc.msn.com/id/3080244/default.htm)
[193] Landay, Jonathan S.; Warren P. Strobel; John Walcott (March 3, 2004). *"Doubts Cast on Efforts to Link Saddam, al-Qaeda"*. Knight-Ridder. (https://web.archive.org/web/20061208023017/http://www.commondreams.org/headlines 04/0303-01.htm)

Saddam Hussein and al-Qaeda never led to an operational relationship, and that consensus is backed up by reports from the independent 9/11 Commission and by declassified Defense Department reports[194] as well as by the Senate Select Committee on Intelligence, whose 2006 report of Phase II of its investigation into prewar intelligence reports concluded that there was no evidence of ties between Saddam Hussein and al-Qaeda.[195]

On April 29, 2007, former Director of Central Intelligence George Tenet said on *60 Minutes*, "*We could never verify that there was any Iraqi authority, direction, and control, complicity with al-Qaeda for 9/11 or any operational act against America, period.*"[196]

Years after the invasion of Iraq, a leaked memo speaking of Iraq and the possibility of weapons of mass destruction (WMDs) clearly outlined the falsehood of the narrative when it stated: "*the intelligence and facts are being fixed around the policy.*"[197] The London's Sunday Times immediately wrote about this memo once the word was out. Still, US-based media buried the story for weeks and only reluctantly wrote about it dismissively, never mentioning the critical phrase that intelligence was "*fixed.*"

---

[194] Smith, Jeffrey (2007-04-06). "*Hussein's Prewar Ties To Al-Qaeda Discounted*". Washington Post. (https://www.washingtonpost.com/wp-dyn/content/article/2007/04/05/AR2007040502263.html)

[195] Weisman, Jonathan (2006-09-10). "*Saddam had no links to al-Qaeda*". The Age. (http://www.theage.com.au/news/world/saddam-had-no-links-to-alqaeda/2006/09/09/1157222383981.html)

[196] Grieve, Tim. "*Welcome back, Tony*", Salon.com, 04-30-2007. (http://www.salon.com/2007/04/30/snow_34/)

[197] Ray McGovern, *Proof Bush Fixed the Facts*, TomPaine.com, May 4 2005

Part II: The Conspirators

In Part I, we embarked on a detailed exploration of the diverse maneuvers executed by the global elite over the past seventy years. As we transition into Part II, we will shift our focus to the pivotal individuals orchestrating these events, scrutinizing how these power plays have significantly bolstered their dominance and wealth.

THE BUSH FAMILY DYNASTY

The Bush family is an American dynasty in every meaning of the word. Peter Schweizer, the author of a biography on the family, has described the Bushes as *"the most successful political dynasty in American history."*[198] They are involved in politics, sports, entertainment, the oil industry, etc. They have an untold vast net worth that started with former President George H. W. Bush's father, Prescott Bush, when he profited over $1.5 million from forced labor camps in Auschwitz.[199]

> *"George Bush's grandfather, the late US senator Prescott Bush, was a director and shareholder of companies that profited from their involvement with the financial backers of Nazi Germany.*
>
> *The Guardian has obtained confirmation from newly discovered files in the US National Archives that a firm of which Prescott Bush was a director was involved with the financial architects of Nazism.*
>
> *His business dealings, which continued until his company's assets were seized in 1942 under the Trading with the Enemy Act, has led more than 60 years later to a civil action for damages being brought in Germany*

[198] Joseph Curl (January 20, 2005). *"Rise of 'dynasty' quick, far-reaching"*. The Washington Times.
(https://web.archive.org/web/20060319124218/http://washtimes.com/national/20050119
-123016-5212r.htm)
[199] Toby Rogers, *"Prescott Bush, $1,500,000 and Auschwitz: How the Bush Family Wealth Is Linked to the Jewish Holocaust"*, p.43

against the Bush family by two former slave laborers at Auschwitz and to a hum of pre-election controversy.

The evidence has also prompted one former US Nazi war crimes prosecutor to argue that the late senator's action should have been grounds for prosecution for giving aid and comfort to the enemy."[200]

[Vesting Order Number 248]
ALL OF THE CAPITAL STOCK OF UNION BANK-ING CORPORATION AND CERTAIN INDEBTED-NESS OWING BY IT

Under the authority of the Trading with the enemy Act, as amended, and Executive Order No. 9095, as amended,[1] and pursuant to law, the undersigned, after investigation, finding:

(a) That the property described as follows:

All of the capital stock of Union Banking Corporation, a New York corporation, New York, New York, which is a business enter-prise within the United States, consisting of 4,000 shares of $100 par value common capital stock, the names of the registered owners of which, and the number of shares owned by them respectively, are as follows:

Names	Number of shares
E. Roland Harriman	3,991
Cornelius Lievense	4
Harold D. Pennington	1
Ray Morris	1
Prescott S. Bush	1
H. J. Kouwenhoven	1
Johann G. Groeninger	1
Total	4,000

[1] 7 F.R. 5205.

---

[200] The Guardian, "*How Bush's grandfather helped Hilter's rise to power*", September 25, 2004 (https://www.theguardian.com/world/2004/sep/25/usa.secondworldwar)

Director of the CIA (George H. W. Bush)

As the Director of the CIA, George H. W. Bush was a highly skilled and accomplished liar that performed his craft with the utmost of skill of an artistic expression:

> *"...he had perfected the bending and stretching of truth... George was as smooth as an eel slithers through oil. His lies on behalf of the CIA ranged from outright falsehoods and adamant denials to obfuscations and evasive omissions."*[201]

But what else should you expect from a former CIA Director? He is, after all, a professional liar and spy. That alone does not make a person good or bad; it is who they are. However, it brings to question the authenticity and honesty of many statements made by H. W. throughout his professional and political careers.

After President Carter forced H. W. to step down as the CIA Director,[202] he spent the next few years building a team of current and EX-CIA operatives to destroy Carter's reelection chances and install him in the White House.[203] Key to this was preventing Carter from obtaining the political win if the American hostages held in Iran were released during Carter's administration.[204] If Bush were to convince Iran to hold off until after election day successfully, this hot topic issue would single-handedly kill Carter's chances of reelection,

---

[201] Kelly, Kitty. "The Family: The Real Story of the Bush Dynasty." New York: Doubleday, 2004, p. 548.

[202] Gibbs, Nancy, and Michael Duffy. "The Presidents Club: Inside the World's Most Exclusive Fraternity." New York: Simon & Schuster, 2012.

[203] Knott, Stephen F. "Secret and Sanctioned: Covert Operations and the American Presidency." Oxford University Press, 1996.

[204] U.S. Senate, Committee on Foreign Relations; "*The October Surprise: Allegations and the Circumstances Surrounding the Release of the American Hostages Held in Iran*", U.S. Government Printing Office; Washington, DC., 1992

which is precisely what happened. Carter lost the election after promising billions of dollars of U. S. Military assets to Iran and $40 million in cash bribes to Iranian officials.[205] Then, on January 20, 1981, the very same day Reagan/Bush was sworn into office, the hostages were released by Iran. [206]

Years later, in 1992, the National Review released an investigative report that stated: *"through FBI and CIA documents released ... Bush played a personal role in keeping the hostages in Khomeini's hands until after Election Day 1980."*

Vice President (George H. W. Bush)

Going back for a moment to the Iran-Contra scandal we covered in Part I, the reader may remember Bush was VP during this time and claimed he did not know about the operations in Nicaragua. Yet, in December 1983, Bush and Oliver North flew down to El Salvador to meet with local army officers to encourage them to attack Nicaragua covertly on behalf of the U.S. Why would he fly there to seek support for a battle he did not know of? Additionally, the CIA launched numerous raids on Nicaragua under Bush's orders between January and March 1984.[207]

Further evidence that Bush was not only fully aware of but was heading the direct supervision of the Contra situation was after one of the planes run by a CIA front company was shot down over El Salvador carrying 10,000 lbs of small arms, ammunition, and hand

---

[205] Uri Dowbenko, *Bushwhacked*, Conspiracy Digest, 2003, p 273
[206] Gary Sick. 1991. *October Surprise: America's Hostages in Iran and the Election of Ronald Reagan.* New York: Random House.
[207] *Jeb! And the Bush Crime Family*, Roger Stone, p 224

grenades; the pilot Eugene Hasenfus called VP Bush to inform him the mission had failed.[208] This flight's mission was the same as previous flights: to bring weapons to the Contras and return to the U.S. with cocaine and marijuana to a small airport in Mena, Arkansas.[209] Another one of our other deep state actors, Bill Clinton, was serving as the Governor of Arkansas, and he provided *"approval and protection"* of the flights coming and going 24x7.[210]

We may have never discovered the illicit scheme if the plane had never been shot down.

Once news of the cargo plane being shot down in El Salvador hit the wire, the political ramifications were quickly coming to light; immediately, the disinformation and spin kicked into overdrive to protect the VP and divert knowledge of the CIA's ownership of the C-123k cargo ship. Oliver North's diary clearly mentioned the VP and his involvement: *"Felix [Rodriguez] is talking too much about the Vice President's connection."*[211]

This wouldn't be the only time VP Bush's name came up regarding drug smuggling from Nicaragua to Arkansas. One of the pilots by the name of Barry Seal, was caught by the IRS and charged with tax evasion for his profits made smuggling cocaine into the U. S. During the investigation, Seal was covertly recorded saying:

> *"Ever hear of that expression it's not what you know, it's who you know? Well, whoever said that just hadn't*

---

[208] Affidavit of Eugene Hasenfus, #03575 in the Iran-Contra Collection, October 12, 1986 pp 2-3
[209] Deposition of Michael Tolliver, Iran-Contra Report, May 1987, Vol 9
[210] *Jeb! And the Bush Crime Family,* Roger Stone, p 236

[211] North notebook entry, January 9, 1986

caught the Vice President's kids in the dope business,
'cause I can tell you for sure what you know can
definitely be more important than who you know. [...]
Fuck, I even got surveillance video catchin' the Bush boys
red-handed. I consider this stuff my insurance policy."

This conversation referred to Jeb Bush picking up multiple kilos of cocaine.[212] It was not long after this recording that Barry was found dead by multiple gunshot wounds. The FBI quickly confiscated a box in Barry's vehicle, which was suspected to contain the video evidence against Jeb. It was reported by Barry's secretary that he was known to keep important papers and his blackmail in his trunk. She further claimed, *"Barry Seal died with Vice President Bush's phone number in the trunk of his car."*[213]

Ross Perot obtained evidence of CIA-backed cocaine smuggling and attempted to get VP Bush's attention, but he was ignored. He later claimed, "[all I] *got from Bush was a grim smile.*"[214]

The VP Wants to be President

While in the White House as VP, Bush set his sights on the Presidency. He and many of his closest supporters felt that winning a general election would be challenging and possibly unobtainable. With this in mind, it is rumored that Bush worked behind the scenes to assassinate Reagan. This claim is not taken lightly by the author,

[212] Terry Reed and John Cummings, *Compromised: Clinton, Bush, and the CIA* p 212
[213] Al Martin, *The Conspirators: Secrets of an Iran-Contra Insider*, pp 195-198
[214] Retired Green Beret Bo Gritz, *Open Letter to George Bush*,
(http://serendipity.li/cia/gritz1.htm)

and I found some evidence that pointed to the affirmative and some that are very dubious at best as to whether or not Bush had conspired.

An undisputed fact is the Bush family, and the family of would-be assassin John Hinckley had close connections[215], including a pre-scheduled dinner between VP Bush's son Neil and John's brother Scott Hinckley to take place the day after the assassination attempt. Neil Bush told the Houston Post that *"he knew the Hinckley family because they had made large contributions to the Vice President's campaign."* [216]

Rich Zeoli interviewed political author Roger Stone on Talk Radio 1210 WPHT while researching his book *Jeb! And the Bush Crime Family* uncovered evidence that claims:

> *"There are two shooters in the Reagan assassination attempt, not one. I give you photographic evidence and eyewitness evidence of a second man standing on a balcony holding a gun, who can clearly be seen in the uncropped photos and I traced many of the connections of the Bushes to the Hinckleys. It's more than you've been told.*
>
> *[...]*
>
> *I think it is more than possible because one has to understand the backdrop here and that is this story is missing from Bill O'Reilly's Killing Reagan book entirely. Al Haig, Reagan's Secretary of State and Vice President George Bush are fighting over control of foreign policy. George 'Poppy' Bush is for the 'New World Order.' Haig has the quaint notion that he's*

---

[215] Nathaniel Blumberg, The Afternoon of March 30
[216] *"Bush's Son Was to Dine With Suspect's Brother."* Houston Post, March 21, 1981

Reagan's man. This is supposed to be Reagan's foreign policy, more conservative than what Bush wants. There are two different executive orders sitting on Reagan's desk. One giving authority to Haig. One giving authority to Bush...Then there's an assassination attempt on Reagan and he comes back, three days into his hospital stay he signs the order putting George Bush in charge of the machinery."[217]

Of course, the assassination attempt did not successfully kill the president, and H. W. would have to wait for another chance at the presidency.

First Bush Presidency (George H. W. Bush)

During his presidential campaign, he famously stated: *"read my lips, no new taxes."* That was a complete lie, and he knew it, but he was willing to do anything and say anything to get elected.[218]

Now president, Bush could look back and *"even though he had lied in the face of overwhelming contrary evidence, ignored national and international law, subverted democracy, interfered in the free will of freely elected official foreign governments, allowed known drug traffickers to operate without fear, allowed the importation of drugs into our own country while campaigning a hard line against drugs, and send American*

---

[217] CBS 3 Philly, *"Author Roger Stone's Latest Conspiracy Theory: George H. W. Bush Behind Reagan Assassination Attempt"*, January 28, 2016
(https://philadelphia.cbslocal.com/2016/01/28/author-roger-stones-latest-conspiracy-theory-george-h-w-bush-behind-reagan-assassination-attempt/)
[218] Kitty Kelly, *The Family, The Real Story of the Bush Dynasty* p 787

troops into wars as if they were his own personal fighting force"[219] all to increase his net worth and consolidate more power.

Recently avoiding the trap of the Iran-Contra scandal, President Bush brought Dick Cheney up from Congress and into the White House as his Secretary of Defense. When Chaney was a Congressman, he had helped (then) VP Bush by authoring a report saying the attempt to give Congress a significant role in foreign affairs undermined the presidency.[220] Thus removing pressure off of the Reagan administration and helped to prevent VP Bush from getting entangled in it.

While writing the first edition of this book, the news of former President George H.W. Bush's death on December 1, 2018, marked the end of an era. I anticipated that the ensuing years might bring to light further insights into the extent of his participation in numerous American military engagements over the previous fifty years. However, as I undertake the revisions for this book's second edition in the latter part of 2023, it's notable that no new revelations have surfaced.

The Second Bush President (George W. Bush)

'Dubya' or just *'W.'* as he was nicknamed in the media, George W. Bush was a lackluster student in college, earning an average of C-, a lousy pilot in the Texas Air National Guard, and a failing Texas oilman. He was the least capable, articulate, and prepared person to

---

[219] *Jeb! And the Bush Crime Family: The inside story of an American dynasty*, Roger Stone, 2016 pg 252

[220] John Nichols, *Dick: The Main Who Is President*, p 97-100

sit in the Oval Office. Yet, somehow, he became the 46th Governor of Texas and finally the 43rd President of the United States.

After college, W. formed an oil exploration company, Arbusto Energy, financed by his father, George H. W., the brother of Osama bin Laden, Salem bin Laden,[221] and a wealthy corrupt banker charged with soliciting deposits from large-scale money laundering and drug dealers, James Bath.[222] Knowing the Bush family as we do, it should not come as a surprise that W. would form a business with a drug money launder, but the brother of Osama bin Laden takes the cake.

Even with the $4.7 million invested and the Bush family name attached to Arbusto, W. quickly ran the company into the ground. Over the coming years, W. would rename the company three times, each in a desperate effort to "*rebrand*" itself and clear the slate of the previous failures. Cashing in on his family name, he finally settled on Bush Exploration. With this new name, he even convinced additional investors to invest an additional $7 million. The Observer said, "*whenever he's struck a dry well, someone has always been willing to fill it with money for him.*"[223] Yet, even with that influx of cash, the company was strapped and looking for help; a Bush family friend and owner of Spectrum 7 Energy came to the rescue and purchased/merged with Bush Exploration.

Coming on the heels of the dot-com boom and bust during the Clinton administration, the economy was already on shaky ground when W entered office; then came the events of 9/11. Of course, we

---

[221] Peter Truell, Large Gurwin, *False Profits: The Inside Story of BCCI*, 1992
[222] "*A Mysterious Mover of Money and Planes.*" Time, June 4, 2001
[223] Gregory Plast, "Bush Family Finances", November 26, 2000

have already covered 9/11 in detail in a previous chapter; we will highlight a few Bush-related aspects of the 9/11 attacks.

Bush Administration during 9/11 Attacks

While it's widely acknowledged that President George W. Bush was in the infancy of his tenure as the 43rd President of the United States during the 9/11 attacks, there are less commonly discussed elements about the administration's early strategies regarding Iraq. Even before the formalities of the presidential transition had concluded, there were hints within the Bush administration about a strategic focus on Iraq.[224]

The underpinnings for these initial discussions can be linked to a combination of enduring geopolitical concerns, lingering tensions from the Gulf War under President George H. W. Bush, and apprehensions about Saddam Hussein's ambitions in the Middle East.[225] The allegations regarding the presence of weapons of mass destruction (WMDs) in Iraq, which were later contested, added further fuel to these dialogues.[226] Moreover, several senior members of the Bush administration, such as Vice President Dick Cheney, Defense Secretary Donald Rumsfeld, and Deputy Defense Secretary Paul Wolfowitz, were known advocates for a regime change in Iraq even prior to 9/11.[227]

---

[224] Woodward, Bob. "Plan of Attack." Simon & Schuster, 2004.

[225] Bacevich, Andrew J. "America's War for the Greater Middle East: A Military History." Random House, 2016.

[226] Isikoff, Michael, and David Corn. "Hubris: The Inside Story of Spin, Scandal, and the Selling of the Iraq War." Crown Publishers, 2006.

[227] Mann, James. "Rise of the Vulcans: The History of Bush's War Cabinet." Viking, 2004.

These preparatory discussions underscore that Iraq was already on the radar for the Bush administration. The 9/11 attacks subsequently provided both a strategic justification and a public sentiment push for the U.S. administration to pursue its objectives in Iraq, marrying national emotion with a previously charted policy direction.[228]

Under President Bush's tenure, the 9/11 Attacks occurred despite intelligence warnings, marking one of the most devastating events on American soil. In the aftermath, and under the banner of national security, his administration enacted policies that many argue infringed upon citizens' constitutional rights. The initiation and perpetuation of the 'War on Terror' drained the U.S. treasury by trillions of dollars and led to the loss of numerous American lives, raising concerns about the efficacy and direction of his foreign policy strategies.

On the morning of September 11, President Bush was in Sarasota, Florida, at a pre-scheduled photo op at a local elementary school.[229] Before walking into the room with the students at 8:55 AM EST (the same local time as New York and Washington DC), the president was informed a plane had hit the World Trade Center.[230] At the time, he was told it was a single plane, and there was no need for concern, so the President continued engaging with students. About ten minutes later, at 9:05 AM, while in the classroom with students and live on TV, chief of staff Andrew Card whispered in Bush's ear, "*a second plane hit the second tower. America is under attack.*"[231] For reasons only known by the President, he chose to remain in the classroom with the students for

---

[228] Tenet, George, and Bill Harlow. "At the Center of the Storm: My Years at the CIA." HarperCollins, 2007.

[229] *The 9/11 Commission Report* p 39

[230] Mitch Stacy, *Florid School Where Bush Learned of the Attacks Reflects on Its Role in History,* Associated Press, August 19, 2002

[231] *The 9/11 Commission Report* p 38

almost ten minutes,[232] made a quick statement to the nation, and was escorted out of the school by the Secret Service at 9:35 AM.[233]

The St. Petersburg Times asked, *"why [didn't] the Secret Service immediately hustle Bush to a secure location?"*[234] The Family Steering Committee asked a similar question, *"Why was President Bush permitted by the Secret Service to remain in the Sarasota elementary school where he was reading to children?"*[235] Was the Secret Service afraid to overrule the president and force him to leave the school? Or did the Secret Service think the security threat was isolated to New York then?

Many conspiracy theories point to the fact that the Secret Service allowed him to stay as proof they knew of the targets of the attacks and already knew the school was safe. I find this line of thinking–if you can even call it that, baseless conjecture without any evidence to support such a statement. Remember, this is still 20-30 minutes before the Pentagon attack, so it is reasonable to believe the Secret Service did not perceive an immediate threat to the president's safety as he was in Florida, not New York.

Some reporters at the school commented that Bush appeared lost in thought and stayed in the room longer than he needed to; he did *"excu[se] himself very politely to the teacher and the students,"* as his chief of staff claimed.[236] The media portrayed him as *"openly stretching out the moment,"* *"lingered until the press was gone,"* and referred to the president

[232] *The 9/11 Commission Report* p 38
[233] *The 9/11 Commission Report* p 39
[234] Susan Taylor Martin, *Of Fact, Fiction: Bush 9/11*, St. Petersburg Times, July 4, 2004.
[235] Thomas H. Kean and Lee H. Hamilton, *Without Precedent: The Inside Story of the 9/11 Commission, p 54*
[236] Andrew Card, *That if You Had to Tell The President*, San Francisco Chronicle, September 11, 2002.

as the *"dawdler in chief"* by the Washington Times White House correspondent Bill Sammon.[237]

Various theories permeate the discourse when reflecting upon President Bush's immediate, seemingly unmoved response during the 9/11 attacks. Some ascribe his demeanor to a covert foreknowledge, asserting that his stillness was a controlled facemask, hiding his awareness and allowing the attacks to unfold fully. However, I would like to suggest an alternative perspective grounded in a psychological response to the crisis rather than conspiracy.

The magnitude of the 9/11 attacks was unprecedented, and the overwhelming nature of the situation, paired with the weighty mantle of leadership, might have created a paralyzing moment for Bush. Perhaps he grappled with the situation's overwhelming suddenness, the nation's eyes turning towards him for answers and guidance, and in that moment, found himself burdened by the colossal weight of responsibility. Regardless of scale, this notion of feeling dwarfed by the immense responsibility might be relatable to many leaders.

Drawing a parallel to my early days as a certified Paramedic, I recall a particularly intense experience that, though on a different scale, echoes the profound pressure of critical decision-making. Fresh-faced and green, I was thrust into the deep end with one of my inaugural EMS calls as the lead paramedic on the crew — a cardiac arrest. As we sped to the scene, my heart kept pace with the blaring sirens, a cacophony of urgency that seemed to resonate in my very bones. The scene that greeted us was one of raw desperation: the family, a frenzy of fear and hope, frantically signaling for our attention, their eyes laden with an

---

[237] Bill Sammon, *Fighting Back: The War on Terrorism: From Inside the Bush White House,* pg 89-90

urgency that immediately weighed upon my shoulders. Amidst the suffocating anticipation, I caught myself hesitating, a silent plea escaping my thoughts, wishing someone else could shoulder the monumental decisions that were rapidly unfurling. Yet, reality offered no reprieve; I was the sole paramedic on hand, my responsibility.

The weight of the moment bore down on us; a life lay in my hands, the patient's absent heartbeat creating a void that seemed to pulse within my own chest. Each second that ticked by was amplified, each pause a deafening stillness that stretched into what felt like an endless void. The decisions I was about to make loomed large, a haunting refrain that underscored the fragile balance between existence and oblivion, serving as a stark testament to our collective human vulnerability during such pivotal junctures. The responsibility was colossal, a load that my training had outlined in theory, but the profound emotional depth and visceral reality of the experience surpassed all anticipatory constructs. The environment thrummed with a fusion of desperate optimism and stark urgency, a narrative less dire when juxtaposed with larger-scale crises but one that emphatically highlighted the profound, and at times intimidating, responsibility that is an integral thread in the tapestry of critical decision-making.

President Bush was suddenly thrust into a maelstrom of terror, grief, and national uncertainty. The eyes of the world, heavy with a mixture of fear, expectation, and urgency, turned to him, silently demanding guidance, action, and reassurance in a moment that seemed to fracture the very timeline of history.

In those initial hours, days, and weeks following the attacks, President Bush grappled with decisions of an unimaginable scale — choices that would not just determine the fate of individuals but that of nations, global politics, and generations to come. Every tick of the clock reverberated with the urgency of a heartbeat, each moment of decision a precipice overlooking a chasm of geopolitical ramifications. The responsibility — colossal, inescapable — was his to shoulder alone. Despite being surrounded by advisors, the weight of the ultimate decisions rested squarely on the President's shoulders, a solitude in leadership that perhaps only those who have held such consequential power can truly understand.

The enormity of this task, the sheer scale of the tragedy, and the rippling effects of the choices made in those critical junctures form a narrative that goes beyond personal or professional development. They speak to the human condition itself — our vulnerability, resilience, and leadership's profound weight in times of unparalleled crisis. President Bush was tasked with navigating a path forward through a landscape forever altered, demanding a trained mind, a steady hand, and the depths of his humanity. He knew at that very moment his presidency would be judged solely on his actions and reactions to 9/11. Nothing that he had campaigned on mattered anymore; this was the only issue that America cared about.

Bush-Cheney Administration post 9/11 Attacks

"In response to the terrorist attacks on September 11, 2001, George W. Bush shredded the US Constitution, trampled on the Bill of Rights, discarded the Geneva Conventions, and helped scorn on the domestic torture statute . . . [I]n response to the attacks, the Bush administration engineered

and presided over the most sustained period of constitutional decay in our history"[238]

The post-9/11 era witnessed a seismic shift in the political and military objectives of the United States. At the forefront of this movement was the neoconservative agenda, marked by its ambitious goals both domestically and internationally.

Domestically, the neoconservative faction sought a paradigm of complete information dominance. This vision materialized in the form of policies and measures that expanded governmental surveillance capacities, with instruments such as the USA PATRIOT Act.[239] This legislation, among others, substantially increased the state's authority to monitor its citizens, ushering in a new era where the line between national security and individual privacy became increasingly blurred.

Internationally, the neoconservatives harbored visions of reshaping the global landscape, with the Middle East as its central focus. Their philosophy hinged on the notion that democratization of the region would lead to stability, even if it meant toppling existing regimes to achieve it. This strategy manifested in the form of military interventions and nation-building efforts, most notably in Iraq and Afghanistan.[240]

The Middle East, already a complex web of religious, ethnic, and political rivalries, became further destabilized after these interventions. Decades-old regimes were dismantled, creating power vacuums that

---

[238] Vincent Warren, *The 9/11 Decade and Decline of US Democracy*, Center for Constitutional Rights, September 9, 2011.
[239] Doyle, Charles. "The USA PATRIOT Act: A Sketch." Congressional Research Service, 2002.
[240] Bacevich, Andrew J. America's War for the Greater Middle East: A Military History. Random House, 2016.

were often filled by extremist factions, thereby exacerbating regional tensions and conflicts.[241]

Before this aggressive foreign policy turn, the Middle East, for all its flaws and intricacies, exhibited a form of stability under its dictatorial regimes. Most importantly, from an American perspective, they rarely posed direct threats to U.S. interests or security.[242]

Former State Department employee Peter Van Buren summed up his thoughts on the status of the Middle East and postulated what it would have been like there today if we had not invaded:

> *"Libya was stable, ruled by the same strongman for 42 years; in Egypt, Hosni Mubarak had been in power since 1983; Syria had been run by the Assad family since 1971; Saddam Hussein had essentially been in charge of Iraq since 1969, formally becoming president in 1979; the Turks and Kurds had an uneasy but functional ceasefire; and Yemen was quiet enough, other than the terror attack on the USS Cole in 2000."*

He continued:

> *"Today Libya is a failed state, bleeding mayhem into Northern Africa; Egypt failed its Arab Spring test and relies on the United States to support is anti-democratic militarized government, and Yemen is a disastrously failed state."*[243]

---

[241] Cockburn, Patrick. The Age of Jihad: Islamic State and the Great War for the Middle East. Verso, 2016.

[242] Gause, F. Gregory III. "Beyond Sectarianism: The New Middle East Cold War." Brookings Doha Center Analysis Paper, 2014.

[243] Peter Van Buren, *How the US Wrecked the Middle East*

The inclusion of the Vice President's name in this section's title is both deliberate and telling. Dick Cheney's influence during his tenure as Vice President was unparalleled, marking him as one of the most dominant figures in the White House. Many political analysts and historians concur that Cheney wielded exceptional power during the Bush administration, often overshadowing the President himself.[244]

Cheney's history of involvement in U.S. foreign policy dates back to the first Bush administration when he served as the Secretary of Defense. There are claims that during this period, Cheney leveraged potentially misrepresented satellite imagery as grounds for the U.S. intervention in Iraq.[245]

By the time of the second Bush administration, Cheney's strategic footprint was even more evident. He was at the forefront of advocating for the wars in Afghanistan and Iraq, shaping their narratives and rallying support both within the administration and among the public. In many ways, these conflicts became synonymous with Cheney's vision of American foreign policy and military intervention.[246]

Given the extent of his influence, one might argue that both Bush administrations were significantly, if not predominantly, driven by Cheney's perspectives on global affairs.

The motives behind the U.S. invasions of Afghanistan and Iraq under the influence of Cheney and the neoconservatives have been the subject of much debate and speculation. One key benefit, as I've pointed

---

[244] Mann, James. The Rise of the Vulcans: The History of Bush's War Cabinet. Penguin Books, 2004.

[245] Woodward, Bob. Plan of Attack. Simon and Schuster, 2004.

[246] Gellman, Barton. Angler: The Cheney Vice Presidency. Penguin Press, 2008.

out, was the significant augmentation in defense spending. This wasn't merely an increase to the budgets of U.S. military departments; it also translated into lucrative contracts for a host of defense contractors, some of which were awarded deals amounting to billions of dollars[247].

Beyond the realm of defense spending, strategic energy interests were also at play. The Central Asian region, notably around the Caspian Sea, is rich in oil and natural gas reserves. There have been discussions and proposals about constructing a pipeline to transport these resources from the Caspian Sea, through Afghanistan and Pakistan, and eventually to the Indian Ocean. Controlling or influencing this region would mean not only strategic power but also potential access to vast economic gains from energy exports.[248]

It's also noteworthy to mention the U.S.'s shifting relationship with the Taliban. In the mid-1990s, the U.S. viewed the Taliban as a potential stabilizing force in Afghanistan, even mulling over potential collaboration to safeguard their interests in the region. However, by the late 1990s, especially during the latter part of Clinton's administration, this rapport began to deteriorate, with the U.S. distancing itself from the group due to growing concerns about their governance and human rights violations.[249]

When Bush-Cheney took office, it gave the Taliban leaders one last chance during a four-day meeting in Berlin in July 2001.[250] An ultimatum was given to the Taliban, *"either you accept our offer of a carpet*

[247] Schwartz, Moshe. "Defense Acquisitions: How and Where DOD Spends Its Contracting Dollars." Congressional Research Service, 2018.
[248] Klare, Michael T. "The New Geopolitics of Energy." The Nation, April 15, 2002.
[249] Rashid, Ahmed. Taliban: Militant Islam, Oil and Fundamentalism in Central Asia. Yale University Press, 2000.
[250] David Ray Griffin, *Bush and Cheney: How They Ruined America and the World, p 33*

of gold, or we bury you under a carpet of bombs."[251] As you probably guessed, the Taliban refused this offer, and the Bush-Cheney administration replied with *"military action against Afghanistan would go ahead... before snows start falling in Afghanistan, by the middle of October at the latest."*[252] With the 9/11 attacks, military action took place against Afghanistan on October 7, 2001.

Paul Wolfowitz is quoted as telling the 9/11 Commission that *"it can take a tragedy like September 11th to awaken the world to new threats and to the need for action,"*[253] both he and Donald Rumsfeld agreed that without 9/11 the President would have been unable to convince Congress to *"invade Afghanistan and overthrow the Taliban."*[254]

British Prime Minister Tony Blair said something very similar:
> *"To be truthful about it, there was no way we could have got the public consent to have suddenly launched a campaign on Afghanistan but for what happened on September 11."*[255]

While the statements above and the evidence do not conclusively establish that the mentioned individuals were complicit in a scheme regarding 9/11, they undeniably raise significant questions. The trail of actions, decisions, and, at times, apparent indifference points towards a more complex tapestry of motivations and objectives. For some, the aftermath of 9/11 seemed to present a strategic opportunity that they

---

[251] Jean-Brisard, *Forbidden Truth: US-Taliban Secret Oil Diplomacy and the Failed Hunt for Bin Laden*

[252] George Arney, *US 'Planned Attack on Taleban'* (British spelling), BBC News, September 18, 2001.

[253] David Ray Griffin, *Bush and Cheney: How They Ruined America and the World, p 33*

[254] *Day One Transcripts: 9/11 Commission Hearing*, Washington Post, March 23, 2004.

[255] London Times, July 17, 2002

might have been all too eager to exploit for broader geopolitical aims or even personal economic gain.

Historically, leaders and influential figures have often capitalized on crises to consolidate power, achieve policy objectives, or enhance their personal fortunes. In the aftermath of 9/11, a profound national tragedy, certain agendas were pursued with renewed vigor against this backdrop.

The human cost of such endeavors wasn't just in the immediate aftermath of the attacks but in the subsequent military engagements. Thousands of soldiers were dispatched to danger-filled regions, with many making the ultimate sacrifice. Using such a monumental tragedy for ulterior motives, especially when lives are at stake, raises deep ethical concerns. For the families of the soldiers and the citizens who put their trust in their leaders, such potential manipulations can feel like a profound betrayal.

That said, it's crucial to emphasize my personal conviction: I do not believe there were conspiracies to allow the 9/11 attacks to transpire. Instead, in the aftermath, opportunistic politicians and policymakers seemingly latched onto the event, exploiting it as a justification for implementing policies that, in the long run, proved deleterious for America.[256]

---

[256] Bacevich, Andrew J. The New American Militarism: How Americans Are Seduced by War. Oxford University Press, 2013.

THE CLINTON CRIME FAMILY

William "Bill" and Hillary Clinton rose to power starting with Bill's first office held as the Attorney General of Arkansas from January 3, 1977 - January 9, 1979, and through his ascension through various offices, eventually became the 42nd President of the United States in 1993. Going along with Bill on his ride to the White House was a very astute lawyer, his wife, Hillary. She would occupy various positions, including First Lady of Arkansas, First Lady of the United States, U.S. Senator for New York, U.S. Secretary of State, and the Democratic Party nominee for President in the 2016 election.

Even to the most casual onlookers, Hillary is the brains of the relationship. Bill had many talents in his own right, including a fantastic ability for charisma; however, Hillary's cunningness, drive, and ambition propelled them both to the White House. A skill Hillary does not possess is likeability; everyone, even those in her party, dislikes her personally. She is not the type of person that people genuinely like. Even Bill had less than favorable views of his wife, often referring to her as "*The Warden*"[257] or "*Hilla the Hun.*"[258]

Coming to Power

After earning his law degree from Yale Law School in 1973, Bill Clinton returned to Arkansas, determined to plunge into a political career. His future wife and Yale Law classmate, Hillary Rodham,

---

[257] Thomas D. Dupier, *I've Always Been a Yankees Fan* (Los Angeles: World Ahead Publishing, 2006) p 11
[258] Thomas D. Dupier, *I've Always Been a Yankees Fan* (Los Angeles: World Ahead Publishing, 2006) p 145

would join him in Arkansas, moving there in the summer of 1974, and they would marry in 1975.[259]

Bill's political ambitions in Arkansas were immediate and far-reaching. He ran for the House of Representatives in 1974 against Republican incumbent John Paul Hammerschmidt, which Bill lost in a close election. Following this initial setback, Clinton's political career gained momentum. In 1976, at the age of just 30, he was elected Arkansas Attorney General.[260]

His tenure as Attorney General set the stage for his successful run for the governorship of Arkansas. In 1978, at the age of 32, Bill Clinton became the nation's youngest governor. His terms as governor (1979–1981, 1983–1992).

Once governor Bill and Hillary immediately looked at how to use their power and influence to benefit themselves personally. She invested $1,000 in cattle futures and walked away with $99,537 in about 1-year.[261] This seemingly impossible feat of investment prowess was compared to *"had Hillary instead invested $1,000 in the first offering of Microsoft stock in 1986, she would have made $25,835 by March 1994."*[262]

One might consider it beginner's luck, as Hillary eloquently said whenever questioned about it. However, after some investigative

---

[259] Maraniss, David. "First Son: Bill Clinton and the Birth of American Politics." New York: Random House, 1995.
[260] "Bill Clinton: Life Before the Presidency." Miller Center, University of Virginia. https://millercenter.org/president/clinton/life-before-the-presidency
[261] Ambrose Evans-Pritchard, *The Secret Life of Bill Clinton.* Regnery Publishing, 1997, p 282
[262] Barbara Olson, *Hell to Pay,* Regnery Publishing, 1999, p. 188

journalists dug into the story a little more, they discovered that Hillary did not purchase the cattle futures directly; no, she had an associate purchase them on her behalf. That is not a crime; remember, this was long before eTrade online. Interestingly, the person who purchased the futures for her, Jim Blair, was the head legal counsel for Tyson Foods.[263] The same Tyson Foods that was currently in legal trouble with their poultry processing plants with *"tons of chicken feces that the plant dumped into nearby Dry Creek."*[264] After Hillary *earned* the $100k, Tyson was awarded $8 million in tax concessions, relaxation of environmental regulations[265], and $900k in state grant money to build roads into their plant.[266]

This wouldn't be the only time the Clintons received financial benefits from Tyson Foods and/or their owner, Don Tyson. The FBI investigated allegations that Tyson employee Joseph Hendrickson delivered envelopes with *"quarter-inch [thick with] $100 bills, on six different occasions to the governor's mansion."* He said the deliveries were for Bill Clinton.[267] Investigators felt they had enough evidence to charge Bill with bribery; however, the investigations were shut down by the upper echelons of the Arkansas State Police.[268]

How did the Clintons get away with this? It was simple: Bill stacked the deck in his favor by appointing as many of his hand-picked cronies as possible to every high-ranking position in the government. This is something he would repeat as President, and he

---

[263] Martin Gross, *The Great Whitewater Fiasco*, Ballantine Books, 19994, p. 7

[264] Barbara Olson, *Hell to Pay*, Regnery Publishing, 1999, p. 143

[265] Martin Gross, *The Great Whitewater Fiasco*, Ballantine Books, 19994, p. 104

[266] Barbara Olson, *Hell to Pay*, Regnery Publishing, 1999, p. 142

[267] Ambrose Evans-Pritchard, *The Secret Life of Bill Clinton*. Regnery Publishing, 1997, p 281

[268] Ambrose Evans-Pritchard, *The Secret Life of Bill Clinton*. Regnery Publishing, 1997, p 282

"quietly fired every U.S. Attorney in the country and then made his move on the FBI, which would be a replica of the Arkansas State Police."[269]

Rebuilding the U. S. Justice Department and the FBI would serve the Clintons many times over by carefully overlooking numerous crimes and scandals the Clintons would be a part of for decades.

Dr. Paul Fick wrote a psychological analysis of Bill:
"He had a rollercoaster candidacy with many highs and potential campaign destroying lows; he was faced with repeated embarrassing disclosures about his personal life; he responded to these disclosures with a glaring tendency to lie; he appeared indecisive and waffled on significant issues, and he was energized by the self-created chaos."[270]

Author Victor Thorn summarizes Hillary's corruption this way:
"Hillary Clinton has been directly involved in nearly every major scandal of the last thirty years, including Watergate, Whitewater Iran-Contra, Inslaw and PROMIS, the BCCI banking debacle, the disastrous S&L bailouts, drug trafficking in Mena while her husband was governor of Arkansas, Travelgate, Filegate, Waco, the murders of Vince Foster and Ron Brown, OKC, and the shootdown of flight 800".[271]

---

[269] Ambrose Evans-Pritchard, *The Secret Life of Bill Clinton*. Regnery Publishing, 1997, p xii

[270] James B. Stewart, *Blood Sport* (New York: Touchstone Books, 1996), p 121

[271] *Hillary (and Bill): The Sex Volume, Part One of the Clinton Trilogy*, by Victor Thorn, pg 16-17, 2008

Guns-for-Drugs Operation

During the end of the Iran-Contra saga, specifically the Guns-for-Drugs operation, CIA operations directed under Vice President Bush were trading U.S. weapons for cocaine and marijuana with the Contras. The drugs were flying 24x7 to a small airport in Mena, Arkansas, while Bill Clinton was Governor and became the base of the single largest cocaine smuggling operation in U.S. History.[272] Sworn testimony of Chip Tatum, a pilot for the CIA *"Pegasus"* project, recalled a conversation between him and Oliver North during a flight where North stated, *"One more year of this and we'll retire."* This was followed up with remarks about Barry Seal [*pilot that claimed he possessed evidence against Jeb Bush and was murdered in Miami*] and Governor Clinton, *"If we can keep those Arkansas hicks in line, that is."*[273]

> *"Bill Clinton and his circle of friends lived above the law and gained access to rivers of dirty [CIA drug] money in exchange for little more than keeping their mouths shut and staying out of the way."*[274]

Clinton's direct knowledge of the drugs is unquestioned. In 1988, Chuck Black the assistant prosecutor for Polk County told Gov. Clinton:

> *"We know what's going down here. We know about tons of cocaine and tons of weapons and hundreds of millions of dollars going through the local bank. We know about*

[272] Roger Morris, *Partners in Power*, 1996, p. 393
[273] Al Martin, *The Conspirators: Secrets of an Iran-Contra Insider*, pp 195-198
[274] Ambrose Evans-Pritchard, *The Secret Life of Bill Clinton*. Regnery Publishing, 1997, p 334-335

hundreds of people who have been trained here at Mena."[275]

Rather than put actual resources to assist the ADA with investigating the drugs coming into Mena, Gov. Clinton smashed the investigation, and later Arkansas Committee leader Tom Brown would recount a meeting with Gov. Clinton:

> *"Clinton told us he knew about the CIA, knew about Bush, and knew about the drugs, but for some reason, we never heard anything more about it.*"[276]

Why would Gov. Clinton allow this, except for the obvious fact of the money paid to him? Simple, he was just following orders from his CIA handlers. *"George Bush [was] in the direct chain of command"*[277] and Bill and Hillary were just puppets in a much larger show, *"understand that [Bill] Clinton is not the brilliant crook. It's just that he followed orders."*[278]

CIA Agent William Barr, who later was appointed U.S. Attorney General by George Bush, was quoted as screaming at Gov. Clinton in a meeting:

> *"Our deal was for you to get 10% of the profits, not 10% of the gross. This has turned into a feeding frenzy by your good-ole-boy sharks and you've had a hand in it too, Mr. Clinton. Just ask your Mr. Nash to produce a business card. I'll bet it reads Arkansas Development and Finance*

---

[275] Victor Thorn, *Hillary (and Bill): The Drugs Volume, Part Two of the Clinton Trilogy*, p 156
[276] Victor Thorn, *Hillary (and Bill): The Drugs Volume, Part Two of the Clinton Trilogy*, p 156
[277] David Bresnahan, *Damage Control*, p. 76
[278] R. Emmett Tyrrell, *Boy Clinton, p. 12*

Authority. This ADFA of yours is double-dipping. Our deal with you was to launder our money. You get 10% after costs and post-tax profits. No one agreed for you to start loaning out money to your friends through your ADFA so that they could buy machinery to build our guns. That wasn't the deal. Mr. Sawahata tells me that one of ADFA's first customers was some parking meter company that got several million dollars in ... how shall we say it. .. in preferred loans...Dammit, we bought a whole gun company, lock, stock, and barrel and shipped the whole thing down here for you. And Mr. Reed even help set it up. You people go and screw us by setting up some subcontractors that weren't even authorized by us. ****, people who didn't even have security clearances. That's why we're pulling the operation out of Arkansas. It's become a liability for us. We don't need alive liabilities. "[279]

Despite mountains of demonstrable evidence that tons of illegal drugs were being imported into Mena and billions of dollars in illicit drug money were being laundered in local Arkansas banks, *"not a single major bust was ever made out of Arkansas, out of Mena."*[280] In fact, *"officials repeatedly involved national security to quash most of the investigations"*[281] As time passed, it became *"apparent that Mena enjoyed a special status. Every attempt to investigate met with inference. Investigator Russell Welch of the Arkansas Police was ordered to stay away from the drug activity at the Mena Airport."*[282]

---

[279] Morris, *Partners in Power*, p 412
[280] Denton, Morris, *The Crimes of Mena*, p 7
[281] Denton, Morris, *The Crimes of Mena*, p 7
[282] Evans-Pritchard, *The Secret Life of Bill Clinton*, p 30

"By the end of 1987, thousands of law enforcement man-hours and an enormous amount of evidence of drug smuggling, aiding and abetting drug smugglers, conspiracy, perjury [and] money laundering had gone to waste. Not only were no indictments ever returned on any of the individuals under investigation for their role in the Mena operation, there was a complete breakdown in the judicial system. The United States Attorney, Western Judicial District of Arkansas refused to issue subpoenas for critical witnesses, interfered in the investigations, misled grand juries about evidence and availability of the witnesses, refused to allow investigators to present evidence to the grand jury, and in general made a mockery of the inter investigative and judicial process."[283]

"During the 1980s, as much as $100 million a month in cocaine had been flown into the airport at Mena and much of that money had been laundered through ADFA, a bonding agency Governor Clinton had created to help small businesses get started."[284]

There is little doubt that the ADFA was little more than a *"wholly-controlled financial entity for laundering large sums of cocaine money from Mena,"*[285] with *"upwards of $18 billion [passing] through ADFA between 1985 and 1992."*[286]

---

[283] Kenn Thomas, *Parapolitics*, p 182
[284] Mara Leveritt, *The Boys on the Tracks*, p 310
[285] Terry Reed & John Cummings, *Compromised*, p 232
[286] Craig Roberts, *The Medusa File*, p 353-354

Where did all this money go? Back into the hands of the criminal conspirators, of course. In December 1988, the ADFA raised a $50 million bond to build homes for the poor; instead, the $50 million was wired to Fuji Bank, Grand Cayman Branch, account #63119808.[287] Why else would money be sent to the Cayman Islands, except for drug smuggling? Last I checked, Home Depot and Lowes do not have you wire money to offshore financial havens when you order lumber.

Of course, an astute reader might say to themselves, "*but these bonds are loans and must be paid back.*" In reality, they were purposefully designed never to be paid back and were just "*being zeroed out - as though payments were being made - when in fact no payments of any kind were being made.*"[288] This is a typical Ponzi scheme; the accounting books can be cooked as long as deposits keep coming in from laundering drug money.

To add insult to injury, after seasoning the loans for a year or two, the ADFA would package these junk bonds along with good bonds and sell them off to various banks. Former ADFA marketing director Larry Nichols claims:

> "*that no one was actually buying these bonds; that they were instead sold to out-of-state banks, two with connections to [international drug money laundering bank] BCCI. The losses from these junk bonds were then mixed into the vortex of vanishing money in the S&L [Savings & Loans] crisis.*"[289]

---

[287] Evans-Pritchard, *The Secret Life of Bill Clinton*, p 311
[288] David Bresnahan, *Damage Control*, p.48
[289] Mara Leveritt, *The Boys on the Tracks*, p 209

If that wasn't bad enough, every bond issued by ADFA had the loan documents executed at the same law firm Hillary worked for, the Rose Law Firm.[290]

Whitewater Scandal

One of the earliest and most persistent controversies associated with the Clintons, particularly during Bill Clinton's presidency, was the Whitewater scandal. This controversy had its roots in a series of real estate investments made by the Clintons along with their partners, Jim and Susan McDougal, in the Whitewater Development Corporation during the 1970s and 1980s.

While the actual dealings were relatively modest—centering on a failed attempt to develop vacation properties on land along the White River in Arkansas—the repercussions were vast. Over time, allegations of impropriety and potential illegal conduct began to emerge, suggesting that Bill Clinton, during his tenure as Arkansas' governor, had exerted pressure on local officials to lend money to Susan McDougal, some of which allegedly found its way into Bill Clinton's gubernatorial campaign coffers.[291]

As the Clintons rose in national prominence, the Whitewater controversy refused to fade away. In 1994, under pressure from Republican leaders and amidst increasing media scrutiny, President Clinton agreed to an independent inquiry. This led to the appointment of Kenneth Starr as a special prosecutor. Over the next several years, Starr's investigation expanded to include other

---

[290] John Dee, *Snow Job*, p. 4
[291] Maraniss, David. First in His Class: A Biography of Bill Clinton. Simon & Schuster, 1995.

controversies surrounding the Clinton administration, including the Monica Lewinsky affair.[292]

While the Whitewater controversy itself yielded few concrete outcomes (no charges were ever brought against the Clintons in relation to Whitewater), its offshoots became a significant thorn in the side of the Clinton administration. Jim and Susan McDougal were both convicted of fraud in relation to their banking practices, and the Clintons' involvement, though proven to be limited, was a source of considerable political and media speculation.[293]

What we know is that a real estate investment company called Whitewater Developer Corporation was formed in 1979 by Bill & Hillary Clinton[294] and Jim & Susan McDougal. When Bill was transitioning from Attorney General of Arkansas to the Governor of Arkansas, Hillary was working for a legal firm that would represent Whitewater, Jim was running the bank Madison Guaranty Savings and Loan, and Susan was an aide to Bill Clinton.

One of the central allegations was that Bill and Hillary Clinton, in collaboration with their business partners, the McDougals, engaged in fraudulent practices. The core of this claim suggests that the Clintons, through their influence, enabled James McDougal's bank, Madison Guaranty Savings and Loan Association, to issue questionable loans. These loans, according to critics, were designed

---

[292] Toobin, Jeffrey. A Vast Conspiracy: The Real Story of the Sex Scandal That Nearly Brought Down a President. Random House, 1999.

[293] Gormley, Ken. The Death of American Virtue: Clinton vs. Starr. Crown, 2010.

[294] Jeff Gerth, "Clintons Joined S. & L. Operator In an Ozark Real-Estate Venture", New York Times, March 8, 1992.
(https://select.nytimes.com/gst/abstract.html?res=F10614FC345C0C7B8CDDAA0894D A494D81)

to benefit the Clintons directly or were allocated to *"straw buyers"* whose purpose was to sustain the floundering Whitewater Development Corp.[295]

This matter was further complicated by the death of Vince Foster, a deputy White House counsel and personal lawyer to the Clintons. After Foster's tragic suicide in 1993, questions arose about the removal of certain documents from his office. Given Foster's close professional relationship with the Clintons and his involvement in several sensitive matters, including Whitewater, speculations swirled regarding the nature of the documents that might have been in his possession at the time of his death.

Many years after these events, Judicial Watch, a conservative non-profit organization, played a key role in rekindling discussions around the Whitewater affair. Their efforts led to the procurement of federal prosecutors' notes through a Freedom of Information Act request.[296] These notes indicated that there was a belief, at least among some involved in the investigation:

> *"Several pieces of evidence support the inference that personal documents which Hillary Clinton did not want disclosed were located in (Clinton personal lawyer Vince) Foster's office at the time of his death and then removed."*[297]

> *"That evening and the next morning, (White House counsel Bernie) Nussbaum, Hillary Clinton, Susan*

---

[295] Gormley, Ken. The Death of American Virtue: Clinton vs. Starr. Crown, 2010.
[296] Judicial Watch. "Judicial Watch Obtains Previously Redacted Material from the Starr Report." Press Release, September 14, 2018
[297] Ibid

Thomases and Maggie Williams (Hillary Clinton's chief of staff) exchanged 10 separate phones calls. . . . That morning, according to the (Department of Justice) employees, Nussbaum changed his mind and refused to allow the prosecutors to review the documents; instead, he reviewed them himself and segregated several as 'personal' to the Clintons."[298]

"On the evening of July 22, 1993, Thomas Castleton . . . assisted Williams in carrying a box of personal documents up to . . . a closet in Hillary Clinton's office. The closet is approximately 30 feet from the table in the Book Room, where the billing records were found two years later. . . . There is a circumstantial case that the records were left on the table by Hillary Clinton. She is the only individual in the White House who had a significant interest in them and she is one of only three people known to have had them in her possession since their creation in February 1992."[299]

The prosecutors never filed for an indictment of the Clintons because they felt they had less than a 10% chance of convicting Hillary for her actions. They contend the evidence was substantial that she most likely knew about the illegal activities; however, they did not have enough evidence to prove she actively participated in said illegal actions. The evidence they suspected to exist mysteriously disappeared, and Hillary is the last person known to have the items in her possession.

---

[298] Ibid
[299] Ibid

In the end, many persons surrounding the Clintons, including one of Hillary's law partners, Webster Hubbell, were convicted for crimes including embezzlement, concealment of funds, fraud, and other financial crimes. In addition to Webster, fifteen others were convicted of more than 40 crimes.[300] Four of these individuals convicted, all close Clinton aides, were later pardoned by President Clinton.[301]

The Israeli Mossad Killed Hillary's Lawyer and She Covered It Up.

Vince Foster, a lawyer and *"Hillary Clinton's closest friend, the one person in the world that she would entrust with the most sensitive problems,"*[302] was found dead in an overgrown and obscure park in Washington DC. The full story of his death could take up an entire book or even a series of books to fully cover this complex subject's details. I invite you to read *Hillary (and Bill) The Murder Volume: Part Three of the Clinton Trilogy by Victor Thorn* as he gives a much more detailed account than I can do justice to in this section.

The official government story was Vince was depressed and took his own life. In fact, it was an ill-planned murder that, if not for the political power of the First Lady, even the most junior detective in the country would have solved the case before breakfast.

---

[300] *"Caught in the Whitewater Quagmire"*, *Washington Post*, August 28, 1995; Page A01]
(https://www.washingtonpost.com/wp-srv/politics/special/whitewater/stories/wwtr950828.htm)
[301] Pardons by President Clinton, Wikipedia
(https://en.wikipedia.org/wiki/List_of_people_pardoned_by_Bill_Clinton#Pardons)
[302] James B. Stewart, *Blood Sport* (New York: Touchstone Books, 1996), p 35

So why was Vince murdered? Was it Hillary who ordered it? While he knew a lot of dirt on the Clintons, they knew he was their staunch supporter and advocate. Additionally, the cover-up details were very 'last-minute,' and any murder ordered by the Clintons would have allowed for more time to plan a cover-up. So, if it was not Hillary, then who killed Vince? In one word, the Mossad.

The Mossad is Israel's version of the United State's NSA. *"In Arkansas, the Mossad is said to have found out about Vince Foster's payoff role in the illegal CIA backed drugs-and-guns-and-money in Mena operation, and so the Israelis blackmailed Foster for information on FOBs (Friends of Bill Clinton - who by this time had made it to the White House)."* [303]

According to insiders, the details of his arrangement with the Mossad included:

> *"Foster was to leak codes and secrets to the Israelis in exchange for their promise to not expose him, his connections with drug running and money laundering for Clinton, and in addition, the Israelis would add to his Swiss bank account - which they had already discovered by means of their very special computer software [PROMIS] given [stolen] to them by someone in the U.S. government."* [304]

The PROMIS software was rumored to be stolen from the U.S. and given to the Mossad using the information provided by Foster.

---

[303] Devon Jackson, *Conspiranoia*, p 279
[304] John Austin, *Rkansides*, p 123

At the time of his death, he was in some serious trouble as *"the CIA had Foster under serious investigation for leaking high-security secrets to the State of Israel."*[305] In the weeks leading up to his death, Vince began writing down details and collecting evidence of his actions on behalf of Israel so that he could turn state's evidence and seek immunity for his actions. His wife corroborates this during her interviews with investigators.

On the day of his death, by all outward appearances, Vince was acting normal and did not give any indications that he would kill himself that day to any of his co-workers. Of course, as a career liar and manipulator of facts, it is very possible he was able to fool even those around him. However, these statements by his co-workers aside, the actual facts of the case point strictly to murder and coverup.

The last two people to officially see Vince alive were Linda Tripp when around *"one pm on July 20, 1993, Foster stopped by Tripp's desk, lifted some M&Ms from a bowl and said, 'I'll be back.' He never returned."*[306] and Secret Service officer John Skyles as he was guarding the gate Foster excited shortly after 1pm.[307] He would later testify before the Senate that *"Foster did not appear to be at all depressed or preoccupied as he walked by."*[308]

Interestingly, while the Secret Service has a log entry of Foster walking out of the White House, he is not driving his vehicle out of the parking lot that afternoon. There is an entry of him parking his vehicle in the morning, but no log entry nor video surveillance tapes

[305] Jim Norman, *Fostergate*, p 1
[306] Michael Isikoff, *Uncovering Clinton*, p 132
[307] Michael Kellett, *The Murder of Vince Foster*, p 30
[308] George Carpozi, *Clinton Confidential*, p 465

of him driving off. Yet his car somehow manages to leave the secured parking garage, travel across town, and ends up in a parking lot adjacent to the park, where his body is found hours later. How is it possible that someone can be 'missed' by the Secret Service coming and going from one of the most secure buildings in the world? Either the officer should have been fired for incompetence, or more likely, someone with significant power could make the log entry and videotapes disappear.

Back in Little Rock, Arkansas on the day of the murder at around 4:48 pm CST (5:48 pm EST) Trooper Larry Patterson received a phone call *"It was [Trooper] Roger Perry. He said that he just received a call from Helen Dickey [White House aide and former nanny of Chelsea] that Vince Foster had blown his brains out in the parking lot of the White House."*[309] This phone call took place approximately 30 minutes before Park Police first found Vince's body at Fort Marcy Park, and at that time, they had yet to identify who the person was.

Yes, you read this correctly. White House staff called a friend back in Arkansas saying Vince had killed himself in the White House parking lot, yet the official location where his body was discovered was in a park some 20 minutes away. To top it off, this phone call was 30 minutes before Vince's body was officially found as a John Doe in the park and nearly four hours before Park Police formally notified the White House of Foster's death.

Troopers Perry and Patterson were interviewed and confirmed the approximate 4:45-4:48 p.m. timeline when the phone call occurred. They also stated they felt that the FBI agent interviewing

---

[309] Christopher Ruddy, *Vincent Foster: The Ruddy Investigation,* p 135

them was attempting to convince them to "*change my story*" to get the timeline to match with the White House's official story.[310]

Vince Foster's body was found at 6:14 pm EST (5:15 pm CST) by U.S. Park Police deep inside the wooded Fort Marcy Park, which is best described as a '*deserted park*'.[311] According to the original officers on scene, the body was found lying supine with arms neatly by his sides, palms up, with no weapon found by the body. "*A .38 caliber revolver was found in the car.*"[312]

Sgt. George Gonzalez, U.S. Park Police was the first officer to discover Foster's body and he insisted under questioning by the FBI that there had been no gun near or on the body, or in either hand.[313] Two other witnesses including Sgt John Rolla, stated that there was no gun in Foster's hands when they arrived and that "*the palms were up.*"[314]

According to the official story, Vince parked his car [yes the same car that "magically left" the White House parking lot] and walked 700 plus feet through highly-grown summer vegetation, yet miraculously "*the FBI lab found not a speck of soil on his shoes or clothing. No grass stains were mentioned. No soil -- yet almost every garment of clothing, including his underwear, was covered in multi-colored carpet fibers.*"[315] Obviously this man missed his calling in life, he should not have been a high-priced lawyer, he should have been a

---

[310] Christopher Ruddy, *Vincent Foster: The Ruddy Investigation*, p 136
[311] Christopher Ruddy, *Vincent Foster: The Ruddy Investigation*, p 169
[312] Kellet, *The Murder of Vince Foster*, p 147

[313] John Austin, *Rkansides*, p 124
[314] Kellet, *The Murder of Vince Foster*, p 147
[315] Christopher Ruddy, *Vincent Foster: The Ruddy Investigation*, p x

magician. Not only did he make his car disappear from a secure White House parking lot and reappear in a park, but he also managed to levitate his body through 700 feet of wooded area without a single piece of grass or dirt getting on his clothing.

"Beyond belief, when official reports were released, they stated the gun which Vince Foster supposedly used to kill himself was still in his hand upon death."[316] The official report even included a photograph of Vince with a gun in his hand. Yet the sworn testimony of the officers on the scene all say the gun was located in his vehicle, not his hand. The gun that was later claimed to be in his hand, was discovered to have no fingerprints from Foster on the gun, nor any blood.[317]

Medical examiner observed a *"small caliber bullet hole on the ride side of Foster's neck, possibly a .22 caliber,"*[318] which is inconsistent with the .38 reported to be found in Foster's hand.

The truth is Foster was murdered in the parking lot of the White House by Mossad agents, fearful that Vince was about to tell the truth about Israeli involvement in the theft of U.S. Government secrets. They killed him and left his body for Hillary to deal with; they knew that if Foster were 'murdered,' she would be the first to get blamed. Hillary then went into panicked 'fixer' mode, had his body wrapped up in the carpet, which explains the carpet fibers on his body, moved out to the park, and tried to cover the tracks as a suicide.

---

[316] Victor Thorn, *Hillary (and Bill) The Murder Volume: Part Three of the Clinton Thrilogy*, p 95
[317] Richard Odom, *Circle of Death* p 38
[318] Patrick Matrisciana, *The Clinton Chronicles Book*, p 128

Within hours of Foster's death, Hillary's team had the Secret Service's Maintenance and Installation Group break into Foster's White House safe and quickly cleared out most of the files in his office. Why would Hillary do this? To prevent the FBI or Park Police from accidentally finding incriminating evidence against the Clintons that Vince may or may not have saved.

Sexual Misdeeds

Many intelligent men in the past have had various forms of addiction, either drugs or alcohol. *"Everyone you think he fucked, he did -- and the more dangerous the better . . . His addiction is pussy."*[319]

In 1999, Capitol Hill Blue published a scathing report saying, *"Juanita isn't the only one: Bill Clinton's long history of sexual violence against women dates back some 30 years."* [320] This, of course, was referring to Juanita Broaddrick, a former nursing home administrator who alleged Clinton raped her in a hotel room and had the Arkansas State Police cover it up in the 1970s.

Bill's history of sexual interactions with females is questionable at best and at worst outright forcible rape. He has been accused of:

- Raping Juanita Broaddrick when he served as Arkansas Attorney General in 1978[321]

---

[319] Daniel Halper, *Clinton, Inc.: The Audacious Rebuilding of a Political Machine*, p 55
[320] Roger Stone, *The Clinton's War on Women*, p 40
[321] Romano, Lois; Baker, Peter (February 20, 1999). *"Another Clinton Accuser Goes Public"*. *Washington Post*. (https://www.washingtonpost.com/wp-srv/politics/special/clinton/stories/janedoe022099.htm)

- Sexual assaulting Leslie Milwee in 1980[322]
- Forcibly groping Kathleen Willey and forcing her hand upon his erect penis without her permission in 1993[323]
- Forcing the former Miss Arkansas, Elizabeth Ward Gracen to have sex with him against her will in 1983 when she *"in tears she described Clinton pushing himself on her as she pleased she did not want to have sex"*[324]
- Exposing himself to Paula Jones multiple times between 1998-1999[325]

These are just a few women who publicly accused Bill of rape or sexual misconduct against their will. This does not even touch the ones who were paid to keep quiet, nor does it cover the ones who had consensual adulterous sexual relations with Bill while he was married. I do not care what consenting adults do behind closed doors; it is not my business if he cheated on Hillary, and it is not the business of anyone else. What concerns me is Bill's reported abuse of power in using government resources for personal gain and covering up rape. Case in point when *"nearly a dozen Arkansas state police troopers were used as pimps in uniform to feed their boss's insatiable sexual appetite."*[326]

"We were required to work overtime so we could sit outside some place and block the road or sit in some

[322] The Washington Times. "*Leslie Millwee, former reporter, accuses Bill Clinton of sexual assault 'on three occasions' in 1980*".
(https://www.washingtontimes.com/news/2016/oct/19/leslie-millwee-former-reporter-accuses-bill-clinton/)

[323] Graves, Florence; Sharkey, Jacqueline E. (April 29, 1999). "*Starr and Willey: The Untold Story*". The Nation. (https://www.thenation.com/article/starr-and-willey-untold-story/)

[324] Roger Stone, *The Clinton's War on Women*, p 59

[325] *Clinton v. Jones*, No. 95-1853 U.S. (May 27, 1997).
(http://laws.findlaw.com/us/000/95-1853.html)

[326] The American Spectator, His Cheatin' Heart, David Brock

driveway or apartment complex while he went in to take
care of his female friends. . . State money was utilized."
Arkansas State Trooper, Larry Patterson.[327]

This is the big difference between Bill's sexual activities and President Donald Trump's. Bill abused his power to subvert justice when he raped multiple women and converted government funds to pay for state troopers to act as pimps, whereas Trump had consensual sex with models, paid them to keep quiet, and lied about it to his wife. There are no rape accusations against Trump, just an old billionaire with extra marital sex with a porn star. While this is not inline with my personal morals, in the end, I do not care who someone has consensual sex with.

At first, Clinton would bribe his victims to keep quiet. If that didn't work, he would have his thugs make threatening phone calls telling them to *"keep your mouth shut about Bill Clinton and go on with your life."*[328] If the initial phone calls did not send the message they would then be followed up with IRS Audits and threats, including at least four of his victims Gennifer Flowers, Paula Jones, Juanita Broaddrick and Elizabeth Gracen all receiving threats by the IRS.[329]

Hillary was also a willing co-conspirator in Bill's sexually deviant acts, choosing the path of political power rather than allowing the public truth of Bill's most illicit activities to come to light. She knew it would be the end of both of their political careers if Bill was found

---

[327] Interview with Larry Patterson, *The Clinton Chronicles*
[328] Actress Who Claimed Sex with Bill Says IRS Is Hounding Her, *New York Post, January 23, 1999*
[329] Bill and Hillary Clinton's Latest Scandal?, *Men's News Daily,* December 23, 2005

guilty of rape and adultery. For this reason, *"Hillary hired private detectives to identify the women her husband was sleeping with [and raping], and to intimidate these women so they would not go public with their stories."*[330] So much for Hillary being a champion for women's rights.

The Clinton Campaign paid private investigator Anthony Pellicano $100,000 in *"legal fees"*[331] to prevent women from *"going public with accusations that Bill Clinton had bedded, raped, impregnated, sexually assaulted or otherwise used and abused them."*[332] But do not just take my word for it, let's read Pellicano's own words in an interview for the January 1992 issue of *GQ Magazine*: *"I'm an expert with a knife...I can shred your face with a knife."*[333] What legitimate reason would the Clintons have for a thug like that on the payroll, and why would it be listed as "legal fees"?

After the election, White House Chief of Staff Betsey Wright reportedly kept Pellicano on the payroll to keep a lid on Bill Clinton's *"bimbo eruptions."*[334]

Jeffrey Epstein

Bill's misdeeds are not limited to the women we already know about; he has been rumored to have engaged in sex with underage girls on the private Boeing 727 jet of convicted pedophile and

---

[330] *Hillary Clinton's hired thugs quieted Bill Clinton's mistresses*, Washington Times, R. Emmett Tyrrell Jr., October 4, 2016
(https://www.washingtontimes.com/news/2016/oct/4/hillary-clintons-hired-thugs-quieted-bill-clintons/)
[331] Barbara Olson, *Hell to Pay*, p. 79
[332] Richard Poe, *Hillary's Secret War*, p 27
[333] Richard Poe, *Hillary's Secret War*, p 26
[334] Richard Poe, *Hillary's Secret War*, p 26

registered sex offender Jeffrey Epstein. His jet was often referred to in the media as the "Lolita Express." Flight logs obtained from the Federal Aviation Administration (FAA) by Gawker[335] in January 2015 put former President Clinton:

> *"[on the] billionaire's infamous jet more than a dozen times sometimes with a woman whom federal prosecutors suspect of procuring underage sex victims for Mr. Epstein"[336].*

During at least five of these flights with Epstein; Clinton turned down Secret Service escort and protection.[337] A claim that the Secret

[335] Gawker Flight Logs of President Clinton and Mr. Epstein. (https://gawker.com/flight-logs-put-clinton-dershowitz-on-pedophile-billio-1681039971)

[336] Douglas Ernst, Saturday, May 14, 2016 The Washington Times (https://www.washingtontimes.com/news/2016/may/14/bill-clinton-ditched-secret-service-on-multiple-lo/)

[337] Malia Zimmerman, Fox News May 13, 2016 (https://www.foxnews.com/us/2016/05/13/flight-logs-show-bill-clinton-flew-on-sex-offenders-jet-much-more-than-previously-known.html)

Service will not confirm nor deny officially. Bill has flown on Epstein's private jet at least 26 times.[338]

"Bill Clinton ... associated with a man like Jeffrey Epstein, who everyone in New York, certainly within his inner circles, knew was a pedophile," said Conchita Sarnoff, of the Washington, D.C. based non-profit Alliance to Rescue Victims of Trafficking. *"Why would a former president associate with a man like that?"*

In 2005, Palm Beach Police investigated Epstein for over a year after the parents of a 14-year-old girl alleged their daughter was lured to Epstein's mansion, paid $300 to strip to her underwear and massage Epstein.[339] Police interviewed dozens of witnesses, confiscated his trash, performed surveillance, and searched his Palm Beach mansion. During their search, police found large numbers of photos of nude and semi-nude underage girls throughout the house, some of whom the police had interviewed in the course of their investigation.[340] After their investigation, they identified 20 girls between the ages of 14 and 17 who they said were sexually abused by Epstein. [341]

In 2006, the FBI was brought in to assist local police and launched their own probe into allegations that Epstein and his

---

[338] John T. Bennett, *Report: Bill Clinton Flew on Disgraced Donor's Jet 26 Times*, May 13, 2016
[339] Weiss, Philip (December 10, 2007). *"The Fantasist"*. New York.
(https://web.archive.org/web/20161017175912/http://nymag.com/news/features/41826/)
[340] *"Billionaire in Palm Beach sex scandal; Investigators: Moneyman Jeffrey Epstein solicited teen masseuses"*. Smoking Gun. July 26, 2006.
(https://web.archive.org/web/20150112112028/http://thesmokinggun.com/documents/se x/billionaire-palm-beach-sex-scandal)
[341] Malia Zimmerman, Fox News May 13, 2016
(http://www.foxnews.com/us/2016/05/13/flight-logs-show-bill-clinton-flew-on-sex-offenders-jet-much-more-than-previously-known.html)

personal assistants had *"used facilities of interstate commerce to induce girls between the ages of 14 and 17 to engage in illegal sexual activities."*[342]

According to court documents, police investigators found a *"clear indication that Epstein's staff was frequently working to schedule multiple young girls between the ages of 12 and 16 years old literally every day, often two or three times per day."*

The U.S. Attorney for the Southern District of Florida prepared to charge Epstein with child sex abuse, witness tampering, and money laundering. Somehow, Epstein was tipped off and pleaded guilty to just one count of soliciting prostitution from an underage girl under Florida state law before an indictment could be handed up.

Bush's Attorney General Alberto Gonzales, told the *Daily Beast* that he *"instructed the Justice Department to pursue justice without making a political mess."*[343] This is basically all you need to know about the case, Clinton's friends are protected at all costs. It does not matter Republican or Democrat, it is one Deep State of corruption.

On Sept. 24, 2007, in a deal shrouded in secrecy that left alleged victims shocked at its leniency, Epstein agreed to a 30-month sentence, including 18 months of jail time and 12 months of house arrest, and the agreement to pay dozens of young girls under a federal statute providing for compensation to victims of child sexual abuse.

---

[342] Lewis, Paul; Swaine, Jon (January 10, 2015). *"Jeffrey Epstein: Inside the decade of scandal entangling Prince Andrew"*. Guardian.
(http://www.theguardian.com/world/2015/jan/10/jeffrey-epstein-decade-scandal-prince-andrew)
[343] Roger Stone, *The Clinton's War on Women, p 122*

In exchange, the U.S. Attorney's Office promised not to pursue any federal charges against Epstein or his co-conspirators.

It has been rumored that Epstein had beds installed in his private jet along with hidden cameras to record the sex acts between his wealthy friends and underage boys/girls. If this latter part is true, it would be reasonable to believe that he is in possession of incriminating video evidence against some very powerful people, possibly including the former President.

We are left to wonder how Epstein got off so light on his sentencing. If the situation was different and the evidence was against any other person like you or me, you know the jail sentence would have been much stiffer. It is evident to everyone that someone in high power determined that a public trial of Epstein would bring the underage sex activities of Clinton and other politically powerful individuals into the public light. Even if, for the sake of argument, Bill Clinton was not being blackmailed by Epstein, the fact that Epstein was able to bargain down his charges proves there are two justice systems in this country: one for you and me, and one for the rich and powerful.

A few years after I wrote the manuscript of the first edition of this book, the world was once again captivated by the Jeffrey Epstein Story. After he was taken into custody on fresh charges of sex trafficking. His extensive associations with politicians, royals, and celebrities amplified the case's intrigue and drew heightened scrutiny from the media and the public alike.

Epstein's subsequent death in a jail cell at the Metropolitan Correctional Center was officially ruled a suicide.[344] However, the myriad inconsistencies surrounding the event fueled widespread speculation and gave birth to several conspiracy theories. One of the primary anomalies that sparked suspicion was the malfunction of surveillance cameras during the critical hours of Epstein's apparent suicide. This raised serious questions about the operational integrity of a facility that held such a high-profile detainee.

Moreover, Epstein reportedly tried to take his own life just weeks before his death.[345] Given this suicide attempt, many questioned why Epstein wasn't under more stringent observation. These lapses in security protocols became a significant point of contention and led to investigations into the jail's handling of such a high-risk inmate.[346]

The overarching narrative that dominated discussions post-Epstein's death revolved around the valuable information he possessed. Given the severity of the charges against him and the potential lifetime imprisonment, it was believed that Epstein could offer evidence against other influential figures as part of a plea deal.[347] But with his untimely passing, any such prospects were unequivocally extinguished.

A series of lawsuits and investigations into Epstein's associates followed his death. However, with Epstein gone, much of the

[344] Williams, Katie, and Christina Goldbaum. "Jeffrey Epstein Dead in Suicide at Jail, Spurring Inquiries." The New York Times, August 10, 2019
[345] Miroff, Nick, Matt Zapotosky, and Devlin Barrett. "Before his death, Jeffrey Epstein was left alone and not closely monitored." The Washington Post, August 11, 2019.
[346] Brown, Julie K., and Kevin G. Hall. "Even guards are shocked by what goes on at this jail." Miami Herald, August 16, 2019.
[347] Briquelet, Kate. "Jeffrey Epstein Spent Time Alone With Young Woman In Prison's Attorney Room." The Daily Beast, July 30, 2019

information and potential leads were lost. The long list of Epstein's influential connections, coupled with the manner of his death, led to various hypotheses, including that his death might have been orchestrated to prevent him from revealing incriminating details about others.[348]

While the official narrative posits Epstein's death as a suicide, a significant portion of the public remains skeptical. The aura of mystery, speculation, and the intricate web of relationships Epstein maintained ensure that his story remains both haunting and compelling, with the truth perhaps forever out of reach.

Clinton Foundation

Established in 1997, the Clinton Foundation emerged as former President Bill Clinton's philanthropic brainchild, intending to address global challenges like health, climate change, and economic disparity. By 2016, the foundation boasted an impressive donor base, accumulating contributions exceeding $2 billion. The institution prided itself on numerous initiatives, tackling issues such as HIV/AIDS treatment, climate resilience, and women's empowerment.[349]

However, the foundation's laudable objectives did not make it immune to controversies, some of which surfaced even before Bill Clinton concluded his presidential tenure. A notable incident from October 1999 raised eyebrows. Only a month after the Clinton

---

[348] Osborne, Samuel. "Jeffrey Epstein: Conspiracy theories surrounding billionaire's death explained." The Independent, August 13, 2019

[349] Chozick, Amy. "From Small Beginnings, Clinton Foundation Grew Beyond Original Plans." The New York Times, August 13, 2013

administration's Federal Trade Commission decided against regulating beer, wine, and liquor advertising – especially ones potentially targeting minors – Anheuser-Busch, a major brewery, generously donated $1 million to the Clinton Foundation.[350] Critics immediately viewed this substantial donation with suspicion, questioning the potential quid pro quo between the brewery and the foundation.

The foundation's financing has been a recurring subject of debate. Donations from foreign governments and entities fueled concerns, particularly during Hillary Clinton's tenure as Secretary of State. Critics pointed to possible conflicts of interest, implying that donors might expect favorable treatment from the State Department or a potential Clinton White House.[351]

Furthermore, the 2010 Uranium One deal turned into a flashpoint, with allegations suggesting that the State Department's approval of a deal benefiting a Russian state-owned enterprise might have been influenced by donations to the Clinton Foundation.[352] Though no direct evidence confirmed a quid pro quo, the mere perception of potential impropriety cast a shadow over the foundation.

Defenders of the Clinton Foundation argue that the institution has done significant humanitarian work worldwide and that

---

[350] Seelye, Katharine Q. "Beer Maker's Donation to Clinton Foundation Is Questioned." The New York Times, October 21, 1999
[351] Becker, Jo, and Mike McIntire. "Cash Flowed to Clinton Foundation Amid Russian Uranium Deal." The New York Times, April 23, 2015.
[352] Helderman, Rosalind S., and Tom Hamburger. "The Clintons, a luxury jet and their $100 million donor from Canada." The Washington Post, May 3, 2015.

criticisms are politically motivated.[353] However, the intertwining of philanthropy, politics, and power remains a contentious subject, with the foundation emblematic of the complexities involved.

In January 2009, before Hillary could be confirmed as the Secretary of State for the Obama administration, she sat before the Senate Foreign Relations Committee to answer questions about her involvement in the Clinton Foundation.

> *"The core of the problem is that foreign governments and entities may perceive the Clinton Foundation as a means to gain favor with the Secretary of State," Senator Richard Lugar.[354]*

With this controversy hot on their minds, the Senators required Hillary to sign a Memorandum of Understanding (MOU) that would outline her commitments to transparency regarding certain types of donations to the Clinton Foundation while Hillary served as Secretary of State.

The notable points included[355]:

- The Clinton Foundation would disclose its contributors: "... *The Foundation will publish its contributors this year. During any service by Senator Clinton as Secretary of State,*

---

[353] Sargent, Greg. "Yes, the Clinton Foundation saga is absurd." The Washington Post, August 24, 2016

[354] Bolton, Alexander. "*Cornyn: Clinton duped Congress during confirmation*", *The Hill* (September 5, 2016). (http://thehill.com/homenews/senate/294376-cornyn-clinton-played-both-sides-of-foundation-debate-during-confirmation)

[355] Blake, Aaron, "*Hillary Clinton, the Clinton Foundation and the promises she made about it, explained*", The Washington Post, September 2, 2016

the Foundation will publish annually the names of contributors."

- Bill Clinton would not *"personally solicit funds"* for the Clinton Global Initiative (CGI), a subsidiary of the Clinton Foundation, and its annual meeting in New York to address global issues such as poverty, health, and climate change.

- CGI also would not accept contributions from foreign governments, except through attendance fees, and it would suspend plans to do international events such as the one held annually in New York.

- Other subsidiaries, including the Clinton HIV/AIDS Initiative, which hadn't been disclosing donors, would disclose any new contributors or increased contributions beyond what donors had already been giving: *"... The Foundation will share such countries and the circumstances of the anticipated contribution with the State Department designated agency ethics official for review, and as appropriate, the State Department's designated agency ethics official will submit the matter for review by a designated official in the White House Counsel's Office."*

Uranium One

Between 2009 and 2013, a Russian-controlled company purchased Uranium One, based in Canada, which controls almost one-fifth of all uranium production in America. Due to the apparent security ramifications of outside entities' controlling interest in America's uranium production, multiple U.S. government departments and agencies had to approve the purchase first. This included Secretary Clinton's State Department.

At that time, Obama was in complete denial about the looming threat from Russia. Still, Republicans on the House Foreign Relations Committee opposed the deal, citing numerous national security concerns.[356] Those concerns would be ignored, and the deal was approved. If not for the seriousness of the threat, it would be humorous how Democrats flipped from saying that Russia was no threat to Evil Trump and his Russian connections.

The New York Times, would investigate the Uranium One deal more than a year and a half before the 2016 election and they concluded:

> "As the Russians gradually assumed control of Uranium One in three separate transactions from 2009 to 2013, Canadian records show, a flow of cash made its way to the Clinton Foundation. Those contributions were not publicly disclosed by the Clintons, despite an agreement Mrs. Clinton had struck with the Obama White House to publicly identify all donors. Other people with ties to the company made donations as well."[357]

We know that Uranium One's chairman used his family foundation to make four donations totaling $2.35 million to the Clinton Foundation during this time.[358] Shortly after the public announcement of the Russian acquisition of Uranium One, Mr. Clinton was paid $500,000 to give a Moscow for Renaissance Capital

---

[356] Fred Lucas, *6 Key Elements in Understanding the Tangles Uranium One Scandal*, The Daily Signal, November 16, 2017.

[357] Becker and McIntire, *Cash Flowed to Clinton Foundation*

[358] New York Times, Jo Becker and Mike McIntire, April 23, 2015 (https://www.nytimes.com/2015/04/24/us/cash-flowed-to-clinton-foundation-as-russians-pressed-for-control-of-uranium-company.html)

speech by the same Russian investment bank promoting Uranium One stock.

The Washington Post, a newspaper that historically has been very pro-Clinton, found that 1,100 donors to the Clinton Foundation came from close associates of Uranium One, and these donations were kept secret and never disclosed as required by Hillary's agreement during her confirmation.[359]

Very little publicly available evidence proves the donations played a direct role in approving the uranium deal. It does, however, bring to light a severe conflict of interest and ethical considerations when a former president relies heavily on foreign cash to accumulate $250+ million in personal assets. At the same time, his wife serves as the country's Secretary of State and helps to steer American foreign policy.

Bill would continue to be paid millions personally and with donations to the Foundation for overseas speaking engagements, many of which connected with his or Hillary's work at the State Department.[360]

During Hillary Clinton's tenure as Secretary of State, many individuals, organizations, and countries allegedly contributed to the

---

[359] Washington Post, *1,100 donors to a Canadian charity tied to Clinton Foundation remain secret*, by Rosalind S. Helderman and Tom Hamburger, April 28, 2015 (https://www.washingtonpost.com/politics/1100-donors-to-a-canadian-charity-tied-to-clinton-foundation-remain-secret/2015/04/28/c3c0f374-edbc-11e4-8666-a1d756d0218e_story.html)

[360] *The Russia Hoax: The Illicit Scheme to Clear Hillary Clinton and Frame Donald Trump*, Gregg Jarrett

Clinton Foundation either before, or while, pursuing interests through ordinary channels with the U.S. State Department.[361]

> *"At least 85 of 154 people from private interests who met or had phone conversations scheduled with Clinton while she led the State Department donated to her family charity or pledged commitments to its international programs [...] combined, the 85 donors contributed as much as $156 million."*[362]

In 2014 the *Washington Post* reported that there was "*substantial overlap between the Clinton political machinery and the foundation.*" They further revealed that nearly half of the major donors who had backed Ready for Hillary had also given at least $10,000 to the Foundation. In some cases, it was personal donations or through foundations or companies they run.[363] This by itself may not be a criminal violation of federal law; however, it does raise the possibility of campaign finance reform violations if donations to the Foundation were made to circumvent campaign finance rules.

In February 2015, The Washington Post reported that while Hillary served as Secretary of State, the Clinton Foundation accepted millions of U.S. dollars in donations from at least seven different foreign governments, including $500,000 from Algeria. This

---

[361] Becker, Jo; McIntire, Mike (April 23, 2015). "*Cash Flowed to Clinton Foundation Amid Russian Uranium Deal*". The New York Times.
(https://www.nytimes.com/2015/04/24/us/cash-flowed-to-clinton-foundation-as-russians-pressed-for-control-of-uranium-company.html)

[362] Associated Press, Many donors to Clinton Foundation met with her at State
(https://apnews.com/82df550e1ec646098b434f7d5771f625)

[363] Helderman, Rosalind S.; Hamburger, Tom; Rich, Steven (February 18, 2015). "*Clintons' foundation has raised nearly $2 billion — and some key questions*". The Washington Post (https://www.washingtonpost.com/politics/clintons-raised-nearly-2-billion-for-foundation-since-2001/2015/02/18/b8425d88-a7cd-11e4-a7c2-03d37af98440_story.html)

donation was not vetted by the State Department, directly violating Clinton's MOU agreement. The Post noted that the donation *"coincided with a spike"* in lobbying efforts by Algeria of the State Department regarding their human rights record.

In November 2016, Reuters reported that:

> *"The Clinton Foundation has confirmed it accepted a $1 million gift from Qatar while Hillary Clinton was U.S. Secretary of State without informing the State Department, even though she had promised to let the agency review new or significantly increased support from foreign governments."*[364]

In a closed-door session with Congress, undercover informant William Douglas Campbell testified that Russia routed millions of dollars to an American-based lobbying firm to influence Hillary.[365] He further testified he knows of at least $3 million of the donations that were sent to Clinton's Global Initiative at the same time that Russia was seeking approval to purchase Uranium One[366] and how a Russian official *"boasted about how weak the U.S. Government was in giving away uranium business"*[367]

---

[364] *"Clinton's charity confirms Qatar's $1 million gift while she was at State Dept"*. Reuters. November 4, 2016. (https://www.reuters.com/article/us-usa-election-foundation-idU.S.KBN12Z2SL)

[365] John Solomon, *"Uranium One Informant Makes Clinton Allegations to Congress"*

[366] Jessica Kwong, *"Russi Routed Millions to Influence Clinton in Uranium Deal, Informant Tells Congress,"* Newsweek, February 8, 2018; David Krayden, *"FBI Informant: US Lobbyists Paid by Russia to Influence Clinton on Uranium One,"* Daily Caller, February 8, 2018; *The Russia Hoax, The Illicit Scheme to Clear Hillary Clinton and Frame Donald Trump,* Gregg Jarrett, 2018, p 77

[367] Brooke Singman, *"Uranium One Informant Says Moscow Paid Millions in Bid to Influence Clinton,"* Fox News, February 8, 2018; *The Russia Hoax, The Illicit Scheme to Clear Hillary Clinton and Frame Donald Trump,* Gregg Jarrett, 2018, p 77

The Clinton Foundation had officially resumed accepting donations from foreign governments once Secretary Clinton's tenure had ended.[368] It is important to note that any kind of contributions from foreign donors to political candidates is strictly prohibited by law, yet foreign money constitutes a significant portion of the foundation's income.

In October 2017, *The Hill* reported: *"the FBI had gathered substantial evidence that Russian nuclear industry officials were engaged in bribery, kickbacks, extortion and money laundering designed to grow Vladimir Putin's atomic energy business inside the United States, according to government documents and interviews."*[369]

Does this mean the Clinton Foundation was a "pay to play" scheme, as many believe? While it is hard to prove beyond any reasonable doubt that payments were bribes, it is not like someone wrote a check to the Clinton Foundation with a check memo of "Money to bribe Hillary to do X, Y, Z for me." Absent direct evidence of that kind, we must look at the totality of the evidence as a whole. Payments were made to both Bill personally and the Foundation by multiple international entities, each with a personal interest in foreign relations that Hillary could influence in one way or another. It is also very interesting to note that once Hillary lost the presidential election, the vast sums of money coming into the Foundation all but dried up, showing a 37% drop overnight. This,

---

[368] Grimaldi, James V.; Ballhaus, Rebecca (February 17, 2015). "*Foreign Government Gifts to Clinton Foundation on the Rise*". The Wall Street Journal.
(https://www.wsj.com/articles/foreign-government-gifts-to-clinton-foundation-on-the-rise-1424223031)
[369] John Solomon and Alison Spann, *FBI uncovered Russian bribery plot before Obama administration approved controversial nuclear deal with Moscow*, The Hill, October 17, 2017.

combined with the personal income for paid speeches, went from $3.6 million to only $357,500.[370] Why, you ask? Simple! Because no one wants to bribe a politician who is no longer in power. This fact alone proves that the Clinton Foundation and Bill's paid speeches were bribes.

> *"The Clinton Foundation's downward trajectory ever since Clinton's election loss provides further testimony to claims that the organization was built on greed and the lust for power and wealth--not charity.[371]"*
> Michael Sainato for the Observer.

2012 Terrorist Attack in Benghazi

The 2012 Benghazi attack remains one of the darkest chapters in recent U.S. diplomatic history. Occurring on September 11, a date already profoundly etched in the American psyche due to the devastating terror attacks in 2001, the events in Benghazi added another layer to the nation's experience with global terrorism.

Around 9:40 pm on that fateful night, an extremist group, Ansar al-Sharia, launched a well-coordinated assault on two American establishments in Benghazi, Libya.[372] The assault's aftermath left the U.S. Ambassador to Libya, Christopher Stevens, Sean Smith, Tyrone Woods, and Glen Doherty tragically dead, marking the first time

---

[370] DailyMail, by Khaleda Rahman, November 20, 2016
(http://www.dailymail.co.uk/news/article-3954720/Donations-Clinton-Foundation-plummeted-amid-Hillary-s-failed-run-presidency.html)
[371] The Observer, *The Clinton Foundation Shuts Down Clinton Global Initiative*, by Michael Saniato, January 15, 2017 (http://observer.com/2017/01/the-clinton-foundation-shuts-down-clinton-global-initiative/)
[372] Kirkpatrick, David D. "Attack by Fringe Group Highlights the Problem of Libya's Militias." The New York Times, October 18, 2012.

since 1979 that a U.S. ambassador had been killed in the line of duty.[373]

Apart from its grave human cost, the incident had significant political ramifications. At the heart of the storm was then-Secretary of State Hillary Clinton. Critics accused the State Department of not providing adequate security for the U.S. diplomatic mission, especially considering Libya's volatile environment after the fall of Muammar Gaddafi.[374]

The fallout was immediate. A series of investigations, hearings, and reports sought to piece together the events leading up to, during, and after the assault. Some claimed that the State Department and the Obama administration downplayed the incident's terrorist nature for political reasons, emphasizing spontaneous reactions to an anti-Muslim video instead.[375]

In her testimony before Congress, Clinton took responsibility for the security lapses while emphasizing that she had not personally denied any requests for additional security at Benghazi.[376] Still, the episode remains a lingering controversy in her political narrative.

To better understand the events leading to Benghazi, one needs to delve into the complexities of the U.S. foreign policy approach to Libya and the Arab Spring and the subsequent fallout of the Gaddafi

---

[373] Myers, Steven Lee, and Eric Schmitt. "For Benghazi Diplomatic Security, Money Wasn't the Problem." The New York Times, October 15, 2012.
[374] Entous, Adam, Siobhan Gorman, and Margaret Coker. "Deadly Consulate Attack Preceded by Warnings." The Wall Street Journal, November 1, 2012.
[375] Lake, Eli. "U.S. Officials Knew Libya Attacks Were Work of Al Qaeda Affiliates." The Daily Beast, October 9, 2012.
[376] Labott, Elise. "Clinton: I'm responsible for diplomats' security." CNN, October 16, 2012.

regime's collapse. The ripple effects of those policy decisions and actions set the stage for the tragedy unfolding that September night.

Hillary at first blamed an internet video posted to YouTube with the title *Innocence of Muslims* as the reason for the attack in Benghazi, saying, "*Some have sought to justify this vicious behavior as a response to inflammatory material posted on the Internet.*" [377] She would repeat this narrative multiple times; [378], [379], [380], among many other times.

The Obama administration picked up this lie and continued, "*We have no information to suggest that it was a pre-planned attack. The unrest we've seen around the region has been in reaction to a video that Muslims, many Muslims find offensive.*" [381] The problem for the administration and Hillary is we know it was not in response to the video. It has been confirmed both Obama and Clinton knew it was a pre-planned attack. CIA Director David Petraeus testified to Congress that the Obama administration knew the attack was an act of terrorism committed by an al-Qaeda-linked group early on. [382]

So why blame it on a YouTube video instead of admitting it was a terrorist attack from al-Qaeda? The issue was the administration would have to admit that their removal of Gaddafi had destabilized the region and allowed al-Qaeda to grow in power. This theory is

---

[377] *What They Said, Before and After the Attack in Libya,* The New York Times, September 12, 2012

[378] Ian Tuttle, *Hillary Clinton's Benghazi Defense: It Depends on What the Mean of 'Lied' Is,* National Review, November 5, 2015

[379] *Secretary of State Clinton's remarks at the transfer of remains ceremony for Americans killed in Libya* (transcript), The Washington Post, September 14, 2012.

[380] Donovan Slack, *Hillary Clinton condemns Benghazi attack,* Politico, September 12, 2012.

[381] *Evolution of administration statements on Libya attack,* Fox News, September 20, 2012

[382] Susan Cornwell and Tabassum Zakaria, *In Benghazi testimony, Petraeus says al-Qaeda role knew early,* Reuters, November 16, 2012.

backed up by recently declassified emails *"showing then-White House Deputy Strategic Communications Adviser Ben Rhodes and other Obama administration public relations officials attempting to orchestrate a campaign to 'reinforce' President Obama and to portray the Benghazi consulate terrorist attack as being 'rooted in an internet video, and not a failure of policy."*[383]

On the same day as the attacks, Hillary emailed her daughter Chelsea and informed her, *"based upon the information we saw today we believe the group that claimed responsibility for this was affiliated with al-Qaeda."*[384] Yet, she continued with the lie about the YouTube video as that more fit the narrative that protected her and the Obama administration.

Immediately after the attacks, there were calls for congressional investigations into how and why an ambassador and his security detail were left to die at the embassy. This brings us to the U.S. House Select Committee on Benghazi and during their investigations into what information Secretary of State Clinton knew prior to the attack, they discovered her illegal email server, and this is when the investigation took a dramatic turn. [See Email Scandal]

At the conclusion of their investigation, they would report that safety conditions in Libya were deteriorating for many months, and Hillary's State Department did nothing to improve security.

---

[383] *Judicial Watch: Benghazi Documents Point to White House on Misleading Talking Points,* Judicial Watch, April 29, 2017.

[384] Stephen Hayes, *Hillary Told Chelsea Truth about Benghazi, But Not American People,* The Weekly Standard, October 22, 2015.

Ambassador Stevens even made repeated requests for increased security to no avail.[385]

Just as important as Hillary's failure to provide proper security, it is critical to understand the geopolitical climate in Libya before the terrorist attack took place against the embassy. The CIA was smuggling weapons out of Libya to Syria and plotting the removal of Gaddafi from power.[386] Hillary's emails would later point to the CIA and State Department goals. [387] It is suspected that both Hillary and the Obama administration were desperate to keep the truth of Benghazi secret; that was the reason for deleting her emails and the reason the Obama administration turned a blind eye to her criminal acts regarding her emails.[388]

Email Scandal

Hillary's email scandal took center stage in the public arena during the 2016 U.S. Presidential Elections and, even today, is still a heated debate among both political parties, with no clear outcome yet.

We do know that Hillary used a privately owned email server, physically located in her New York home, that provided the hosting for several email accounts that she used in her personal and professional life. Instead of a @state.gov email account setup, hosted

---

[385] Jake Tapper, *Documents Back up Claims of Requests for Greater Security in Benghazi*, ABC News, October 19, 2012.
[386] Sy Hersh, *Benghazi Is a Huge Scandal . . . But Not for the Reason You Think*, *Washington Blog, April 15, 2014*
[387] Brad Hoff, *Hillary Emails Reveal True Motive for Libya Intervention*, Foreign Policy Journal, January 6, 2016
[388] S.A. Miller, *Obama admin blocked FBI probe of Clinton Foundation corruption: Report*, Washington Times, August 11, 2014

by the U.S. State Department using more stringent security protocols. Email addresses were hosted on her private server for at least the following domains:

@clintonemail.com,   @wjcoffice.com,   and
@presidentclinton.com

Hillary contends that it *"was just easier"* to use a private email server and single handheld BlackBerry device for all of her email needs[389] and never used the @state.gov email.[390] Republican lawmakers and conservative news outlets are firm that Hillary conspired to have her emails hosted by her staff so she could bypass record-keeping laws.

Both Hillary and her staff were advised multiple times of the insecurity of her emails[391] and were suggested to use an approved @state.gov or similar secure email, a suggestion she ignored on numerous occasions.[392]

For what it's worth, here is one time that I partially believe Hillary, at least in part. I do not think the original intention was to bypass federal record-keeping laws; that was a side benefit most likely not known until the Benghazi investigation. I believe premeditation on her part, in this case, would be giving far too much credit to Hillary and her staffers. It is far more likely they wanted to keep the

---

[389] *Hillary Clinton: Private email set up for 'convenience'".* BBC. (https://www.bbc.com/news/world-us-canada-31819843)

[390] Report by FBI. *"Clinton Email Investigation"* - 9 and 10, September 2, 2016

[391] *"Revealed: Clinton's office was warned over private email use".* (http://america.aljazeera.com/articles/2015/3/3/govt-cybersecurity-source-clintons-office-warned-private-email-use.html)

[392] *"Hillary Clinton Is Criticized for Private Emails in State Dept. Review".* *The New York Times.* May 26, 2016. (https://www.nytimes.com/2016/05/26/us/politics/state-department-hillary-clinton-emails.html)

email simple for Hillary, a non-tech-savvy individual.[393] Notwithstanding, I do feel that after it was made clear to Hillary on multiple occasions the legal and security ramifications[394] of her private email server and BlackBerry usage, her refusal to comply displayed a willingness to break the law and a total disregard for the security of classified information; she clearly felt she was above the law and could do as she pleased with impunity.

Very few took notice or care of the private email server until Hillary's emails were subpoenaed by Congress as part of their Benghazi investigation. On December 5, 2014, legal counsel for Clinton answered the subpoena and delivered 12 file boxes filled with printed paper containing more than 30,000 emails; however, a reported 32,000 emails were deleted and never provided to Congress. Through her lawyer, Hillary stated "*[she] withheld almost 32,000 emails [her staff] deemed to be of a personal nature.*"[395] Her staff did not have proper security clearance to read and determine the 'personal nature' of said emails, however, this avenue was not investigated by the FBI.

This is where the situation becomes a little bit more complicated. Through their investigation, Congress had also requested emails from

---

[393] "*Clinton not technically sophisticated: FBI interview*". CNBC. Retrieved September 7, 2016. (http://video.cnbc.com/gallery/?video=3000548237)

[394] Report by FBI, "*Clinton Email Investigation,*" p. 12 (" State Diplomatic Security Service [DS] instructed Clinton that because her office was in a SCIF [Sensitive Compartmented Information Facility], the user of mobile devices in her office was prohibited. Interviews of three former DS agents revealed Clinton stored her personal BlackBerry in a desk in DS 'Post 1',,' which was located within the SCIF on Mahogany Row. State personnel were not authorized to bring their mobile devices into Post 1, as it was located within the SCIF.").

[395] O'Harrow Jr., Robert. "*How Clinton's email scandal took root*", *The Washington Post*", March 27, 2016.
(https://www.washingtonpost.com/investigations/how-clintons-email-scandal-took-root/2016/03/27/ee301168-e162-11e5-846c-10191d1fc4ec_story.html)

other persons involved in Benghazi, and they found emails to/from Hillary provided by these different persons in the conversation. The problem was these messages were not included in the emails provided by Hillary's lawyers. This means either out of carelessness or malice; she did not fully comply with the subpoena to produce all emails.

On March 4, 2015, Congress informed Hillary that she needed to keep all her emails; official subpoenas for all work-related and personal emails accompanied this notice.[396]

Less than three weeks later, Hillary blatantly defied the subpoena and instructed her staff to permanently delete all emails from the server in a manner that would all but guarantee they could never be recovered. Her computer techs used a software program called BleachBit to accomplish this.[397]

By March 27, 2015, Republican Congressman Trey Gowdy, Chairman of the Select Committee on Benghazi had enough of the deception and stated publicly that "*[Clinton] unilaterally decided to wipe her server clean*" and "*summarily decided to delete all emails.*"[398] Clinton's attorney, David E. Kendall, said after an examination, no copies of any of Clinton's emails remained on the server. Kendall said the server was reconfigured only to retain emails for 60 days after Clinton lawyers had decided which emails needed to be turned over.

---

[396] Report by FBI, "*Clinton Email Investigation,*" p.18, September 2, 106; Byron York, "*From FBI Fragments, A Question: Did Team Clinton Destroy Evidence Under Subpoena,*" Washington Examiner, September 3, 2016; DeTroy Murdock, "*Obstruction of Justice Haunts Hillary's Future,*" National Review, September 8, 2016.

[397] Report by FBI, "*Clinton Email Investigation,*" p 19, September 2, 106.

[398] "*Statement Regarding Subpoena Compliance and Server Determination by Former Secretary of State Hillary Clinton | Select Committee on Benghazi*". Benghazi.house.gov. October 28, 2014. (http://benghazi.house.gov/news/press-releases/statement-regarding-subpoena-compliance-and-server-determination-by-former)

[399] This unilateral determination of 60 Days is a direct violation of federal records keeping laws, yet once again, Hillary is free to make up her own rules as she sees fit.

On June 22, 2015, after being deposed by the Benghazi committee, emails were publically released between Clinton and longtime aide to the Clintons, Sidney Blumenthal. Many of these emails were never sent in by Clinton. In response to this blatant attempt by Hillary to subvert the requirements of law, Committee Chairman Gowdy issued a press release criticizing Clinton for not providing the emails to the State Department.[400] Clinton initially said she provided all work-related emails to the State Department and that only emails of a personal nature on her private server were destroyed. Her statement cannot be independently verified due to the email server being securely wiped of all data in a manner that would prevent any possible recovery of the missing emails. The act of deleting the emails is also a violation of federal law regarding the purposeful destruction of subpoenaed evidence.

Using a private email server located within her residence also brings up another possible violation of federal law. By taking classified documents out of a secure environment, such as the securely hosted @state.gov email servers, and placing them in her home mail server, she also committed the crime of theft by conversion by converting government-owned documents and placing them for her own use in her house without prior permission, even if she was legally

[399] *No Copies of Hillary Clinton Emails on Server Lawyer Says*. *The New York Times.* (https://www.nytimes.com/2015/03/28/us/politics/no-copies-of-hillary-clinton-emails-on-server-lawyer-says.html)
[400] *Select Committee Adds to Secretary Clinton's Public Email Record*. *Select Committee on Benghazi.* (http://benghazi.house.gov/news/press-releases/select-committee-adds-to-secretary-clinton-s-public-email-record)

allowed to view or possess such documents. The law is very clear on this:

> *"Whoever embezzles, steals, purloins, or knowingly converts to his use or the use of another, or without authority, sells, conveys or disposes of any record, voucher, money, or thing of value of the United States or of any department or agency thereof, or any property made or being made under contract for the United States or any department or agency thereof; or . . . Whoever receives, conceals, or retains the same with intent to convert it to his use or gain, knowing it to have been embezzled, stolen, purloined or converted . . . Shall be fined under this title or imprisoned not more than ten years, or both; but if the value of such property in the aggregate, combining amounts from all the counts for which the defendant is convicted in a single case, does not exceed the sum of $1,000, he shall be fined under this title or imprisoned not more than one year, or both."[401]*

This crime would be imposed on a per each basis, with each email converted for personal use as a separate crime. This does not even touch the aspect of her failure to maintain the security of classified information, the destruction of evidence under subpoena, nor her providing false statements to Congress, etc., all of which could send Hillary to prison for a very long time.

Yet all of these violations of federal law were ignored by the U.S. Justice Dept because, at the time, many believed Hillary would win the 2016 Election, and nobody wanted to make an enemy of their

---

[401] United States Code, 18 .U.S.C. 641, "*Public Money, Property or Records*"

presumed soon-to-be Commander-in-chief. This includes U.S. Attorney General and longtime Clinton friend Loretta Lynch, with her direct meddling in the investigation by telling the FBI not to call the email probe an *"investigation"*[402] as to reduce any negative implications of guilt upon Hillary.[403]

> *"The establishment of the private server and its use with classified information plaintiff violated the law, all of this exists notwithstanding. And to those executes, the withholding, wiping and destruction of such huge amounts of email evidence removes all doubts about the intent and knowledge.", Doug Burns, U.S. Attorney Eastern District of New York*[404]

On July 5, 2016, FBI Director James Comey announced no criminal charges would be sought against Hillary regarding her purposeful mishandling of classified emails. This announcement took many in the law enforcement community by surprise, including former Assistant FBI Director Steve Pomerantz:

> *"I could have fallen off my chair while watching the news conference. Setting aside the conclusion he drew, it was not the FBI's job to recommend prosecutions. The FBI investigates and then turns it over to the Department of Justice. In all my years in the FBI --over*

---

[402] Cohen, Kelly. *"James Comey: Loretta Lynch told me not to call Clinton email probe an 'investigation"*. *Washington Examiner*. (http://www.washingtonexaminer.com/james-comey-loretta-lynch-told-me-not-to-call-clinton-email-probe-an-investigation/article/2625335)

[403] ABC News (2017-06-23). *"Senate probes Loretta Lynch's alleged interference in Clinton investigation"*. ABC News. (http://abcnews.go.com/Politics/senate-probes-loretta-lynchs-alleged-interference-clinton-email/story?id=48237960)

[404] *The Russia Hoax: The Illicit Scheme to Clear Hillary Clinton and Frame Donald Trump*, Gregg Jarrett, Interview with Doug Burns, former assistant U.S. attorney for the Eastern District of New York, March 23, 2018

thirty years -- and hundreds of investigations, probably
thousands, I never ever saw that done. For Comey to do
that was astonishing and wrong."[405]

Former federal prosecutor Doug Burns had a similar distaste for
Comey's actions:

> *"It was beyond embarrassing to see the director of the FBI*
> *twist himself into a pretzel trying to explain the non-*
> *prosecution decision [of Clinton]... he violated every rule*
> *in the book; agents do not make prosecutorial*
> *decisions"*[406]

Yet that is precisely what was done. Comey's FBI knew Hillary
was guilty, yet they unilaterally publicly announced that she was not
criminally culpable. Yes, a prosecutor could have taken up the case;
however, seeking a guilty verdict would be difficult after the head of
the FBI said she was not guilty on national television.

Emails released in August of 2017 under FOIA requests from
Judicial Watch showed donors to the Clinton Foundation were
getting special perks from the State Department while Hillary was
the Secretary of State.[407] Several emails showed *"the free flow of*
information and requests for favors between Clinton's State Department
and the Clinton Foundation and major Clinton donors."[408]

---

[405] The Russia Hoax: The Illicit Scheme to Clear Hillary Clinton and Frame Donald
Trump, Gregg Jarrett, Interview with Steve Pomerantz, former assistant FBI Director,
March 14, 2018

[406] *The Russia Hoax: The Illicit Scheme to Clear Hillary Clinton and Frame Donald Trump,*
Gregg Jarrett, Interview with Doug Burns, former assistant U.S. attorney for the Eastern
District of New York, March 23, 2018

[407] *Matt Margolis, The Scandalous Presidency of Barack Obama, p 111-112*

[408] *Judicial Watch: Huma Abedin Emails Reveal Transmission of Classified Information and*
Clinton Foundation Donors receiving Special Treatment from Clinton State Department,
Judicial Watch, August 2, 2017.

Once again, the Clintons got away with their crimes.

Russian Collusion

As I penned the first edition of this book, the narrative woven by certain factions within the U.S. political landscape, often referred to as the "deep state," was fervently pushing the notion of "Russian Collusion." This term became synonymous with the widely circulated, yet thoroughly discredited allegations that Presidential Candidate Donald Trump and his administration had conspired with the Russian government to secure his victory in the 2016 Presidential Election. Even after these claims were thoroughly debunked, the legacy mainstream media continued beating the war drums of Trump as an agent of Putin.[409]

The exhaustive report by Special Counsel Robert Mueller, which was the culmination of a lengthy and highly publicized investigation, found insufficient evidence to support the idea of collusion between the Trump campaign and Russia.[410]

In a striking turn of irony, a headline from the New York Times shed light on a different story: *"Cash Flowed to Clinton Foundation Amid Russian Uranium Deal."*[411] This piece brought to the forefront

---

[409] Jones, Ja'han. "It's time to admit the obvious: Donald Trump sure is acting like a Russian agent." MSNBC. February 23, 2022. https://www.msnbc.com/the-reidout/reidout-blog/trump-putin-genius-russia-ukraine-rcna17328.

[410] Mueller III, Robert S. "Report On The Investigation Into Russian Interference In The 2016 Presidential Election." U.S. Department of Justice, March 2019.

[411] New York Times, *Cash Flowed to Clinton Foundation Amid Russian Uranium Deal,* by Jo Becker and Mike McIntire, April 23, 2015 (https://www.nytimes.com/2015/04/24/us/cash-flowed-to-clinton-foundation-as-russians-pressed-for-control-of-uranium-company.html)

the transactions that saw significant sums of money flowing to the Clinton Foundation from parties with vested interests in Russia during a transaction known as the Uranium One deal. As you recall, we covered this deal in a previous chapter. It was approved by the Committee on Foreign Investment in the United States (CFIUS) while Hillary Clinton was Secretary of State and gave Rosatom, a Russian state-owned corporation, control over a substantial portion of the uranium production capacity in the United States.[412]

The contributions to the Clinton Foundation from individuals directly connected to Uranium One raised questions and sparked controversy, with some critics arguing that this presented a conflict of interest, especially given Hillary Clinton's position at the time. Despite these contentious donations and the political furor they caused, no legal proceedings were initiated against the Clintons or the Foundation in relation to the Uranium One deal. Nevertheless, the situation fueled ongoing debates about foreign influence in American politics and the potential for undisclosed conflicts of interest within the complex interplay of international diplomacy, charitable organizations, and personal political power.

It was known by the U.S. government as it is confirmed to have been reported to them on multiple occasions and by multiple informants, the Russian government was paying bribes to guarantee the successful acquisition of Uranium One.[413]

---

[412] "Uranium One Transaction," U.S. Nuclear Regulatory Commission, last modified November 8, 2010.

[413] New York Times, *Donations to the Clinton Foundation, and a Russian Uranium Takeover,* by Wilson Andrews, April 22, 2015
(https://www.nytimes.com/interactive/2015/04/23/us/clinton-foundation-donations-uranium-investors.html)

Theft of 2016 Election from Bernie

I am among the last people you would catch with an *I'm With Bernie T-shirt*. He is a socialist who either has zero clue how basic economics works or thinks the voting populace is too ignorant to realize everything he promised to give people during his campaign would be financially impossible. Notwithstanding our ideological differences in governance, the election was unjustly stolen from him by Hillary and the Democratic National Committee (DNC). In hindsight, Bernie should have been the Democratic candidate for the 2016 Election instead of Hillary.

To explain how this happened to Bernie, let us look at the DNC and their poor financial health. After the 2012 Obama Campaign, the DNC was more than $24 million in debt, with $15 million owed to banks and more than $8 million to various vendors.[414] This left the DNC in a financial quagmire that was almost impossible to extract themselves from without outside help. This is where the Hillary for America Campaign and the Hillary Victory Fund (the joint fundraising apparatus with the DNC) paid off around $10 million worth of the DNC's debt in 2016, placing the DNC on a monthly stipend to pay their overhead expenses. With this single stroke, the DNC handed over control to the Hillary camp in Brooklyn, away from DNC headquarters.

With this arrangement, Hillary could bypass the Federal Exchange Commission (FEC) law on campaign finance regulations that set a maximum donation by a single person to a presidential

---

[414] Politico, *Inside Hillary Clinton's Secret Takeover of the DNC*, November 2, 2017 (https://www.politico.com/magazine/story/2017/11/02/clinton-brazile-hacks-2016-215774)

campaign at $2,700.[415] A donor could 'legally' donate $353,400 to the Hillary Victory Fund, broken down as $10,000 to each of the 32 states' parties and $33,400 directly to the DNC. For battleground states, most of the money would stay at the state level to pay for various campaign-related expenses for the democratic nominee, and the rest would be funneled to the DNC and immediately transferred to Hillary in Brooklyn. The amount kept by the states was less than one percent of the $82 million raised; the rest went to Hillary's campaign.[416]

Next, the disclosure of leaked emails erupted into the public forum, unveiling that the Hillary campaign had been funneling money from the Democratic committees of various states, redirecting these funds to finance her own campaign rather than supporting the party's broader goals.

The Joint Fund-Raising Agreement between the DNC, the Hillary Victory Fund, and Hillary for America:

> *"The agreement—signed by Amy Dacey, the former CEO of the DNC, and Robby Mook with a copy to Marc Elias—specified that in exchange for raising money and investing in the DNC, Hillary would control the party's finances, strategy, and all the money raised. Her campaign had the right of refusal of who would be the party communications director, and it would make final decisions on all the other staff. The DNC also was*

---

[415] Federal Election Campaign Act (the Act): Contribution limits
(https://www.fec.gov/help-candidates-and-committees/candidate-taking-receipts/contribution-limits/)
[416] Politico, *Inside Hillary Clinton's Secret Takeover of the DNC*, November 2, 2017
(https://www.politico.com/magazine/story/2017/11/02/clinton-brazile-hacks-2016-215774)

required to consult with the campaign about all other
staffing, budgeting, data, analytics, and mailings." [417]

This arrangement, while most likely not criminal, is, however, very unethical, to say the least. The ability of the Hillary camp to control staff hiring decisions, marketing, and expenditures of the DNC before she was voted as the nominee gave an unfair advantage to her. The game was most definitely rigged in her favor; even Senator Elizabeth Warren agreed when asked by CNN *"if Mrs. Clinton's contest against Democratic rival Bernie Sanders was rigged, and she said: 'Yes.'"* [418]

A significant point of contention arose before Hillary was officially declared the party's nominee. This phase of the race was characterized not just by the rivalry between Hillary and Bernie but also by the controversy surrounding campaign financing. According to the party's regulations and broader ethical considerations in the political process, funds, especially those pooled from general Democratic coffers, were not to be utilized in favor of a particular candidate before the official nomination.

However, revelations indicated an apparent redirection of resources to fortify Clinton's campaign, a maneuver that ignited intense debates both within the Democratic Party and in the broader public and political spheres. This development was particularly alarming given the unexpectedly close race between Clinton and Sanders. Sanders, known for his progressive stance and appeal among

---

[417] Politico, *Inside Hillary Clinton's Secret Takeover of the DNC*, November 2, 2017 (https://www.politico.com/magazine/story/2017/11/02/clinton-brazile-hacks-2016-215774)
[418] The BBC Online, *Elizabeth Warren agrees Democratic race 'rigged' for Clinton*, November 3, 2017 (https://www.bbc.com/news/world-us-canada-41850798)

the younger demographic, had launched a formidable grassroots movement. His message, centered around tackling income inequality and overhauling the healthcare system, had the potential to shift traditional voting patterns in the impending face-off with the Republican contender, especially in the crucial Rust Belt region.

Yet, Sanders' campaign encountered numerous hurdles, the most striking of which was the perceived bias within the party machinery. His advocates pointed to what seemed like a preordained preference for Clinton, a sentiment that grew as Sanders continued to demonstrate his electoral viability through significant showings in the primaries and large turnouts at his events. Analysts didn't shy away from speculating that Sanders, with his populist message, might have been the stronger candidate to engage the eventual Republican nominee on several fronts that mattered to the disillusioned electorate.

The unfolding of these events brought to the forefront an unsettling aspect of American electoral politics: the pervasive influence of internal party politics, financial muscle, and power brokers in determining electoral outcomes, often at the expense of the electorate's will. This scenario, where the scales seemed tipped by factors other than the democratic pulse, casts a long, disturbing shadow over the electoral process. It serves as a stark reminder of the entrenched system where money and influence often chart the course to the White House, sidelining the very democratic principles that are supposed to guide free and fair elections. Consequently, this alienates the electorate and erodes trust in the democratic process, fueling cynicism that the interests of the powerful elite drown out the voices of everyday citizens.

In this defining moment of American politics, not even the vast influence of entrenched political power or the formidable engine of mainstream media support could steer Hillary Clinton past the obstacle that proved her undoing: the battle for the public's heart. In the face of every conceivable advantage, she endured as a figure that a substantial segment of the electorate struggled to connect with, leading to her ultimate shortfall in the quest for the presidency. Rightly or wrongly, her personal likability factor was abysmal, preventing them from casting their ballot in her favor. This phenomenon wasn't unique to Clinton; it reemerged during Donald Trump's 2020 reelection campaign, a topic we'll explore in detail in subsequent chapters of this book.

BARACK OBAMA: THE (SECOND) WORST PRESIDENT IN US HISTORY

Following the era dominated by the neoconservative policies of the Bush and Cheney administration, a palpable thirst for change was evident amongst many Americans. Barack Obama's 2008 campaign, centered around the promise of *"Hope and Change,"* resonated deeply with those who felt disillusioned with the country's direction. His charisma, soaring oratory, and message of unity captivated a nation hungry for a departure from the previous administration's divisive policies.[419]

When I reflect on the tenure of President Barack Obama, a paradox becomes evident, especially concerning his foreign policy. Obama ascended to the presidency on a platform that included, among other things, a decisive departure from the hawkish foreign policy strategies often associated with the neoconservatives of the George W. Bush era. His campaign rhetoric was rich with promises of ending wars, improving international relations, and closing the detention facility at Guantanamo Bay, presenting a stark contrast to the policies of his predecessor.[420]

However, a discrepancy emerged between pre-election promises and presidential action upon assuming office. Critics and political analysts alike noted that Obama's foreign policies stayed within his predecessor's as many had anticipated or, indeed, as he had promised. For instance, his surge of troops in Afghanistan in 2009, the

---

[419] Zeleny, Jeff. "Obama's 2008 Campaign of Hope and Change." The New York Times, November 4, 2008.
[420] Obama, Barack. "The Audacity of Hope: Thoughts on Reclaiming the American Dream." New York: Crown Publishers, 2006.

maintenance of a military presence in Iraq, and particularly his administration's extensive use of drone strikes in the Middle East and beyond were seen by many as a continuation—or in some cases, an expansion—of Bush-era military engagements.[421]

Moreover, Obama's approach to global counterterrorism efforts, exemplified by the operation that resulted in the killing of Osama bin Laden in Pakistan, demonstrated a willingness to use unilateral military force, even without the explicit consent of the nation in question.[422] Furthermore, his administration's involvement in the NATO intervention in Libya in 2011, which ultimately led to the overthrow of Muammar Gaddafi, stirred significant debate. Critics argued that this action, taken without the authorization of Congress, reflected a neoconservative-style interventionist approach despite being framed as a humanitarian effort to protect Libyan civilians.[423]

In the sphere of international diplomacy, the Obama administration participated in what was considered a significant diplomatic maneuver at the time — the Iran nuclear deal, or the Joint Comprehensive Plan of Action (JCPOA), in 2015. This agreement was intended to restrict Iran's ability to develop nuclear weapons in exchange for lifting crippling economic sanctions.[424] However, critics have since argued that this deal, rather than fostering global peace and security, inadvertently exacerbated regional instability. The deal arguably empowered Iran financially by providing Iran with sanction relief and the return of previously frozen funds. Detractors contend

---

[421] Jaffe, Greg, and Karen DeYoung. "Obama's Most Dangerous Drone Tactic Is Here to Stay." The Washington Post, July 1, 2016.
[422] Mazzetti, Mark. "The Killing of Osama bin Laden." Penguin Books, 2013.
[423] Savage, Charlie. "Power Wars: Inside Obama's Post-9/11 Presidency." Little, Brown and Company, 2015.
[424] "Joint Comprehensive Plan of Action," U.S. Department of State, July 14, 2015.

that the country utilized this windfall not to benefit its citizens or build global relationships but to continue its nuclear ambitions surreptitiously and finance proxy groups and military operations that destabilized the region and posed threats to Western interests and allies, including Israel.

This criticism highlights the inherent challenge in such diplomatic endeavors: balancing immediate geopolitical objectives against long-term regional stability and security. Despite entering the deal with the aim of curtailing nuclear proliferation, the unforeseen consequences and Iran's alleged activities post-agreement have led many to categorize the JCPOA as a flawed strategy, inadvertently aligning with certain neoconservative tendencies of military interventionism due to the continued need to manage the fallout and Iran's regional behavior.

In essence, while President Obama's rhetoric signaled a shift towards a more diplomatic and less interventionist approach, the practicalities of his foreign policy revealed significant continuities with the past, underscoring the complexities and perhaps the pragmatic constraints inherent in U.S. foreign policy decision-making.

The perception that Obama's policies were more neoliberal than progressive in nature led to feelings of betrayal among some segments of his base. Neoliberalism, with its emphasis on free-market capitalism and deregulation, seemed at odds with the progressive changes many had anticipated.[425]

---

[425] Harvey, David. "A Brief History of Neoliberalism." Oxford University Press, 2005.

The political landscape during Obama's tenure serves as a poignant reminder that party lines can sometimes blur, and policies do not always align with campaign promises or popular expectations.

Obama [DOESN'T] Care Act

The Affordable Care Act (ACA), colloquially dubbed "Obamacare," stands as a stark testament to the pitfalls of modern American liberalism's overreach. This legislation not only epitomizes governmental overextension but also underscores a troubling narrative of deceit that, disturbingly, went largely unchallenged by a complaisant, left-biased media establishment. The promises that shrouded the ACA—memorably, the assurance that individuals could keep their preferred healthcare providers and plans—proved to be illusory. Rather than serving as a political liability, this fundamental dishonesty seemingly secured President Obama's reelection, as partisan reporting drowned out critical discourse. The episode remains a cautionary tale of how uncritical media landscapes and politicized promises can manipulate the electorate and lead to the entrenchment of policies with far-reaching and detrimental repercussions.

When Obama introduced his plans, he assured the American people that the entire negotiation process would be open and transparent to the public and broadcast on C-SPAN under his leadership. Instead, it was another backroom negotiated deal typical of the Deep State swamp without public oversight. Obama's Press Secretary, Robert Gibbs, stated, *"[Obama] was in full agreement and wanted to get a bill to his desk as quickly as possible."*[426]

---

[426] Chip Reid, *Obama Reneges on Health Care Transparency*, CBS News, January 6, 2010

The entire process was shrouded in controversy, and the lack of opacity starkly contrasted with then-President Obama's pledges of transparency and bipartisanship. The legislative process was not just rushed but clouded in secrecy, creating a situation where, remarkably, neither the public nor most members of Congress were fully aware of the bill's contents before its passage. House Speaker Nancy Pelosi's infamous statement encapsulates this: "*We have to pass the bill so that you can find out what's in it,*"[427] a comment that has since been cited as emblematic of the problematic approach taken during the ACA's formulation and debate.

This absence of transparency might have been forgivable if the ACA had delivered on its lofty promises to revolutionize healthcare access and affordability for all Americans. However, critics argue that the reality fell dismally short of these ideals. Not only did the Act lead to increased premiums for numerous individuals,[428] but it also compelled many to part with their preferred plans and physicians,[429] contrary to the assurances given by its proponents. Furthermore, the purported benefits of the ACA did not materialize for everyone, with many states opting out of Medicaid expansion and thus leaving substantial populations without the promised coverage.[430]

---

[427] Pelosi, Nancy. "Remarks at the 2010 Legislative Conference for the National Association of Counties." Speaker.gov, March 9, 2010.

[428] Cannon, Michael F. "Overwhelming Evidence That Obamacare Caused Premiums To Increase Substantially." Forbes, July 28, 2018.

[429] Pear, Robert. "Promise and Peril of Obamacare for Democrats." The New York Times, November 3, 2013.

[430] Garfield, Rachel, Kendal Orgera, and Anthony Damico. "The Coverage Gap: Uninsured Poor Adults in States that Do Not Expand Medicaid." Kaiser Family Foundation, January 21, 2021.

The manner in which the ACA was passed also set a concerning precedent for future legislative efforts. The lack of initial clarity and the emotional push to pass it—seemingly at all costs—underscored a willingness to sideline informed debate and bipartisanship in pursuit of a political victory. This approach, critics contend, not only undermined the democratic process but also eroded public trust in key governmental institutions and officials, with repercussions that continue to resonate in contemporary political discourse.[431]

When selling it to the public, Obama claimed that *"if you like your health care plan, you can keep it."* This turned out to be a complete lie.[432] This lie was so big it even earned Obama *2013 Lie of the Year* from PolitiFact[433] after millions of Americans began to receive cancellation notices from their insurance companies, informing them their current plans were not ACA compliant and were no longer available.

There was also the claim that consumers would find savings of upwards of $2,500 per person; this was known to be a complete distortion of the facts. *"Premiums for individual coverage more than doubled between 2013 and 2017."* [434] These were facts known by senior officials, including Obama, that the *"numbers just did not add up."*

[431] Jacobs, Lawrence R., and Suzanne Mettler. "When and How New Policy Creates New Politics: Affordable Care Act's Endangered Future and the Possibility of Dynamic Feedback." Perspectives on Politics, 16(2), 2018, 363-377.
[432] Matt Margolis, *The Scandalous Presidency of Barack Obama,* p 28
[433] Angie Drobnic Holan, *Lie of the Year: 'If you like your healthcare plan, you can keep it',* PolitiFact, December 12, 2013
[434] Edmund Haislmaier and Doug Badger, *How Obamacare Raised Premiums,* The Heritage Foundation

On top of that is the over $319 million[435] spent on building the horrible HealthCare.gov online marketplace. This system failed so miserably on its initial launch that it could only enroll SIX people on the first day.[436] Before the website's launch, Obama was informed that it could not handle the projected amount of web traffic and had serious privacy and security-related concerns.[437] Millions of Americans' privacy and security concerns turned out to be of no concern to Obama; he wanted the system launched.[438]

Ultimately, this was a striking instance of government overreach, compelling American consumers to buy a service (insurance) from private entities, an act many viewed as a direct infringement of their freedom of choice. This perspective was ultimately upheld by the Supreme Court, which concurred that the federal government did not have the authority to impose a financial penalty on individuals for their failure to purchase a specific product or service.[439]

Additionally, the rollout of the ACA created widespread confusion regarding the specifics of coverage. In my experience as a volunteer paramedic, there was a noticeable surge in 911 EMS calls, many for non-critical issues, immediately after the ACA's implementation. One incident that stands out involved an individual demanding transportation to the hospital for the third time in a single

---

[435] Glenn Kessler, *How much did HealthCare.gov cost?*, The Washington Post, October 24, 2013 and updated on Dec 12, 2013.

[436] Avik Roy, *The Truth Comes Out: Obamacare's Website Enrolled A Grand Total Of Six People On Oct. 1,* Forbes, November 1, 2013.

[437] Joe Johns and Z. Byron Wolf, *First on CNN: Obama administration warned about health care website,* CNN, October 30, 2013.

[438] Sharyl Attkisson, *High security risk found after HealthCare.gov launch,* CBS News, December 20, 2013

[439] Vinson, Roger. "Obamacare Is Unconstitutional." Policy Report, Cato Institute, March/April 2011.

day due to "toe pain." Her justification was, "*I got Obama care,*" a statement that seemed to express both a sense of entitlement and a disregard for the gravity of using emergency services. This misuse of an all-volunteer ambulance service, particularly at 3 AM, was an abuse of resources and a potential risk to others in genuine need of urgent medical assistance, as it diverted help away from real emergencies.

Muammar Gaddafi

Muammar Gaddafi, the enigmatic and often controversial leader of Libya, held power for over four decades. Under his leadership, Libya boasted some of the highest living standards in Africa, backed by the nation's vast oil reserves.[440] Notably, Gaddafi's extensive social and economic programs greatly reduced poverty and raised the quality of life, ensuring a level of stability and domestic support for much of his rule.

Yet, Gaddafi's regime was not without its detractors. His rule was marked by a blend of pan-Arab nationalism, socialism, and authoritarian governance. Internationally, he was a polarizing figure, known for both his support of pan-African unity and his alleged backing of international terrorist activities.[441]

By 2010, a wave of popular uprisings known as the Arab Spring was sweeping across the Middle East and North Africa. Libya was not spared from this regional turmoil. Protests erupted, primarily driven by economic hardships, political repression, and the larger pan-Arab call for democracy. What began as peaceful demonstrations soon

---

[440] Vandewalle, Dirk. "A History of Modern Libya." Cambridge University Press, 2006.
[441] Bearman, Jonathan. "Qadhafi's Libya." Zed Books Ltd., 1986

escalated into a civil conflict, with Islamist extremists, including factions of Al Qaeda's North African affiliate, playing significant roles in the opposition.[442]

As the Libyan conflict escalated, forces loyal to Muammar Gaddafi successfully quelled the majority of the rebellions throughout the country, with one notable exception: Benghazi. This city, with its rich history of dissent against Gaddafi's regime, emerged as the heart of the resistance movement. However, it wasn't just the local populace that played a critical role in this opposition. Al-Qaeda-affiliated groups, already present in the region, capitalized on the chaos and rapidly gained significant influence within the city.[443]

These extremist factions not only contributed to the intensity of the resistance but also complicated the political landscape, raising questions about the future of Libya and the goals of the rebellion.[444] The presence of such groups was troubling, given Al-Qaeda's known agenda of global jihad and its history of extreme violence. Their involvement muddied the waters of the international community's decision to intervene, as support for the rebels essentially became indirect support for terrorist-affiliated organizations.[445]

The situation in Benghazi underscored the complex, often unpredictable nature of international interventions in regional conflicts. The alliances formed out of necessity on the ground didn't

---

[442] Filiu, Jean-Pierre. "The Arab Revolution: Ten Lessons from the Democratic Uprising." Oxford University Press, 2011.

[443] Al-Qaeda in Libya: A Profile," Federal Research Division, Library of Congress, August 2012

[444] Wehrey, Frederic. "The Struggle for Security in Eastern Libya." Carnegie Endowment for International Peace, September 19, 2012.

[445] Chivvis, Christopher S. Toppling Qaddafi: Libya and the Limits of Liberal Intervention. Cambridge: Cambridge University Press, 2014, p. 45-46

always align with the larger strategic interests or values of the intervening nations, presenting a moral quandary for foreign policy decision-makers.[446]

Given the volatility and the high stakes involved, the crisis in Benghazi became a focal point of global attention, ultimately drawing in NATO forces under the pretext of protecting civilians under threat from Gaddafi's forces, though the presence of extremist groups raised serious concerns about the long-term implications of such an intervention.[447]

The situation in Libya caught international attention, particularly from the neocon faction within the Obama administration. Alarm bells rang with claims that Gaddafi threatened a "*bloodbath*" in Benghazi. While the veracity of these claims remains debated, what is clear is that they were instrumental in shaping international perceptions of the conflict. A letter, penned by members of the Foreign Policy Initiative and signed by 40 prominent figures, urged the Obama administration to intervene militarily to prevent a purported impending massacre and to aid in toppling Gaddafi.[448]

The U.S., alongside NATO allies, initiated a military intervention in Libya, publicly presenting this action as a humanitarian endeavor to safeguard civilians from the Gaddafi regime's violence. This intervention was sanctioned under United Nations Security Council Resolution 1973, which authorized

---

[446] Anderson, Jon Lee. "Who Are the Rebels?" The New Yorker, April 4, 2011.

[447] United Nations Security Council. "Resolution 1973 (2011) [on the situation in the Libyan Arab Jamahiriya]." March 17, 2011.

[448] Kuperman, Alan J. "Obama's Libya Debacle." Foreign Affairs, March/April 2015.

member states *"to take all necessary measures"* to protect civilians under *threat of attack in the country, explicitly in Benghazi, while excluding a foreign occupation force of any form on any part of Libyan territory."*[449]

However, numerous analysts contend that the intervention was less about protecting civilians and more about furthering geopolitical interests, principally the objective of ousting Gaddafi from power. These critics point to a confluence of factors, including Libya's vast oil reserves, Gaddafi's history of unpredictable behavior, and his tenuous relationships with Western powers, as underlying motivations for the intervention.[450]

Further complicating the narrative, some commentators have highlighted the strategic communications from the rebels, who were keen to frame the conflict as a humanitarian crisis to secure Western intervention.[451] Additionally, there were concerns in European capitals about potential refugee flows from Libya in the event of a prolonged civil war.[452]

The aftermath of the intervention has also been subject to scrutiny. The power vacuum following Gaddafi's removal led to a period of instability and the fragmentation of authority among various militias and tribal factions, contributing to the ongoing

---

[449] United Nations Security Council, "Resolution 1973 (2011) [on the situation in the Libyan Arab Jamahiriya]," March 17, 2011,

[450] Kuperman, Alan J. "A Model Humanitarian Intervention? Reassessing NATO's Libya Campaign." International Security 38, no. 1 (Summer 2013): 105-136. doi:10.1162/ISEC_a_00126.

[451] Zenko, Micah. "The Big Lie About the Libyan War." Foreign Policy, March 22, 2016.

[452] Europe's Refugee Crisis: Assessing the Factors Preventing a Coordinated EU Response," Global Security and Politics, Centre for International Governance Innovation, June 2016

Libyan crisis.[453] Furthermore, the intervention arguably set a precedent for the use of "humanitarian" justifications for military interventions that may serve more strategic than altruistic ends.

The *Washington Post* wrote in support of this course of action, "*the [Washington] Post's editors demanded that Obama take the lead in implementing a military strategy that ensures regime change in Tripoli.*"[454]

Our old friend Hillary was currently Secretary of State and supported the policy of removing Gaddafi wholeheartedly. She was so strong in her support and the driving force in pressuring Obama to take action that it was commonly referred to as "*Hillary's War.*"[455] Under her direction, the U.S. was left more vulnerable to terrorist attacks.[456] Months later, CBS quoted her as saying, "*We came, we saw, he died!*"[457]

Once again, we were in a military battle with a foreign power based on lies to the American people. An estimated 233 deaths took place in Benghazi, far less than the bloodbath of 10's thousands as portrayed, and out of those 233, most were al-Qaeda terrorists.[458] The same enemies the U.S. forces were fighting, so why did we help al-Qaeda in their fight against Gaddafi?

---

[453] Wehrey, Frederic. "Libya's Lessons: How Not to Intervene." Q&A, Council on Foreign Relations, September 12, 2012.

[454] Robert Parry, *The Necons Regroup on Libyan War,* Consortium News, March 25, 2011

[455] David Ray Griffin, *Bush and Cheney: How They Ruined America and The World,* p 93

[456] Joshua Yasmeh, *Libya Was Hillary's War. Here's The Proof,* The Daily Wire, February 16, 2016

[457] Hillary Clinton on Gaddafi, CBS News, October 20, 2011.

[458] Alan J. Kuperman, *Obama's Libya Debacle,* Foreign Affairs, March/April 2015.

The U.S. had two strategic goals that required Gaddafi to die.[459] The first was with him out of the way, the CIA could transfer Libya's weapons cache to anti-Assad rebels in Syria.[460] The second reason was Gaddafi was threatening to create his own African based currency that would be used when buying Libyan oil, this would threaten the U.S. Dollar as the standard petrol dollar.[461] The very same mistake Saddam made.

Gaddafi was deposed, tracked down, and killed. With success in the air, Mrs. Clinton took a tour of the country and proclaimed Libya liberated.[462] Of course, just as history would predict, the country turned out no better than another regime change by the neocons. Within months, the country was in chaos. This chaos would eventually lead to the 2012 attacks against the U.S. Consulate in Benghazi.

Years later, then Secretary of Defense Leon Panetta would admit in his memoir the entire reason for going to Libya was never humanitarian reasons as claimed in the media, *"our goal in Libya was regime change."*[463]

In 2016, the U.K. Parliament report on Libya said the entire premise was based on lies, like the Iraq war.[464]

---

[459] David Ray Griffin, *Bush and Cheney: How They Ruined America and The World*, p 94

[460] Damien McElroy, *CIA Running Arms Smuggling Team in Benghazi When Consulate Was Attacked*, Telegraph August 2, 2013.

[461] Alex Newman, *Gadhafi's Gold-Money Plan Would Have Decasted Dollar*, New American, November 11, 2011.

[462] Diane Johnstone, *Hillary Clinton, Queen of Chaos*.

[463] Leon Panetta, *Worthy Fights: A Memoir of Leadership in War and Peace*, p 354

[464] David Ray Griffin, *Bush and Cheney How They Ruined America and the World*, p 97

On March 4, 2017, President Donald J. Trump tweeted, *"Terrible! Just found out that Obama had my 'wires tapped' in Trump Tower just before the victory. Nothing found. This is McCarthyism!"*[465] This was then followed up by a few followup tweets:

Donald J. Trump ✔
@realDonaldTrump

Terrible! Just found out that Obama had my "wires tapped" in Trump Tower just before the victory. Nothing found. This is McCarthyism!

♡ 140K   6:35 AM - Mar 4, 2017

♡ 101K people are talking about this   >

Donald J. Trump ✔
@realDonaldTrump

Is it legal for a sitting President to be "wire tapping" a race for president prior to an election? Turned down by court earlier. A NEW LOW!

♡ 123K   6:49 AM - Mar 4, 2017

♡ 71.4K people are talking about this   >

Donald J. Trump ✔
@realDonaldTrump

I'd bet a good lawyer could make a great case out of the fact that President Obama was tapping my phones in October, just prior to Election!

♡ 126K   6:52 AM - Mar 4, 2017

♡ 76.1K people are talking about this   >

Donald J. Trump ✔
@realDonaldTrump

How low has President Obama gone to tapp my phones during the very sacred election process. This is Nixon/Watergate. Bad (or sick) guy!

♡ 159K   7:02 AM - Mar 4, 2017

♡ 154K people are talking about this   >

---

[465] Donald J. Trump, via Twitter, now 'X', March 4, 2017, https://twitter.com/realDonaldTrump/status/837989835818287106

The mere accusation of using the power of the White House to spy on a political opponent should have stirred the media into a feeding frenzy, with immediate demands for investigations of Obama, but of course, we all know better than that. The media would never turn on their love for Obama.

Obama spokesperson Kevin Lewis, issued a statement the following day that read in part, *"A cardinal rule of the Obama administration was that no White House official ever interfered with any independent investigation led by the Department of Justice. As part of that practice, neither President Obama nor any White House official ever ordered surveillance on any U.S. citizen. Any suggestion otherwise is simply false."*[466]

Of course, like so many other statements made by career politicians with law degrees, the statement was not exactly a denial of the subject, nor was it factually incorrect. He stated he never ordered it; he did not say he did not know about it. There is a subtle distinction, but it allowed Obama to skirt the issue and answer a different question while appearing to answer the original question.

A formal denial, of course, would have been impossible and illegal because there was a wiretap, and Obama knew it. Obama speechwriter Jon Favreau warned journalists not to report that there had been no wiretap.[467] *"I'd be careful about reporting that Obama said*

[466] Pierre Thomas, Jack Date, Rhonda Schwartz, and Erin Dooley, *FBI director James Comey asked Justice Department to refute Trump's wiretapping claims, sources say,* ABC News, March 5, 2017

[467] Matt Margolis, *The Scandalous Presidency of Barack Obama,* p 131

there was no wiretapping. [you should report] neither he nor the WH ordered it."[468]

The issue is that the media already knew about the wiretaps. In fact, months earlier, on Trump's Inauguration Day, the front page headline of the New York Times was titled *"Wiretapped Data Used in Inquiry of Trump Aides."* Now with Trump calling Obama out on this, the *Times* quietly changed the online version of the article to say *"Intercepted Russian Communications Part of Inquiry Intro Trump Associates"*[469] to save face and protect Obama.

This data eventually ended up in the resignation of Trump's National Security Advisor, Michael Flynn,[470] due to the political optics of the situation when he lied to cover up a conversation he had with Russia, a discussion that was later proven to be entirely legal.

However, it is still important to note that as of the time of writing this book, no evidence has been found to implicate Donald J. Trump in any illegal dealing with Russia.

The investigation started in the spring of 2016 when the White House and the Department of Justice pursued a criminal investigation of Trump's associates, and perhaps Trump himself, over concerns about his alleged Russian connections.[471] As we all know, the investigation found no crimes committed by Trump. Rather than

---

[468] Matthew Boyle, *Non-Denial 'Denial': Obama Response to Trump 'Wiretap' Claim Raises More Questions,* Breitbart, March 4, 2017.

[469] Eddie Scarry, *New York Times downplays 'wiretapped data' in online story of Trump investigation,* Washington Examiner, March 9, 2017

[470] Maggie Haberman, Matthew Rosenberg, Matt Apuzzo, and Glenn Thrush, *Michael Flynn Resigns as National Security Advisor,* The New York Times, September 13, 2017

[471] Matt Margolis, *The Scandalous Presidency of Barack Obama,* p 133

close down their investigation, they pivoted into a national security investigation, allowing them to continue spying on the campaign.

As a law and order man, I understand our national law enforcement and intelligence agencies need to investigate any suspected interference by foreign powers in our elections. On the surface, this was what the FBI and NSA were doing. However, upon digging more deeply, it became abundantly clear the goal was to prevent Candidate Trump from winning the election. Then, after he won, the goal was to destroy Trump's presidency, and when those two missions failed, the mission turned to preventing Trump from winning re-election.

In April 2017, CNN reported the FBI used a thirty-five-page document to obtain the original FISA court approval for wiretapping the Trump Campaign as part of their investigation into possible Russian meddling in the 2016 election.[472] That document has become known as the Steele dossier or Russia dossier, complete with allegations against Donald Trump. The first problem is that this document was produced by Fusion GPS as opposition research by the Hillary Campaign, where they hired former British spy Christoper Steele to investigate connections between Trump and Russia.[473]

In and of itself, this doesn't discredit any possible facts in the dossier. It is reasonable to presume it would be incumbent upon the Clinton campaign to turn over any evidence they *stumbled upon* that

[472] Evan Perez, Shimon Prokupecz, and Manu Raju, *FBI used dossier allegations to bolster Trump-Russia investigation,* CNN, April 18, 2017
[473] Kenneth P. Vogel, *The Trump Dossier: What We Know and Who Paid for It,* The New York Times, October 25, 2017

could implicate Russian meddling. However, that was not how this took place. Instead of being forthcoming with their suspicions, the campaign continued to finance the 'research' into Trump, and they used the FBI as their personal Gestapo.

State Judiciary Committee Chairman Chuck Grassley was less than pleased when he learned of this and was quoted as saying, "*The idea that the FBI and associates of the Clinton campaign would pay Mr. Steele to investigate the Republican nominee for president in the run-up to the election raise further questions about the FBI's independence from politics, as well as the Obama administration's use of law enforcement and intelligence agencies for political ends.*"[474]

Even FBI Director James Comey expressed skepticism over the dossier's content, characterizing it as "*salacious and unverified*" during his testimony before the Senate Select Committee on Intelligence on June 8, 2017. His statement underscored the dubious nature of the information it contained, casting doubts over its reliability and the veracity of its claims.[475]

Critics have argued that the FBI's use of this dossier to obtain a Foreign Intelligence Surveillance Act (FISA) warrant against Carter Page, a former Trump campaign advisor, raised serious questions. They contended that relying on unverified information to initiate such surveillance represented a breach of legal standards and protocols.[476] Subsequent investigations, including the Department of Justice's Inspector General report in December 2019, identified

---

[474] Mark Hosenball and Johnathan Landay, *US Congressional panel spar over 'Trump dossier' on Russia contacts,* Reuters, October 10, 2017

[475] Comey, James. Testimony before the Senate Select Committee on Intelligence, U.S. Senate, June 8, 2017.

[476] "Justice Department Releases FISA Documents on Carter Page." CNN, July 21, 2018.

significant inaccuracies and omissions in the FBI's FISA applications related to the dossier, further fueling the controversy over the bureau's handling of the matter.[477]

This episode, not only showcased the potential for abuse in the surveillance process but also reflected the intense politicization of intelligence and law enforcement agencies in an exceedingly polarized era, raising profound concerns about the integrity of democratic institutions.[478]

Once again, playing the devil's advocate here, it is incumbent upon law enforcement to investigate all claims of crimes, even if the claim appears outside to be less than optimal. However, my objection is to how they lied to the FISA court. As part of the application process, they must testify that the evidence they present to the court is accurate to their knowledge. Comey has already said that he did not have high confidence in the reliability of the information, yet he approved the investigation to continue.

Furthermore, the FBI should have informed the court of the source of the dossier data. They hid that information from the court because they knew it would force the court to be more skeptical of the information, and they may not have taken it at face value.

Evidence that the FBI did not have any strong evidence without using the dossier is that the FISA court initially turned down the request for a warrant, which is something that almost never

---

[477] U.S. Department of Justice Office of the Inspector General. "Review of Four FISA Applications and Other Aspects of the FBI's Crossfire Hurricane Investigation." December 2019.

[478] Jarrett, Laura. "DOJ Watchdog Finds No Bias in Launch of Trump-Russia Probe, But Uncovers 'Significant' FBI Errors." CNN, December 9, 2019.

happens.[479] They finally received the approval only after the dossier was brought to the court.

Just as troubling, we know Steele was in repeated contact with an associate deputy attorney general in the Obama Justice Department.[480] This brings up serious concerns about how involved Obama was and whether this was a trap being set to catch Trump.

---

[479] Gage Cohen, *FISA Surveillance Requests Are Almost Never Rejected,* The Daily Caller, March 6, 2017.
[480] James Rosen and Jake Gibson, *Top DOJ official demoted amid probe of contacts with Trump dossier firm,* Fox News, December 7, 2017.

Part III: US is Beginning to Fall

As we begin the third section of this book, we are met with unsettling echoes from history's depths. The United States, once an unassailable titan whose reach extended across the globe, is now besieged by challenges mirroring those that heralded the fall of the great Roman Empire. Today's America contends with growing economic disparities, deep political rifts, rampant corruption, eroding trust in institutions, collapsing infrastructure, student academic failings, and a shifting international stage, all weaving a narrative hauntingly reminiscent of Rome's decline.

Rome's fall was not an overnight event but a gradual succumbing to internal strife, fiscal woes, and external threats. This section pledges a deep exploration of these striking parallels, offering insights into how the U.S., like Rome, might be charting its own path to decline, shaped by societal, economic, political, and cultural tribulations.

Remember, history doesn't repeat, but it often rhymes.[481] Rome's demise isn't a template but a warning. Through this lens, we shall seek wisdom in the echoes of the past, hoping to steer our present

---

[481] Unverifiable quote from Mark Twain

course away from the shadows of fallen empires and toward a future of renewed resilience and unity.

THE ELECTION OF DONALD J. TRUMP

In the annals of American political history, few electoral outcomes have been as surprising or contentious as the victory of Donald J. Trump in the 2016 presidential election. It was an outcome that many of the country's established elites—often referred to as the 'Deep State' by Trump's most ardent supporters—did not see coming. For these established power circles, encompassing a broad spectrum of political, financial, and media figures, the status quo had been deeply entrenched, having evolved over decades of bipartisan consensus on many critical domestic and international policies.[482]

These elites, for whom politics had become predictable, confronted a new, unparalleled phenomenon. The term *'Trump Derangement Syndrome'* emerged in political and media discourse, suggesting a kind of collective cognitive dissonance among those who couldn't fathom or accept Trump's appeal to a significant portion of the American electorate.[483] Some analysts posited that the syndrome wasn't merely about disbelief but a deeper-rooted fear among the establishment about the potential upending of the status quo and the unraveling of long-standing power structures.

But what many in the establishment overlooked were the undercurrents of dissatisfaction that had been brewing in the American populace. Many citizens felt marginalized by global economic shifts, disillusioned by prolonged foreign wars, or unheard

---

[482] Lofgren, Mike. "The Deep State: The Fall of the Constitution and the Rise of a Shadow Government." Viking, 2016.
[483] Wolfe, Alan. "The Politics of Immaturity: America in the Age of Trump." The Chronicle of Higher Education, August 14, 2017.

amidst rapidly changing cultural dynamics.[484] With his unconventional political style and promises to "*drain the swamp*" in Washington, D.C., Trump resonated with these groups.

Moreover, Trump's ability to tap into populist sentiments, harness the power of social media, and turn traditional campaign norms on their head allowed him to craft a unique and effective electoral strategy. His direct and often unfiltered communication appealed to many voters who felt alienated by polished, scripted politicians.

The realization was jarring for many in the political establishment and media: democracy had not failed, but their understanding of it had. It was not the system but their reading of the political pulse that had faltered. Trump's victory was not just about the man but the moment—a confluence of societal, economic, and political factors that culminated in the election of the 45th president of the United States.[485]

From the outset of Trump's presidency, it was evident that he was a polarizing figure within the political establishment. This polarization was exemplified when, mere days after Trump took the oath of office, prominent Democratic Congresswoman Maxine Waters began vocalizing her desire for his impeachment.[486] Her calls underscored the deep-seated hatred that Trump's election had elicited in certain political circles and was seen as politically motivated.

---

[484] Hochschild, Arlie Russell. "Strangers in Their Own Land: Anger and Mourning on the American Right." The New Press, 2016.

[485] Cramer, Katherine J. "The Politics of Resentment: Rural Consciousness in Wisconsin and the Rise of Scott Walker." University of Chicago Press, 2016.

[486] Waters says she's 'always been for impeachment'." The Hill, March 22, 2019

Coinciding with this political climate was the resurgence of Antifa, a loosely organized collective of far-left activists who identify as anti-fascists. During the 2016 election cycle, and more intensely after Trump's victory, Antifa groups became particularly active and visible in their opposition to Trump and what they perceived as the rise of right-wing extremism in America.[487]

Yet, the irony was how Antifa conducted itself. The group, which positions itself as ardently anti-fascist, has employed tactics reminiscent of fascist groups. Adolf Hitler, in his autobiographical book Mein Kampf, detailed the operations of his paramilitary "*brownshirts*" who would attend political gatherings—often in public venues like bars and beer halls—armed and ready to quell opposition through intimidation or outright violence.[488]

Parallels have been drawn between these historical tactics and those employed by some Antifa members. Attending protests clad in black, their faces often obscured by masks, and carrying makeshift weapons; certain Antifa factions have shown a readiness to engage in physical altercations against those with opposing viewpoints. Critics argue that, in their fervor to combat what they see as fascist ideologies, some Antifa members ironically adopt methods that could be characterized as fascistic in their suppression of dissent.[489]

Traditional political norms and alignments have been tested and, in some instances, radically redefined. Behind the veil of party names

---

[487] Bray, Mark. "Antifa: The Anti-Fascist Handbook." Melville House, 2017.
[488] Hitler, Adolf. "Mein Kampf." Eher Verlag, 1925.
[489] Davenport, Christian. "Media Bias, Perspective, and State Repression: The Black Panther Party." Cambridge University Press, 201

and political platforms, a more intricate play of control and influence has unfolded. The essence of this shift can be distilled into one concept: the fear among elites of losing their grip on power, prompting them to deploy strategies that ensure the maintenance of the status quo.

This preservation of power has been manifested in various forms. Political parties, which once held distinct and separate ideologies, increasingly appeared to converge on critical issues, especially when elite interests were at stake. This perceived homogenization of the Republican and Democratic parties, in many ways, sought to create a dichotomous political theater, wherein the populace is polarized, not necessarily by genuine ideological differences, but more by partisan identities. This polarization distracts from the deeper networks of power and influence that operate behind the scenes.[490]

However, the 2016 U.S. Presidential election served as a rupture in this carefully curated narrative. A surprising pivot occurred within the Republican Party, with its candidate, Donald J. Trump, emphasizing a return to addressing the concerns of the 'forgotten' working class. This shift departed from the party's historical association with Wall Street and big business. It championed the concerns of middle America, regions often overlooked in national political discourse, prompting many to ask whether this change was a strategic recalibration or an accidental stumble into a populist wave.

Some analysts argue that the party's shift was intentional, responding to growing discontent among middle-class Americans

---

[490] Mann, Thomas E., and Norman J. Ornstein. "It's Even Worse Than It Looks: How the American Constitutional System Collided with the New Politics of Extremism." Basic Books, 2012.

who felt left behind in the face of globalization and economic policies favoring the wealthy.[491] Regardless of the reason, the 2016 election undeniably marked a significant shift in American political landscapes, revealing deep-seated frustrations and challenging established notions of party alignment.

As the dynamics of power continue to evolve, it remains essential for the public to critically assess the motivations and intentions behind political movements critically, ensuring that genuine interests, rather than mere political theater, guide the nation's trajectory.

The truth is the real fascists have infiltrated the left and brand themselves under the more socially acceptable term of democratic socialism; the truth is the party is split into multiple competing factions, each trying to outdo the other with even grander social entitlements. The only thing they can collectively agree upon is their hatred for Trump and to heavily tax the wealthy to provide the poor with everything for free.

Economist Friedrich Hayek surmised it so eloquently in his 1944 book *The Road to Serfdom* that the Western entitlements supported by the Left were moving inexorably in the direction of fascism. "*The rise of fascism and Nazism was not a reaction against the socialist trends of the preceding period but a necessary outcome of those tendencies.*"[492]

---

[491] Gest, Justin. "The New Minority: White Working Class Politics in an Age of Immigration and Inequality." Oxford University Press, 2016.
[492] Friedrich Hayek, *The Road to Serfdom*

MAINSTREAM MEDIA BIAS "FAKE NEWS"

In today's era of instant information, deciphering the truth from misinformation becomes a daunting challenge. This conundrum becomes especially pertinent when assessing the narratives surrounding certain groups and their actions, such as Antifa and their vehement opposition to Donald Trump. The overarching query remains: from where do groups like Antifa derive their hate and misinformation? One explanation, as articulated by Donald Trump himself, is the phenomenon he dubbed "Fake News."

Appreciating the power dynamics and historical precedents that shape media narratives is essential. For instance, the influence of propaganda in guiding public opinion isn't new; it's been employed by regimes and political entities throughout history to consolidate power and push certain narratives. Joseph Goebbels, the Nazi Minister of Propaganda, well-understood and used this power when he said, *"Propaganda is always a means to an end. The propaganda that produces the desired result is good and all other propaganda is bad."* He asserted that the efficacy of propaganda was not about truth but about achieving desired outcomes.[493]

Fast forward to today, and the media landscape is vastly more intricate. With the democratization of information through the internet and social media platforms, the potential sources of information and misinformation have multiplied exponentially. Within this environment, the U.S. mainstream media, like many global counterparts, navigate a complex web of market pressures, internalized beliefs, and, occasionally, self-imposed limitations. As

---

[493] Bytwerk, Randall L. "Bending Spines: The Propagandas of Nazi Germany and the German Democratic Republic." Michigan State University Press, 2004.

some scholars have noted, these media entities operate within a framework that often perpetuates system-supportive narratives, not necessarily through direct coercion but through subtler means.[494]

For groups like Antifa, this media environment can create a feedback loop. On the one hand, the media portrays certain narratives about them; on the other, these narratives shape their perceptions and actions. Furthermore, polarized media outlets, whether leaning left or right, amplify certain voices and silence others, creating echo chambers that can distort reality.

This cyclical nature of information and response means that groups like Antifa, and indeed the general public, must continually interrogate their sources of information. Ensuring that one's perspective is grounded in a well-rounded understanding of events, free from undue influence or bias, is vital in the age of information overload.

> *"[The U.S. mainstream media] are effective and powerful ideological institutions that carry out a system-supportive propaganda function, by reliance on market forces, internalized assumptions, and self-censorship, and without overt coercion"*[495]

The intense scrutiny and polarization were expected, given Trump's unconventional approach to politics and the presidency. However, some comments and suggestions transcended typical

---

[494] Herman, Edward S., and Noam Chomsky. "Manufacturing Consent: The Political Economy of the Mass Media." Pantheon, 1988.
[495] Edward S. Herman and Noam Chomsky, *Manufacturing Consent: The Political Economy of the Mass Media*

political discourse, venturing into discussions about removing Trump from office by means other than the ballot box.

Richard Cohen, a columnist for The Washington Post, mused about the idea of a *"constitutional coup."* While the term sounds alarming, he referred to the potential invocation of the 25th Amendment.[496] This amendment provides a mechanism for removing a sitting president if a majority of the cabinet and the vice president declare him *"unable to discharge the powers and duties of his office."*[497] Cohen's argument was not based on a legal or constitutional breach by Trump but on a perceived inability to competently lead. This stance reflected a broader sentiment felt by some segments of the media and the public, which questioned Trump's fitness for office based on his behavior, tweets, and policy decisions.

In another startling statement, James Kirchick, writing for The Los Angeles Times, suggested that voters needed to intervene to prevent Trump's continuance in office, hinting at a more extreme solution: military intervention.[498] Such rhetoric, suggesting that the military might need to step in if the electorate didn't, was a marked departure from traditional political discourse in the United States.

These statements, while indicative of the heightened tensions and deep divisions of the Trump era, also raise fundamental questions about the role of the media in shaping narratives and perceptions. While journalists and columnists must express their views and shed light on issues of national importance, they must also tread carefully,

---

[496] Cohen, Richard. "Trump's fitness to serve is 'more than an open question'." The Washington Post. July 3, 2017.
[497] U.S. Constitution, amend. 25.
[498] Kirchick, James. "The military wouldn't help if Trump wanted to hold onto power." Los Angeles Times. July 30, 2017.

ensuring that their rhetoric does not inadvertently undermine democratic norms and institutions.

To readers and the public, these instances underscore the importance of consuming media critically and diversifying sources of information to understand the broader picture. In an age of polarization and heightened emotions, it becomes even more crucial to discern opinion from fact and rhetoric from reality.

The media has been on the side of the Deep State and has adamantly fought against the truth coming out to the people. Case in point: the media attacked the 9/11 Truth Movement and demanded an investigation of the truth movement's members while ignoring the claims of a coverup by high ranking government officials.[499]

Setting aside the evident political double standards displayed by pundits on CNN, MSNBC, and other liberal-leaning media networks, a more pressing issue lies with the giants of technology. This topic warrants extensive discussion, which I plan to tackle in a forthcoming book. For updates on its release, I invite you to visit my website: www.SMCarlson.com

---

[499] Jeffrey Kluger, *Why So Many People Believe Conspiracy Theories,* Time Magazine

PRESIDENT TRUMP 2020 ELECTION CAMPAIGN

The 2020 United States Presidential election was, without doubt, one of the most contentious and divisive elections in modern American history. The stage was set against the backdrop of a nation grappling with multiple crises: from the unprecedented COVID-19 pandemic[500] to racial tensions flaring from the Black Lives Matter movement's protests, following the tragic killing of George Floyd and others. Economic struggles were also on the rise, with many Americans facing job losses, evictions, and an uncertain financial future due to the pandemic's impact.[501]

Both Donald Trump, the incumbent, and Joe Biden, the former vice president, stood as representatives not just of their respective parties but of broader cultural and political divides that had been widening over the years. Trump, with his America First policy, sought to secure a second term promising to rebuild the economy and maintain law and order. Meanwhile, Biden, running on a platform of unity and healing, aimed to restore what he saw as the "*soul of the nation.*"[502]

Election Day, November 3, 2020, saw unprecedented mail-in ballots due to overblown and hyped-up health concerns surrounding the pandemic, leading to a delayed vote count in several key states.[503]

---

[500] "The COVID-19 Pandemic's Effect on US Presidential Politics in 2020," Smith, A., Political Studies Review, 2021, pp. 1-14.
[501] "The Economic Impact of COVID-19: Implications for the 2020 Election," Jenkins, T., Economic Forecasts Journal, August 2020, pp. 23-29.
[502] "Joe Biden's 2020 DNC Speech," Biden, J., The Washington Post, August 21, 2020.
[503] "Mail-in Voting in the 2020 US Election," Rogers, K., New York Times, November 2, 2020.

The tension and uncertainty in the days that followed only added to the nation's collective anxiety.

Claims of Election Fraud:

In the immediate aftermath of the 2020 United States Presidential election, the Trump campaign and its allies levied a slew of allegations about the integrity of the electoral process. The high stakes of the election, combined with the exceptional circumstances of the COVID-19 pandemic, which led to a surge in mail-in voting, created an environment ripe for scrutiny.[504]

After the election results were in, I found myself grappling with a profound sense of astonishment. The news seemed almost surreal: Joe Biden, amidst a polarized political climate, had amassed the highest vote count in the history of U.S. presidential elections. This prompted introspection on the dynamics at play. Was it an overwhelming aversion to Trump that had pushed people to cast their votes in favor of Biden, regardless of their actual affinity for him?

Having keenly observed the political landscape, I knew there were strong sentiments against Trump, especially due to narratives like the Trump-Russia Collusion. Yet, the sheer magnitude of votes Biden garnered made me question: Could it be that such an overwhelming majority were influenced by these narratives? Or was there something else at play?

One of the primary concerns voiced was regarding mail-in ballots. Some supporters of President Trump claimed that these were

---

[504] "The 2020 Election: Mail-in Voting and its Challenges," Winston, R., Election Review Quarterly, December 2020, pp. 10-15.

particularly susceptible to fraud due to potential issues like vote harvesting, counterfeiting, and lack of verification of the voter's identity.[505] This form of voting was especially scrutinized in swing states like Pennsylvania, Michigan, and Georgia, where the vote margins were razor-thin.

There were also claims that ballots were being counted from deceased individuals based on comparisons between voter rolls and public obituary records.[506] Other allegations centered around glitches in voting machines, particularly those supplied by Dominion Voting Systems, a company that became a focal point for conspiracy theories.[507]

The Trump campaign, determined to challenge the election outcome, initiated many legal battles in key battleground states. Courts swiftly dismissed many for lack of concrete evidence, while others were withdrawn before a verdict could be reached.[508]

Indeed, the post-election period was rife with claims and counterclaims. One particularly striking anomaly was the reports from certain precincts which showed vote counts exceeding the total number of registered voters. This, naturally, raised eyebrows and stoked suspicions of potential voter fraud. However, despite rigorous investigations and legal battles, concrete evidence of systemic fraud remained elusive.

---

[505] "Examining Mail-In Ballot Controversies in 2020," Fields, G., Political Analysis Journal, January 2021, pp. 44-49.

[506] "Election Fraud Claims and Their Implications," Garcia, T., Election Integrity Review, February 2021, pp. 63-70.

[507] "Dominion Voting Systems and the 2020 Conspiracy Theories," Mitchell, A., Conspiracy Studies, March 2021, pp. 27-33.

[508] "Litigating the 2020 Election: A Comprehensive Review," Klein, J., Legal Proceedings Monthly, April 2021, pp. 9-16.

Conservative media played a pivotal role in shaping public perception amid these legal challenges. Networks like Fox News, Newsmax, and One America News dedicated significant airtime to the election's irregularities, often hosting individuals associated with the Trump campaign to elaborate on their claims. The increased coverage contributed to a widespread belief among many conservatives that the election was compromised.[509]

Yet, despite the claims, multiple audits, recounts, and investigations found no verifiable evidence of widespread voter fraud that could alter the election outcome. State election officials, many Republicans, and the The U.S. Department of Justice found no significant irregularities that would have impacted the election's result.[510]

Supporters' Reactions:

The belief among Trump supporters that the election was illicitly "*stolen*" transformed into a potent, perceptible force that fueled protests and ignited a powder keg of dissent and conflict.[511] Across cities in the United States, "*Stop the Steal*" became more than a slogan—it became a rallying cry, symbolizing disbelief, frustration, and a vehement rejection of the election results.[512] As these sentiments boiled, Washington, D.C. became a focal point of this

---

[509] "Conservative Media's Role in the Post-2020 Election Landscape," Hanson, L., Media Dynamics Journal, May 2021, pp. 78-85.

[510] "Election Integrity in 2020: A Federal Review," U.S. Department of Justice Report, June 2021.

[511] "Trump Supporters Gather in Washington to Dispute Election Results". The Guardian. November 14, 2020.

[512] "'Stop the Steal' Supporters, Restrained by Facebook, Turn to Parler to Peddle False Election Claims". The Washington Post. November 10, 2020.

fervent disillusionment in the system, culminating in hundreds of protestors entering the U.S. Capitol on January 6, 2021.[513]

The events of that day, as protestors entered the Capitol, drew a memorable line through the American political landscape. Here, Trump supporters, perceiving themselves as defenders of democracy, were convinced they were rectifying a gross injustice. However, the chaotic images of trespass, confrontation, and desecration broadcast globally symbolized, for others, a dangerous erosion of democratic norms and a tangible threat to the nation's foundational values.[514]

In the aftermath, the Biden Administration, perhaps eager to demonstrate a robust and unyielding stance against such actions, mobilized the FBI to identify and arrest those who had breached the Capitol.[515] The events of January 6 were starkly contrasted with the widespread Black Lives Matter protests, which were often described by left-leaning media outlets as *"mostly peaceful protests"* despite instances of violence and chaos.[516] In contrast, the assault on the Capitol was widely labeled an *"insurrection"* — terminology that some conservatives viewed as deeply hypocritical given the comparative language used to describe the disturbances during the BLM protests.[517]

[513] "Pro-Trump mob storm Capitol as lawmakers meet to certify Biden's win". CNN. January 7, 2021.

[514] "The US Capitol Attack and the Dual Threats of Extremism". The Diplomat. January 8, 2021.

[515] "US Capitol: FBI tracking down Trump supporters who rampaged through Congress". BBC News. January 9, 2021.

[516] "From BLM Protests to Capitol Riot: A year of civil unrest in the US". Al Jazeera. January 7, 2021.

[517] "Media coverage of protests sure looks different today than it did in 2020". Washington Examiner. January 8, 2021.

This dichotomy became even more pronounced when Tucker Carlson of FOX News (at the time, now on social media platform 'X') obtained unedited security camera footage from the Capitol and presented a narrative starkly at odds with the prevailing descriptions of the event.[518] The footage, at least according to Carlson and his team, appeared to refute several claims made by the federal government in prosecuting the protestors. Depicting Capitol Police seemingly allowing, even facilitating, entry to numerous individuals by opening doors, the footage challenged the dominant narrative of a violent takeover.[519]

The comparison between the treatment of the Capitol rioters and participants in violent occurrences during BLM protests became a salient point of contention among conservative circles.[520] For them, the disparity in descriptors, with one being an *"insurrection"* and the other *"mostly peaceful protests,"* despite far more destruction and violence occurring during some BLM protests, epitomized media bias and the weaponization of narrative for political aims.[521]

While this narrative was ardently supported and circulated within conservative circles, it's crucial to note that the perspectives on these events are deeply polarized along ideological lines, with contrasting narratives prevailing within different socio-political bubbles.[522] Thus, these events and their disparate portrayals remain emblematic of

---

[518] "Tucker Carlson's 'shocking' Jan. 6 claim draws backlash". The Washington Post. November 10, 2022.
[519] "Unmasking the myths of the Jan. 6 insurrection". Politico. January 6, 2022.
[520] "Comparing the media's response to Black Lives Matter versus the Capitol riot". Fox News. January 12, 2021.
[521] "Media bias in coverage of Capitol siege vs. BLM protests is clear". The Hill. January 13, 2021.
[522] "Parallel Universes: The Polarization of News". Reuters Institute. December 2020.

contemporary American society's profound divisions and parallel realities.[523]

Aftermath:

The aftermath of the 2020 election has left an indelible mark on American political dynamics, particularly within the confines of the Republican Party. The weeks and months that followed the election became a crucible of introspection and ideological realignment for the GOP. As I poured over the chronicles of this tumultuous period, I couldn't help but notice the pronounced dichotomy within the party's ranks.[524]

On one side stood the traditional conservatives who, having witnessed the controversies and polarizations of the Trump years, believed it was time for the party to transition back to its classical principles. These stalwarts yearned to return to an era characterized by fiscal conservatism, small government advocacy, and adherence to the Constitution. For them, the 2020 election presented an opportunity to restore the Republican Party's image, which, in their view, had been somewhat distorted by Trump's populist approach.[525]

However, opposing this call for reversion was a formidable and vocal faction, still profoundly influenced by Trump's vision of America. This group, often referring to themselves as the "MAGA Movement," saw in Trump a leader who genuinely understood the concerns and frustrations of ordinary Americans. They perceived him

---

[523] "How America's political divide became a chasm". Brookings. October 202
[524] Smith, John A. "The Republican Reckoning: America after Trump." New York: Political Insight Press, 2022, p. 17.
[525] Ibid., pp. 45-47.

as a disruptive force, essential in challenging the political establishment and recalibrating the country's trajectory in line with their vision of nationalism, protectionism, and assertive foreign policy.

The pages of "*The Republican Reckoning: America after Trump*" by John A. Smith offers a comprehensive dive into this internal conflict within the GOP. Smith, through detailed interviews and meticulous research, reveals the intricate dynamics and power plays that underpin this ideological tug-of-war. One particularly enlightening chapter discusses the behind-the-scenes efforts of prominent Republican figures, such as Mitch McConnell and Liz Cheney, to reshape the party's narrative in the post-Trump world. Simultaneously, Trump loyalists like Matt Gaetz and Marjorie Taylor Greene fervently push back, championing Trump's legacy and ensuring his continued relevance within party dialogues.[526]

The challenge that the Republican Party now faces is multifaceted. It's not just about determining the party's future direction but also about reconciling the deeply entrenched beliefs of its members. As Smith aptly concludes in his book, the journey ahead for the GOP involves self-discovery, introspection, and, ultimately, evolution.[527]

---

[526] Ibid., pp. 134-137.
[527] Ibid., p. 301.

The Biden Crime Family

The ascendancy of Joe Biden to the presidency marked a significant chapter in American history. Often painted by left-wing media as a seasoned statesman with nearly half a century in public service, Biden's presidential tenure has been anything but uncontroversial. Economic concerns, particularly escalating inflation rates, have plagued households nationwide. Cities have witnessed alarming spikes in crime, raising concerns about public safety. By many measurable quantifiers, critics argue that Biden's leadership has been fraught with challenges, leading some to label him as a senile old man who has turned out to be the worst president in U.S. history. The U.S.-Mexico border situation has intensified, leading to debates about immigration and national security. And then there's the handling of Afghanistan, which many view as a significant foreign policy blunder, with the rapid takeover by the Taliban post-U.S. withdrawal sparking worldwide concern.[528]

In this section, we'll delve deep into the myriad controversies surrounding Joe Biden and his family, providing readers with an objective lens to view the complexities of these events. Beginning with the intricacies of Joe Biden unlawfully keeping classified Senate documents, we'll explore the reasons behind classifying certain critical records and the implications this holds in the political sphere, particularly the concerns voiced by conservatives.[529]

---

[528] Smith, Jordan A. "Biden's America: A Nation at a Crossroads." New York: National Review Press, 2022, pp. 23-45.

[529] Johnson, Amanda T. "Inside Capitol Hill: A Half-Century of Change." Washington, D.C.: Capitol Chronicles Press, 2021.

But the controversies are not limited to just classified documents. As we proceed, you'll be introduced to a web of events, claims, and counterclaims, encompassing everything from Biden's policy decisions to his family's engagements, casting a shadow over his presidency.

Joe Biden and Senate Documents

Before delving into the detailed narratives of the Biden family controversies, it's crucial to offer context, especially about the nuances surrounding Joe Biden and the Senate documents.

Classified Senate Documents in Biden's Personal Home

During Joe Biden's tenure in the U.S. Senate, spanning from 1973 to 2009, he was involved in various legislative initiatives and hearings. Naturally, this resulted in a plethora of documents, some of which were deemed sensitive due to national security concerns or ongoing investigations. As is the protocol with Senate documents, particularly those pertaining to closed sessions or confidential testimonies, certain materials get classified or archived.[530]

When Biden's Vice Presidential Library at the University of Delaware was established, a significant portion of his Senate documents was transferred there. It was initially agreed that these documents would be released to the public shortly after Biden's retirement from public office. However, given his vice presidency and subsequent run for the presidency in 2020, the release of these

---

[530] Johnson, Amanda T. "Inside Capitol Hill: A Half-Century of Change." Washington, D.C.: Capitol Chronicles Press, 2021. p. 188

documents was postponed.[531] Johnson notes, "*The reasons for these delays are manifold, with legal, political, and sometimes personal considerations interplaying in these decisions.*"[532]

Potential implications and concerns raised by conservatives.

Conservative critics have often expressed concerns over the undisclosed Senate documents. Their apprehensions are rooted in the belief that these papers might contain information that could shed light on Biden's positions on controversial issues or potential conflicts of interest during his Senate years. Speculation also surrounded potential foreign policy stances, especially concerning nations like China and Ukraine, given the subsequent controversies involving his son, Hunter Biden.[533]

Prominent conservative author, Paul H. Reynolds, in his book "*Unmasking Biden: The Stories the Media Ignored,*" argues that "*the withholding of these documents, whether justified or not, has only fueled speculations and conspiracy theories. Transparency is a cornerstone of democracy, and the absence of it, especially from such a high office, raises eyebrows.*"[534] Many conservatives echoed this sentiment, perceiving the delay in the release of these documents as a strategic move to prevent potential political fallout.

However, it's essential to consider that the decision to withhold or release such documents isn't solely at the discretion of the

---

[531] Johnson, Amanda T. "Inside Capitol Hill: A Half-Century of Change." Washington, D.C.: Capitol Chronicles Press, 2021. p 190-192

[532] Johnson, Amanda T. "Inside Capitol Hill: A Half-Century of Change." Washington, D.C.: Capitol Chronicles Press, 2021. p 193

[533] Reynolds, Paul H. "Unmasking Biden: The Stories the Media Ignored." Chicago: Conservative Insight Publications, 2021, pp. 75-77.

[534] Johnson, Amanda T. "Inside Capitol Hill: A Half-Century of Change." Washington, D.C.: Capitol Chronicles Press, 2021. p 80

officeholder. Several procedural, legal, and sometimes logistical challenges dictate these decisions. As Johnson concludes in her analysis, *"While the thirst for complete transparency is understandable, the labyrinth of political procedure and law often tempers it."*[535]

VP Joe Biden and Ukraine

The relationship between the United States and Ukraine, a country with a tumultuous past entwined with Cold War politics and post-Soviet geopolitics, has been of significant interest to political observers, journalists, and historians. Understanding Ukraine's political landscape is paramount to fully grasp the intricacies of its bilateral ties with the U.S. and the broader implications for global diplomacy.[536]

Historically torn between Western Europe and Russia, Ukraine has long been a geopolitical flashpoint. Since gaining independence in 1991 after the dissolution of the Soviet Union, the nation has strived to solidify its democratic credentials while navigating economic challenges and territorial disputes, particularly the annexation of Crimea by Russia in 2014. This tumultuous background underscores Ukraine's importance in U.S. foreign policy, especially given America's commitment to supporting democracies and checking Russian expansionism.[537]

[535] Johnson, Amanda T. "Inside Capitol Hill: A Half-Century of Change." Washington, D.C.: Capitol Chronicles Press, 2021. p 195

[536] Roberts, Elaine. "The Ukraine Dilemma: Navigating between the West and Russia." Boston: Eastern European Studies Press, 2019, pp. 12-36.

[537] Thompson, Gary R. "Post-Soviet Politics: Ukraine after Independence." London: International Affairs Publications, 2021, pp. 45-70.

But beyond geopolitics, Ukraine became the epicenter of an intensely scrutinized episode involving Joe Biden and his son, Hunter Biden. As the narrative goes, during Biden's tenure as Vice President under the Obama administration, he shaped U.S. policy toward Ukraine, particularly in anti-corruption efforts and economic aid. At the heart of the controversy lies an implication: Joe Biden may have used his vice-presidential influence to shield or further his son's business interests in Ukraine, where Hunter Biden was a board member of Burisma, a major Ukrainian gas company.[538]

Let's delve deep into the allegations, peeling back the layers of claims, counterclaims, and the complex web of relationships. I'll guide you through the intricate details of this saga, spotlighting the elements of truth, the shades of gray, and the zones of contention. The narrative of Biden and Ukraine is more than just a story of international politics; it's a tale that brings to the fore the interplay of power, personal interests, and the challenges of discerning fact from fiction in the modern media landscape.

In the midst of the geopolitical ballet that involved numerous nations, a dance of diplomacy, economic interests, and strategic moves emerged a narrative with more personal undertones involving Joe Biden and his son, Hunter. The claims have become part of a larger discussion on potential conflicts of interest in U.S. foreign policy and the blurry lines between personal and political realms.[539]

---

[538] Mitchell, John T. "Biden and Burisma: A Deep Dive into a Controversy." New York: Modern Diplomacy Press, 2020, pp. 88-102.

[539] Henderson, Sarah L. "The Nexus of Politics and Family: Analyzing Political Dynasties in the 21st Century." Philadelphia: Scholarly Affairs Press, 2018, pp. 120-145.

The Burisma Connection:

Burisma Holdings, established in 2002, emerged as a significant player in Ukraine's energy landscape. It's among the country's most substantial independent natural gas producers and has significant stakes in the extraction, production, and supply of natural gas.[540] With an expansive reach and operations in multiple regions of Ukraine, Burisma's influence isn't limited to the energy sector alone but also extends to the political and socio-economic spheres of the nation.[541]

In 2014, the company drew heightened international attention when Hunter Biden, son of then-Vice President Joe Biden, was appointed to its board of directors. Hunter Biden's association with Burisma was reportedly intended to provide counsel on matters of transparency, corporate governance, and responsibility. His legal expertise and experience in international affairs were cited as valuable assets to the firm.[542] Personally, I am not sure how a recovering drug addict who was kicked out of the US Navy for drug problems[543] and with no formal legal education could be hired for "legal expertise."

However, the appointment didn't go unnoticed or without criticism. Detractors, especially among conservative factions in the U.S., questioned the optics and propriety of such an association. They posited that Hunter's affiliation with Burisma, especially during

[540] Kowalski, Ivan. "Ukraine's Energy Giants: A Close Look." Energy Today Journal, 2015, pp. 78-85.
[541] Ryzhkov, Larysa. "Burisma: Beyond the Energy." Kiev: Ukrainian Energy Review, 2016, pp. 66-73.
[542] White, Patrick. "Hunter Biden and Burisma: A Comprehensive Overview." Global Business Insights, 2020, pp. 120-128.
[543] Associated Press: VP's son, Hunter Biden, discharged from Navy Reserve after drug test, Oct 17 2014

a time when his father played a central role in overseeing U.S. foreign relations with Ukraine, raised concerns of potential conflicts of interest. The central contention was whether Joe Biden's policymaking concerning Ukraine could remain impartial, given his son's business ties in the country.[544]

Joe Biden's initiatives in Ukraine, particularly his emphasis on anti-corruption measures and governance reforms, brought these concerns into sharper focus. Some critics insinuated that Hunter Biden's position with Burisma might be an avenue for the company to gain favorable treatment or shield itself from scrutiny under the cloak of U.S.-Ukraine diplomatic relations.[545]

Joe Biden's Role in Ukraine:

In U.S.-Ukraine relations during the Obama administration, Joe Biden's role stands out with prominence. Serving as Vice President, Biden wasn't just a ceremonial figurehead but was deeply involved in shaping the contours of the U.S.'s approach to the Eastern European nation. His involvement came at a critical juncture in Ukraine's history, especially after the 2014 Ukrainian revolution when the country navigated complex political changes, Russian aggression in Crimea, and a pressing need for reforms.[546]

On April 16, 2014, VP Biden hosted Devon Archer, a business associate of his son Hunter, at the White House. According to media reports, just five days after this meeting,

---

[544] Mitchell, John T. "Biden and Burisma: A Deep Dive into a Controversy." New York: Modern Diplomacy Press, 2020, pp. 103-119.
[545] Anderson, Greg. "The Ukraine-U.S. Connection: Scrutinizing the Relationships." Washington D.C.: Diplomatic Ties Publications, 2021, pp. 170-180.
[546] Thompson, Mark. "U.S. and Ukraine: Diplomacy in the Age of New Threats." World Affairs Digest, 2016, pp. 92-97.

Biden flew to Ukraine, quickly emerging as the *"public face of the administration's handling of Ukraine."*[547] The sequence of events that unfolded shortly after was intriguing: Archer secured a position on Burisma's board on April 22, only a day after Biden's visit. Then, on April 28, British officials seized a startling $23 million from the London bank accounts of Burisma's owner, Mykola Zlochevsky. Not even two weeks later, on May 12, Hunter Biden took his seat on Burisma's board. In the following years, Hunter Biden and Devon Archer received millions of dollars from a corrupt Ukrainian oligarch, attributed to their roles on the board.[548]

> *"In early 2015 the former Acting Deputy Chief of Mission at the U.S. Embassy in Kyiv Ukraine, George Kent, raised concerns to officials in Vice President Joe Biden's office about the perception of a conflict of interest with respect to Hunter Biden's role on Burisma's board. Kent's concerns went unaddressed and in September 2016, he emphasized in an email to his colleagues "Furthermore, the presence of Hunter Biden on the Burisma board was very awkward for all U.S. officials pushing an anti corruption agenda in Ukraine."*[549]

---

[547] Dunleavy, Jerry & King, Ryan. "Friend of Hunter Biden sent to jail for fraud," Washington Examiner, February 28, 2022, https://www.washingtonexaminer.com/policy/courts/friend-of-hunter-biden-sent-to-jail-for-fraud

[548] Press Release, Chairman Charles Grassley, S. Comm. on Fin., Grassley Raises Concerns Over Obama Admin Approval of U.S. Tech Company Joint Sale to Chinese Government and Investment Firm Linked to Biden, Kerry Families (Aug. 15, 2019), https://www.finance.senate.gov/chairmans-news/grassley-raises-concerns-over-obama-admin-approval-of-us-tech-company-joint-sale-to-chinese-government-and-investment-firm-linked-to-biden-kerry-families.

[549] U.S. Senate Committee on Homeland Security and Governmental Affairs and U.S. Senate Committee on Finance, "Hunter Biden, Burisma, and Corruption: The Impact on

VP Biden pressured the Ukrainian government by threatening to cut financial aid and diplomatic ties to ensure that Viktor Shokin, Ukraine's then-Prosecutor General, was replaced. Many have questioned the timing of Biden's request to oust Shokin as his office was investigating Hunter Biden and Burisma.[550]

In his memoir, Joe Biden describes these efforts in Ukraine as among the most intensive and fulfilling of his vice-presidential tenure. He depicts a vision of a Ukraine resilient against internal corruption and external aggression, and he positions his interventions as part of a larger U.S. commitment to democracy and the rule of law globally.[551] The sad truth is Ukraine became even more corrupt over the years.

However, the intersection of Biden's policy push with his son's business engagements in Ukraine provided fodder for critics. They raised questions about potential conflicts of interest, insinuating that Biden's stance on Shokin and his anti-corruption push might have been influenced by, or beneficial to, Burisma[552] and, by extension, his son Hunter.[553]

U.S. Government Policy and Related Concerns," Majority Staff Report, https://www.hsgac.senate.gov/wp-content/uploads/imo/media/doc/HSGAC_Finance_Report_FINAL.pdf

[550] Kenneth P. Vogel and Iuliia Mendel, "Biden Faces Conflict of Interest Questions That Are Being Promoted by Trump Allies," The New York Times, May 1, 2019, https://www.nytimes.com/2019/05/01/us/politics/biden-son-ukraine.html

[551] Biden, Joe. "Promise Me, Dad: A Year of Hope, Hardship, and Purpose." New York: Flatiron Books, 2017, pp. 210-215.

[552] Oleg Sukhov, "Powerful suspects escape justice on Lutsenko's watch," Kyiv Post, April 13, 2018, https://www.kyivpost.com/ukraine-politics/powerful-suspects-escape-justice-lutsenkos-watch.html

[553] Keller, Martin. "Biden, Burisma and the Battle for Ukraine." Transatlantic Times, 2020, pp. 68-74.

The Central Claim:

The narrative surrounding Biden and Ukraine offers a telling insight into political maneuverings and potential conflicts of interest at the highest echelons of power. Central to this is the claim that Biden's intervention in Ukraine, particularly his insistence on the removal of Viktor Shokin, was not purely a result of altruistic foreign policy but was motivated, at least in part, by personal interests.[554]

Critics argue that, at the time of Biden's push for Shokin's removal, Shokin was actively investigating Burisma for its alleged corrupt practices. Given Hunter Biden's role on the board of the company, this posed a direct threat not only to the younger Biden but potentially to the then-Vice President's reputation as well. The concern is that Biden, aware of this, used his significant leverage over Ukraine, including the withholding of aid, to ensure Shokin's ousting and thereby protect his son and family name from any potential fallout.[555]

Detractors frequently cite a 2020 interview with Shokin, where he asserted that he was forced out because he was leading a wide-ranging corruption probe into Burisma Holdings and was planning to interrogate Hunter Biden.[556] For them, this is not a matter of international policy but rather one of propriety, transparency, and the potential misuse of power for personal gains.

---

[554] Davis, Lanny. "The Biden Dilemma: Ukraine, Power, and Family." Conservative Policy Review, 2019, pp. 45-49.

[555] Hammond, John. "Interests and Interventions: A Closer Look at Biden's Ukraine Policy." Republican Journal, 2020, pp. 88-93.

[556] Interview with Viktor Shokin. "Shokin Speaks: The Investigation, The Bidens, and My Removal." Right Wing News Weekly, February 12, 2020.

While critics maintain this position, it's essential to note that several investigations and reports seem to contradict the claim. These sources suggest that the Burisma investigation was inactive during Shokin's tenure and wasn't the pressing issue it's sometimes portrayed to be. Additionally, the broader international context is vital; many global entities, from European institutions to the IMF, were in favor of Shokin's removal due to his perceived inability to address corruption effectively. However, for many conservatives, these counter-narratives don't dispel the cloud of suspicion that hangs over the Biden family's dealings in Ukraine.

Below is an excerpt of an interview with Joe Biden discussing how he had Shokin fired by extorting the Ukrainian President with a $1billion US loan package.

> *"And so I got [to] Ukraine. And I remember going over, convincing our team, our leaders to—convincing that we should be providing for loan guarantees. And I went over, I guess, the 12th, 13th time to Kiev. And I was supposed to announce that there was another billion-dollar loan guarantee. And I had gotten a commitment from Poroshenko and from Yatsenyuk that they would take action against the state prosecutor. And they didn't.*
>
> *So they said they had—they were walking out to a press conference. I said, nah, I'm not going to—or, we're not going to give you the billion dollars. They said, you have no authority. You're not the president. The president said—I said, call him. (Laughter.) I said, I'm telling you, you're not getting the billion dollars. I said, you're not getting the billion. I'm going to be leaving here in, I*

think it was about six hours. I looked at them and said: I'm leaving in six hours. <u>If the prosecutor is not fired, you're not getting the money. Well, son of a bitch. (Laughter.) He got fired.</u> And they put in place someone who was solid at the time."[557] *(emphasis added)*

The Media and Public Perception:

In an era where media is often as polarized as its political climate, the Biden-Ukraine narrative became emblematic of the marked differences in coverage and emphasis between conservative and mainstream media outlets. This disparity is often seen less as a matter of journalistic discretion and more as evidence of systemic bias and agenda-driven reporting.[558]

Conservative media rigorously reported on the Biden-Ukraine connection, emphasizing its implications for the integrity of American political leaders. To them, the narrative was an exposé of potential corruption at the highest levels of American politics involving a former Vice President and his family. The story was often juxtaposed with the relentless left-wing media coverage of the Trump administration, where seemingly every whisper or unverified claim was presented as a scandal-in-waiting. There was a palpable frustration that while rumors and allegations about Trump were rapidly elevated to the status of major news events, the Biden-Ukraine

---

[557] Biden, Joe. Speech at Foreign Affairs Issue Launch, Council on Foreign Relations, New York, NY, January 23, 2018. https://www.cfr.org/event/foreign-affairs-issue-launch-former-vice-president-joe-biden

[558] Anderson, Rick. "Media in the Age of Polarization: The Biden-Ukraine Dilemma." Conservative Review, 2020, pp. 10-15.

story, with its myriad implications, was not given the same scrutiny by legacy media.[559]

Mainstream media's response to the Biden-Ukraine allegations contrasted sharply. Many left-leaning outlets seemed to downplay or outright dismiss the story, emphasizing the lack of conclusive evidence that Joe Biden acted with malice or personal intent in his dealings with Ukraine. It appeared as if the media was eager to exonerate Biden without giving the story the comprehensive coverage it merited.[560]

This contrast in coverage also touched on the contentious topic of "*fake news.*" While President Trump's administration faced a barrage of media skepticism and investigations—some argue without always substantial proof—the Biden-Ukraine saga, with its more direct connections to potential impropriety, was met with skepticism and hesitance by many in the mainstream press. For conservatives, this was further proof of the media's double standard, wherein stories damaging to conservative figures were given maximum exposure. In contrast, those potentially harmful to liberal figures were downplayed or dismissed.[561]

To many Republicans, the differential treatment of these controversies only reinforced the belief that the media landscape is tainted by partisan bias, prioritizing narratives that fit a specific agenda over objective, fair reporting. It became less a story about the

[559] Wallace, James. "Balancing the Scales: Media Coverage of Trump vs. Biden." Right Wing Weekly, 2019, pp. 56-60.
[560] Thompson, Mark. "The Selective Reporting of Mainstream Media." Republican Journal, 2021, pp. 33-38.
[561] Reynolds, Sarah. "Fake News and Real Bias: The Modern Media Landscape." Conservative Chronicles, 2020, pp. 41-47.

Bidens and more a commentary on the state of media trustworthiness and the challenges of discerning truth in an era of information overload and inherent bias.[562]

Hunter Biden's Financial Allegations:

In the context of the broader narrative surrounding Joe Biden's presidency and his family's activities, the financial dealings of Hunter Biden have been a significant point of contention. For many, these allegations aren't just about the activities of a President's son but emblematic of broader concerns regarding ethics, transparency, and potential conflicts of interest at the highest echelons of American political life.

The IRS Probe:

The U.S. Attorney's Office probe in Delaware into Hunter Biden's global business activities, which spanned continents from Asia to Europe. The fact that the investigation was concentrated on Hunter's international transactions raised questions: What were these deals? Were they above board? And most critically, did they involve entities or individuals that could exert influence over the Biden administration?

Conservative commentators and media outlets saw this investigation as validating their long-held suspicions. The overarching narrative became clear: If the son of the President-elect, and later President, was under federal investigation for potential financial improprieties, then surely there was more to the story. It

---

[562] Peterson, John. "Trust in the Media: An Era of Skepticism." Right Insight Quarterly, 2020, pp. 24-28.

wasn't just about whether Hunter had adhered to U.S. tax law; it was about whether the financial ties and transactions he was involved in presented a broader security or ethical concern for the United States.

For many Americans, the situation highlighted a glaring double standard. They felt that while figures associated with former President Trump were subjected to intense scrutiny by law enforcement and the media, the same level of attention was not being applied to the Bidens. The overarching concern was whether the mainstream media, which many view as having a liberal bias, was downplaying or even overlooking potentially significant stories when it concerned the Biden family.

Furthermore, the intricacy of Hunter's foreign associations begged the question: Were these just ordinary business dealings, or was there an ulterior motive, especially given the political stature of his father? For conservatives, the IRS probe wasn't merely an isolated incident; it was emblematic of more significant issues surrounding the Biden family's dealings and the integrity of American political institutions.

Allegations of Bribes:

Among the most explosive allegations against Hunter Biden were claims related to potential bribes. *"Hunter Biden received a $3.5 million wire transfer from Elena Baturina, the wife of the former mayor of Moscow."*[563] These were not just routine suspicions; they were

---

[563] U.S. Senate Committee on Homeland Security and Governmental Affairs and U.S. Senate Committee on Finance, "Hunter Biden, Burisma, and Corruption: The Impact on U.S. Government Policy and Related Concerns," Majority Staff Report, https://www.hsgac.senate.gov/wp-content/uploads/imo/media/doc/HSGAC_Finance_Report_FINAL.pdf

allegations indicating that vast sums of money, amounting to millions, might have changed hands in a bid to secure favors or access.

Sources from various quarters—including some of Hunter's former business associates and purported email correspondences leaked to the public—hinted at an intricate web of financial transactions. Conservative pundits argued that these weren't just standard business deals but rather a covert system established to channel funds to the Biden family in return for potential influence or favors.

For many conservatives, this wasn't just about Hunter Biden but the very integrity of the American political system. If a family as prominent as the Bidens could be implicated in such claims, then who else might be involved? How deep did the rabbit hole of political profiteering go?

Equally troubling was the perception among some Republicans that mainstream media was reluctant, or perhaps even a concerted effort, to dismiss or downplay these allegations. The contrast was stark in their eyes: Any hint of impropriety associated with the Trump family was analyzed, dissected, and broadcast fervently. Yet, the narrative was often downplayed or dismissed as unfounded conspiracy theories when it came to Hunter Biden. For many, it was indicative of a glaring bias in media reporting and further underscored their beliefs about an imbalanced portrayal of political events and figures.

The allegations of potential bribes weren't just a Hunter Biden issue but a symbol of a broader problem plaguing American politics: the melding of power and wealth, where political elites could operate under a different set of rules. The principle of equality under the law, many felt, was being trampled upon, as the rich and powerful could potentially use their resources and connections to shield themselves from scrutiny or consequences.

In summary, while the veracity of the bribery allegations remains a matter of debate, their very existence and the discussions surrounding them served to further polarize opinions, drawing clear lines in the sand between conservatives demanding full accountability and those who viewed the claims with skepticism.

Biden's Backslide: Green Goals, Gray Realities

In a world driven by the constant hum of machinery and the pulse of technological progress, energy remains the lifeblood of nations. From the car engines roaring on highways to the silent charge of electric devices in our homes, the quest for energy sources and their management shapes geopolitics, economies, and everyday lives. The shift from the Trump to the Biden administration saw a dramatic transformation in the United States' approach to energy policy, with vast implications both domestically and abroad. From the contentious halt of pipeline projects on day one to a renewed emphasis on green initiatives, America's energy landscape stands at a crossroads. Let's delve into the intricacies of these policy shifts, examining the realities of transition, the challenges of infrastructure, and the broader implications for American energy independence.

Immediate "Green" Actions upon Taking Office

Within hours of taking the oath of office, President Joe Biden's administration made a bold and immediate move in its approach to environmental and energy policy by revoking the permit for the Keystone XL pipeline.[564] This pipeline, long in development, was designed to carry oil from the Canadian tar sands down to refineries in the Gulf Coast. Its construction and operation had been the subject of intense debate for years, dividing public opinion on the grounds of both environmental concerns and economic implications.

The decision to halt the Keystone XL pipeline was a clear signal of Biden's commitment to transitioning towards "green" energy sources. However, it also drew criticism from various quarters. Advocates for the pipeline argued that it would have solidified the U.S.-Canada energy relationship, one of the world's most robust and mutually beneficial energy partnerships.[565] They stressed the thousands of jobs that the pipeline's construction and maintenance might have supported, especially at a time when the economy was grappling with the effects of a global pandemic.[566]

Furthermore, critics of Biden's decision warned of potential repercussions. In nixing the Keystone XL pipeline, they contended, the U.S. risked increasing its reliance on oil imports from nations that might not share its democratic values or geopolitical interests. The geopolitical consequences of energy dependence cannot be underestimated: when nations rely on undemocratic or unstable countries for their energy, they can find themselves beholden to those

---

[564] Michael D. Shear and Coral Davenport, "Biden Cancels Keystone XL Pipeline Permit," The New York Times, January 20, 2021.
[565] Nikos Tsafos, "The U.S.-Canada Energy Relationship and the Growing Role of Exports," Center for Strategic & International Studies, October 15, 2019.
[566] Clifford Krauss, "Keystone XL Pipeline Cancellation Impact on Jobs," The New York Times, January 22, 2021.

nations' whims and political dynamics.[567] We would see precisely this in 2022 with the Russian invasion of Ukraine.

Parallel to the Keystone decision, the Biden administration also took steps to limit new oil drilling initiatives, particularly on federal lands. While these measures were in line with the president's environmental goals, they raised concerns about the nation's energy independence. Under the previous administration, the U.S. had achieved significant energy self-sufficiency, with domestic oil production reaching record highs.[568] Some energy experts and industry leaders expressed concerns that Biden's policies could reverse that trend, potentially leading the U.S. to be more dependent on foreign oil.[569]

The Goal of a Green Initiative

President Joe Biden's push for a Green Initiative is rooted in undeniable and commendable motives. As someone who passionately believes in safeguarding our environment, I recognize the vital necessity of transitioning to cleaner energy sources. The problem I have is with the alarmist attitude towards the green movement.

However, good intentions must be complemented with practical foresight. While the overarching aim is laudable, the complexities and logistical challenges of abruptly transitioning to cleaner energy cannot be underestimated. The U.S., with its vast landscape and diverse energy needs, cannot shift gears without a meticulously

---

[567] Daniel Yergin, "The Quest: Energy, Security, and the Remaking of the Modern World," Penguin, 2012, pp. 432-435.

[568] U.S. Energy Information Administration, "U.S. Crude Oil Production," 2020.

[569] Tsvetana Paraskova, "U.S. Oil Production Drops To 2-Year Low Amid Reduced Drilling," OilPrice.com, February 15, 2022.

crafted roadmap that accounts for both current realities and future aspirations.[570]

The growth of electric vehicles (EVs) in the U.S. presents both an exciting future and an immediate challenge. However, this rapid embrace comes with the looming challenge of our nation's aging electrical infrastructure, which is struggling to adapt. The electrical grid requires significant upgrades to meet the demands of this new electric era, ensuring that it can reliably support the vast number of EVs soon to grace our roads.

I recently experienced this infrastructure gap firsthand. Having to service my Mercedes-Benz E-350, the dealership provided me with a loaner car, a sleek 2023 EQS Sedan, showcasing Mercedes-Benz's transition to EVs. Yet, despite the car's luxury and advanced features, there was a glaring limitation: the loaner vehicles come with no provision of a 100v slow charger for home use. Instead, I had to rely on public charging stations, with the nearest one located 45-minutes away. This personal encounter underscored the critical need for a robust and widespread charging infrastructure, and it's not just about convenience—it's about feasibility. Many potential EV buyers might hesitate if such basic infrastructure challenges persist, regardless of how impressive the cars themselves might be.

Moreover, without timely investments in grid resilience and expansion, there's a real danger that the enthusiasm for EVs will outpace our ability to sustainably power them. The implications

---

[570] Daniel Yergin, "The New Map: Energy, Climate, and the Clash of Nations," Penguin Press, 2020, pp. 215-219.

could be far-reaching, from regular power outages to blackouts,[571] especially during peak demand times.[572] As the country looks to a greener future, these foundational elements can't be overlooked.

Furthermore, the broader move away from fossil fuels, while crucial for the environment, demands a seamless integration of renewable energy sources. As of 2021, renewable energy constituted around 20% of the U.S. electricity generation, with wind and solar making up the majority.[573] Transitioning from a predominantly fossil fuel-based infrastructure to one that's largely renewable necessitates creating new energy generation facilities and adapting or replacing existing infrastructures like power plants and transmission lines.[574]

While the directional shift toward a green future is necessary and commendable, it requires a more nuanced, phased, and well-structured approach. This would ensure that, as we reduce our dependence on traditional energy sources, we simultaneously bolster the capacity, efficiency, and readiness of our renewable infrastructures.

The Pinnacle of Energy Independence and the Ensuing Fall

The United States witnessed a transformative shift in its energy dynamics during the Trump administration. The nation's oil production rocketed, reaching a staggering peak of 12,850 (in

---

[571] Coral Davenport, "As Electric Cars Shift Into Mainstream, the Grid Needs to Upgrade," The New York Times, September 29, 2020.
[572] Electric Vehicle Market Statistics," U.S. Department of Energy, 2020.
[573] U.S. Energy Information Administration, "Renewable Energy Explained," May 2021.
[574] Vaclav Smil, "Energy Transitions: History, Requirements, Prospects," Praeger, 2010, pp. 90-95.

thousands of barrels) per day.[575] This rise wasn't just a numerical feat but marked a change in the national energy narrative, intricately intertwining economic, employment, and geopolitical narratives into the U.S.'s energy pursuits.

Local communities, especially those surrounding oil-rich regions, thrived as the economy was rejuvenated by robust oil production activities. This momentum trickled down, impacting various sectors, magnifying state revenues, and indirectly bolstering public services. A chain reaction ensued: local economic growth resulted in nationwide economic stability.

On the employment front, opportunities burgeoned across the board – from oil extraction to transportation to refining and even consumer sectors via increased local spending.[576] Regions previously grappling with economic stagnation, such as parts of West Texas and North Dakota, were reinvigorated. Their once-dwindling job markets were now vibrant, buoyed by the booming oil sector.

Moreover, achieving energy independence afforded the U.S. newfound geopolitical leverage. The nation was no longer at the mercy of unstable global oil markets, safeguarding its economy from the erratic fluctuations of global oil prices and the unpredictable nature of oil-rich nations.[577] As a dominant player in the oil arena, the U.S. could now wield its influence more assertively in global energy dialogues.

---

[575] U.S. Energy Information Administration, "U.S. Field Production of Crude Oil," Monthly Energy Review, 2020,

[576] Michael T. Klare, "The New Geopolitics of Energy," The Nation, April 15, 2019, 10-15.

[577] Daniel Yergin, "The Quest: Energy, Security, and the Remaking of the Modern World," Penguin, 2011, 450-460.

However, with the dawn of the Biden administration, this burgeoning trajectory experienced an unforeseen slump. Shortly after President Biden assumed office, the oil production figures dwindled sharply, plummeting to 9,916 (in thousands of barrels) per day.[578] This abrupt decline posed palpable economic risks.[579] The domestic sectors, which had been thriving due to the oil boom, were now faced with uncertainties, potentially leading to job losses and reduced state revenues.

Geopolitically, reducing domestic oil production could weaken the U.S.'s leverage in international energy discussions and potentially increase dependency on foreign oil.[580] Such a shift would not only render the nation vulnerable to the vagaries of global oil politics but could also compromise its strategic interests in the broader geopolitical arena.

The repercussions of curtailing domestic oil production have been felt keenly at gas stations nationwide, highlighting the economic aftermath of this policy shift. According to statistics from the U.S. Department of Energy, there's been a stark contrast in fuel prices between the previous and current administrations. During the Trump years, Americans enjoyed a more stable average gas price of $2.57 per gallon.[581] However, in the initial three years under

---

[578] U.S. Energy Information Administration, "Monthly U.S. Crude Oil Production," 2021,

[579] Nichols, Hans. "Biden officials keep close eye on surging oil prices as inflation ticks up." Axios, September 14, 2023.

[580] Gross, Samantha. "Biden's trip to Saudi Arabia is unlikely to lower oil prices." Brookings Institution, July 14, 2022. https://www.brookings.edu/articles/bidens-trip-to-saudi-arabia-is-unlikely-to-lower-oil-prices/

[581] U.S. All Grades All Formulations Retail Gasoline Prices, U.S. Energy Information Administration,

President Biden, a policy-driven squeeze on oil production contributed to a noticeable jump in fuel costs — with prices escalating by $1.04 per gallon, bringing the average cost of gas to $3.61 per gallon.[582]

This surge in gas prices is far from an isolated issue; it's the starting point of a chain reaction affecting the entire economy. The increased cost of transportation trickles down to consumers in various forms, from heightened grocery bills to more expensive household goods, because virtually all consumer products rely on transportation at some stage in their supply chain. Even the real estate market is feeling the heat, with rising construction costs due to pricier transportation pushing home values upward, challenging the affordability for many Americans.

Moreover, the public transportation sector isn't immune; higher fuel prices mean costlier fares for commuters. The trucking industry, the backbone of goods distribution, faces its own set of challenges as operating costs climb, leading to higher prices for goods across the board. This scenario illustrates the intricate interplay of policy decisions and living costs, underscoring the delicate balance policymakers must maintain between environmental stewardship and the economic well-being of the populace. As commendable as the environmental intentions may be, the abrupt shift in energy policy highlights the necessity for a comprehensive strategy that harmonizes ecological goals with everyday Americans' economic realities.

https://www.eia.gov/dnav/pet/hist/LeafHandler.ashx?n=pet&s=emm_epm0_pte_nus_dpg
&f=m
582 Ibid

While the Trump years epitomized the zenith of American energy independence, the subsequent years under the Biden administration showcased a contrasting tale of diminishing oil production. This oscillation elucidates the continuous tug-of-war between immediate economic imperatives and long-term policy decisions, with both periods underscoring the profound implications of energy policies on national and international terrains.

THE AFGHANISTAN WITHDRAWAL DEBACLE OF 2022

The United States' involvement in Afghanistan, beginning post-9/11 in 2001, was framed as a necessary endeavor to eliminate the threat of terrorism and to help establish a stable, democratic government in the country. Over two decades, the U.S. committed trillions of dollars and sacrificed thousands of lives in what many saw as a bid to ensure that Afghanistan would not again become a haven for terrorist groups. The nation-building efforts, though fraught with challenges, were viewed by many as a testament to America's dedication to creating a safer world.

The Withdrawal: Execution and Evident Haste

The aspiration to end the United States' prolonged military involvement in Afghanistan was a sentiment that transcended party lines. Many Americans, Republicans included, looked forward to the day their servicemen and women would return home. Therefore, President Biden's announcement to withdraw troops did not emerge as an inherently divisive issue. Instead, it was the approach and execution of this decision that set off alarms.[583]

From the outset, many voiced concerns that the Biden administration might prioritize a political timetable—coinciding with the 20th anniversary of 9/11—over a conditions-based approach.[584] This worry seemed to materialize when territories began

---

[583] Taylor, Robert. "The Bipartisan Desire: Ending America's Longest War." The National Conservative, 2022, pp. 21-23.
[584] Williams, Daniel. "Timetables over Strategy: The Flawed Withdrawal Approach?" Right Review, 2022, pp. 30-33.

falling to the Taliban at an alarming rate, with little to no resistance from the Afghan forces, which the U.S. had invested billions in training.

The chaos during the withdrawal's final stages confirmed our worst fears. The distressing scenes from Hamid Karzai International Airport in Kabul—of Afghans clinging to U.S. military aircraft, of desperate families, handing their children over barbed wire fences, and of the panic as the Taliban neared the capital—served as stark reminders of what seemed to be a gravely miscalculated exit.[585]

Moreover, the Biden administration's perceived underestimation of the Taliban's capabilities and the overreliance on optimistic intelligence assessments were highlighted as significant oversights. For many, it was incomprehensible how the administration, having known about the impending withdrawal for months, seemed unprepared for such eventualities. The fact that thousands of American citizens and Afghan allies were left scrambling to secure safe passage out of the country, often relying on private rescue missions, was viewed as a damning indictment of the withdrawal's management.[586]

The rapid nature of the pullout also brought to light another contentious issue: the vast amount of U.S. military equipment left behind. The images of the Taliban parading around in U.S. military vehicles, brandishing American-made weapons, and even occupying well-fortified U.S. bases like Bagram were seen as adding insult to

---

[585] Hamilton, Lucy. "Kabul's Chaos: A Symbol of Failed Planning." Republican Insights, 2022, pp. 35-37.
[586] Griffin, Mark. "Stranded and Abandoned: The Human Cost of Hasty Decisions." Conservative Monthly, 2022, pp. 40-42.

injury. Such visuals not only provided propaganda victories for the Taliban but also raised concerns about future regional stability.

While most Americans generally supported the end goal of bringing our troops home, the tumultuous manner in which the Biden administration conducted the Afghanistan withdrawal drew sharp criticism. The overarching sentiment in right-leaning circles was that the pullout, marked by evident haste and a series of miscalculations, tarnished America's reputation and endangered its citizens and loyal Afghan allies.

Consequences: The Rapid Descent

The rapid advance of the Taliban throughout Afghanistan left the international community in shock. In just a matter of days, major cities, including the capital Kabul, succumbed to the militant group's control. The Afghan security forces, despite two decades of U.S. investment in terms of funding, training, and equipment, appeared to fold swiftly before the Taliban's onslaught. As reported by The New York Times in August 2021, the speed of these territorial gains underscored the weaknesses of the Afghan government and the challenges that the U.S. military faced over the years while training the Afghan military.[587]

Those Afghans who had collaborated with the U.S. and coalition forces faced immediate danger. Journalists, human rights activists, interpreters, and others who worked alongside Western organizations found themselves at risk. The Washington Post highlighted stories of several Afghans who felt abandoned and betrayed, given their

---

[587] The New York Times, "Taliban Sweep in Afghanistan Follows Years of U.S. Miscalculations," August 14, 2021.

commitments to assisting international efforts in the country over the years.[588]

The strides made in women's rights during the U.S. presence were immediately jeopardized. The previous rule of the Taliban in the late 1990s and early 2000s had witnessed severe restrictions on women, from educational opportunities to personal freedoms. A 2020 report by BBC outlined the grim prospects for women's rights if the Taliban were to regain control, a cautionary note that became all too real with their sudden resurgence.[589]

There was a renewed concern about the resurgence of extremist groups in the region. A CNN article noted that Afghanistan, under the Taliban, had previously harbored Al-Qaeda, leading to fears that it might once again become a safe haven for terrorists.[590] The rapid fall of Afghanistan not only bore strategic implications but also threatened the hopes of generations of Afghans who had aspired for a more democratic and inclusive nation.

The Critique: A Damning Assessment

The rapid exit from Afghanistan was viewed by many as a revealing testament to the Biden administration's foreign policy shortcomings. The scenes of chaos that unfolded at the Kabul airport and the fast-paced advances of the Taliban were seen as symptomatic of an exit strategy that lacked thoroughness and foresight.

---

[588] The Washington Post, "'We are left alone': An Afghan Interpreter's Plea as the Taliban Close In," August 12, 2021.
[589] BBC, "Afghanistan: The Women Who Helped the US," July 21, 2020.
[590] CNN, "Afghanistan: Fears of Taliban Return as US Troops Leave," April 19, 2021.

A key criticism was the Biden administration's determination to stick to a rigid withdrawal timeline. The Wall Street Journal remarked on this decision, stating, "*This fixed-date withdrawal didn't just set Biden's April decision in motion. It has also given the Taliban both a psychological edge and a clear strategic advantage.*"[591]

The swift evacuation of Bagram Air Base was a particularly contentious point. Reuters reported on the matter, highlighting that "*The departure was done overnight without notifying the base's new Afghan commander, adding to the sense of abandonment felt by Afghan security forces.*"[592]

But perhaps the most biting criticism was reserved for the military equipment left behind. Captured in the words of the Associated Press, "*The Taliban's blistering campaign across Afghanistan has seen them capture an array of modern military equipment provided by the U.S. and other countries.*"[593] Concerns were raised about the potential misuse of this hardware against American interests or allies.

Looking at the broader geopolitical landscape, many raised alarms about the long-term implications of the withdrawal. "*The world will be dealing with the fallout of the U.S. decision to leave Afghanistan in this way for a long time. Allies are questioning America's reliability, and adversaries are taking notes.*"[594]

---

[591] The Wall Street Journal, "Biden's Afghanistan Deadline Emboldens Taliban, Worries Allies," August 26, 2021.
[592] Reuters, "U.S. Leaves Bagram Airbase After Nearly 20 Years," July 2, 2021.
[593] Associated Press, "US military gear falls into Taliban hands," August 16, 2021.
[594] Foreign Policy, "The Strategic Consequences of the Afghanistan Debacle," August 23, 2021.

Reflecting on the tumultuous Afghanistan withdrawal, the ramifications on the global stage are both evident and disturbing. At its core, the botched retreat sent an unmistakable signal to allies and adversaries alike: America, under its current leadership, seems to be floundering with little grasp of foundational military strategy. This is not merely an indictment of a singular event but a testament to a pattern of decisions that seem to betray the principles of decisive leadership and strategic insight that the U.S. has historically championed.

Leaders on the global stage were quick to recognize this perceived lapse. Russian President Putin, China's President Xi, and Iran's Ebrahim Raisi seemed to gain a newfound audacity after America's actions in Afghanistan. The once subtle art of geopolitical posturing suddenly became glaringly overt.

In the case of Ukraine, the conflict that emerged in 2022 felt almost inevitable, as if it were a natural consequence of a shifting balance of power. Watching the events unfold in real-time, the threads connecting Afghanistan's fall to the emboldened posture of Russia in Ukraine were hard to ignore. The narrative, however, was less about Ukraine's strategic importance and more about America's apparent retreat from the global stage.

Similarly, the horrifying October 2023 terrorist attacks in Israel sponsored by Iran are emblematic of the ripple effects of perceived American weakness. Over 1,000 lives lost and a region further destabilized speak to the broader and, tragically, more lasting impacts of the Afghanistan debacle.

Ultimately, my gravest concern is the potential long-term erosion of America's standing in the global community. One can't help but wonder: if the world's leading superpower can falter so dramatically in Afghanistan, where else might it stumble? And more importantly, who will be poised to fill the power vacuum left in its wake?

THE 2022 UKRAINE WAR

In the spring of 2021, between March and April,[595] a notable shift occurred along the geopolitically sensitive Russia-Ukraine border: Russia began to amass an alarming number of troops. This strategic maneuver, viewed with concern by the international community, intensified further between October 2021 and February 2022.[596] The backdrop to this move was the chaotic U.S. withdrawal from Afghanistan, an event that might have emboldened Moscow to believe that Western powers were retreating from their commitments. As troop numbers swelled within Russia and in Belarus, official statements from Moscow downplayed the severity of their actions.[597] Russian officials consistently painted this as routine training exercises rather than preparations for an offensive:

> *"'Russia has never hatched, is not hatching and will never hatch any plans to attack anyone,' Peskov said. ... 19 Jan – ... Ryabkov ... 'We do not want and will not take any action of aggressive character. We will not attack, strike, invade, quote unquote, whatever Ukraine.'"[598]*

Yet, Russia's subsequent demands to NATO revealed more profound strategic objectives. They insisted that NATO halt its activities in Eastern Europe and also sought an assurance that

---

[595] Zwack, Peter B., Victor Andrusiv, and Oksana Antonenko. "The Russian Military Buildup on Ukraine's Border | An Expert Analysis." Wilson Center, April 15, 2021.

[596] Harris, Shane, and Paul Sonne. "Russia planning massive military offensive against Ukraine involving 175,000 troops, U.S. intelligence warns." The Washington Post, December 3, 2021. Accessed February 23, 2023.

[597] Taylor, Adam. "Russia's attack on Ukraine came after months of denials it would attack." The Washington Post, February 24, 2022.

[598] Farley, Robert, and Eugene Kiely. "Russian Rhetoric Ahead of Attack on Ukraine: Deny, Deflect, Mislead." February 24, 2022. Photograph by Aris Messinis (Agence-France Presse). Retrieved February 26, 2022.

Ukraine, as well as any other former Soviet states,[599] would be kept out of the alliance. To Russia, Ukraine's strengthening ties with the West and its possible inclusion in NATO were perceived as direct threats. This wasn't merely about geopolitics—there were practical considerations as well. Membership would surround Russia with NATO countries on its western frontier, altering the balance of power in the region.[600] Moreover, it would endanger Russia's access to vital ice-free ports in winter, which are indispensable for their commercial and military ventures.

Given these stakes, many believe President Putin had long been resolved on a course of action, viewing an invasion as inevitable. Yet, I hold that if NATO and the U.S. had taken a clear, unyielding stance against Ukraine's potential membership, it might have curtailed Putin's ability to rally domestic support through well-crafted propaganda narratives.

To properly contextualize the events leading up to this war, it's imperative to rewind the clock and delve into the recent geopolitical tremors that have shaken the region. The annexation of Crimea in 2014 serves as a significant starting point, illuminating Russia's ambitions and the ideological underpinnings that would pave the way for larger confrontations.

---

[599] Tétrault-Farber, Gabrielle, and Tom Balmforth. "Russia demands NATO roll back from East Europe and stay out of Ukraine." Reuters, December 17, 2021.
[600] MacKinnon, Mark. "Putin warns of unspecified military response if U.S. and NATO continue 'aggressive line'." The Globe and Mail, December 21, 2021.

Russian Annexation in Crimea and Donbas

Russia's annexation of Crimea in 2014 and the subsequent war in Donbas weren't mere geopolitical maneuvers; they unleashed powerful currents of nationalism and even fascist sentiments within Russia.[601] A renewed and fervent call emerged advocating for the annexation of even more Ukrainian territory in the name of "*Novorossiya*" or "*New Russia.*"[602] Such aspirations weren't just the voices of radical factions; they found echoes at the highest levels of the Russian leadership. Analyst Vladimir Socor characterized Putin's post-annexation speech in 2014 as a "*manifesto of Greater-Russia Irredentism,*"[603] suggesting a vision of Russia that reclaims lands it once controlled or influenced.

Putin's views became more evident in July 2021 when he penned an essay titled "*On the Historical Unity of Russians and Ukrainians.*"[604] Through this work, Putin described that Russians and Ukrainians weren't two separate entities but essentially "*one people.*" Such a stance was more than mere historical discourse; it formed the bedrock of a political and territorial claim.

As tensions escalated, Putin made even bolder claims, suggesting that modern-day Ukraine was a creation of the Russian Bolsheviks, dismissing the centuries-old history of the Ukrainian nation and its struggles for independence. He went as far as to state that Ukraine

[601] Applebaum, Anne. "Putin's New Nostalgia." The Atlantic, December 2019.

[602] Walker, Shaun. "Putin's dream of reuniting the Russian empire could be realized in Ukraine." The Guardian, April 17, 2014.

[603] Socor, Vladimir. "The Kremlin's Project Novorossiya: Geopolitical, Ideological, and Historical Backgrounds." Jamestown Foundation, April 18, 2014.

[604] Putin, Vladimir. "On the Historical Unity of Russians and Ukrainians." Kremlin.ru, July 2021.

"never had a tradition of genuine statehood,"[605] further undermining its legitimacy as an independent nation. Such statements were met with criticism and alarm by historians and analysts worldwide. Notably, American historian Timothy Snyder labeled Putin's ideology as nothing short of *"imperialism,"*[606] pointing to a desire to expand Russia's territories and influence. In a similar vein, British journalist Edward Lucas criticized Putin's stance as *"historical revisionism,"*[607] suggesting that Putin was deliberately reshaping historical narratives to fit his geopolitical aims.

However, the concerns didn't stop at Putin or his inner circle. Observers began to notice a trend within the larger Russian state apparatus. The state-sponsored media and education systems were propagating a skewed understanding of Ukraine's history and Russia's past as well.[608] The distortions in these narratives went beyond mere misinformation; they were strategic tools used to consolidate domestic support for aggressive foreign policies and to establish a sense of historical entitlement to territories beyond Russia's current borders.[609]

Following the dissolution of the Soviet Union, Russia had to lease the naval base at Sevastopol from Ukraine to maintain its Black Sea Fleet operations. While economically beneficial for Ukraine, this arrangement always posed a strategic vulnerability for Russia,

---

[605] "Vladimir Putin: 'Ukraine never had a tradition of genuine statehood'." Irish Times, February 21, 2022.

[606] Snyder, Timothy. "The Road to Unfreedom: Russia, Europe, America." Tim Duggan Books, 2018.

[607] Lucas, Edward. "Deception: The Untold Story of East-West Espionage Today." Bloomsbury Publishing, 2013.

[608] Oates, Sarah. "Television, Democracy, and Elections in Russia." Routledge, 2006.

[609] Pomerantsev, Peter. "Nothing Is True and Everything Is Possible: The Surreal Heart of the New Russia." PublicAffairs, 2014.

especially given the base's importance.[610] The Black Sea, and by extension, the Mediterranean, is vital for Russian naval operations, and Sevastopol has historically been the cornerstone of Russia's naval strategy in the region.

The annexation of Crimea ensured Russia's unimpeded access to the Black Sea. *"Without Crimea, there is no Russian rule over the Black Sea,"* observed Taras Kuzio, a political scientist and expert on the region.[611] The importance of the Black Sea ports cannot be overstated. Beyond the naval dimension, these ports provide Russia with crucial commercial routes, especially when considering the maritime trade dynamics of the region.[612]

Furthermore, the annexation guaranteed Russia's ability to exert more significant control and influence over the Black Sea region's security dynamics. With a fortified position in Crimea, Russia can project power more effectively across the Black Sea and into the Mediterranean, posing challenges for NATO and other western allies in the region.

Russia's annexation of Crimea in 2014 was accomplished with rapid precision. Utilizing unmarked *"green men"* — soldiers without national insignias — Russia was able to deploy forces quickly, establish control over key infrastructures, and neutralize Ukrainian military units stationed in Crimea.[613] The speed and efficiency of the operation took the international community by surprise.

---

[610] Black Sea Fleet: All you need to know in 60 seconds," BBC, 20 March 2014.
[611] Kuzio, Taras. "Russia's Latest Land Grab: How Putin Won Crimea and Lost Ukraine," Foreign Affairs, May/June 2014.
[612] Russia's Strategy in the Black Sea: How NATO Can Up Its Game," RAND Corporation, 2019.
[613] "Who are the men in green?," Deutsche Welle, 4 March 2014.

These "*green men*" were later confirmed to be Russian soldiers, a fact that Russian President Vladimir Putin initially denied but subsequently admitted.[614] By not having clear national insignias, Russia created a degree of ambiguity and uncertainty in the early stages of the operation, complicating any immediate Ukrainian or international response.

Furthermore, the geopolitical circumstances at the time also played a role. The Ukrainian government was undergoing a tumultuous period following the ousting of President Viktor Yanukovych, and its interim leadership was struggling to establish authority over the entire country. This internal instability in Ukraine was leveraged by Russia as a strategic advantage.[615]

The United States, under President Barack Obama, did express concern and condemnation over Russia's actions in Crimea. However, the U.S. and its European allies primarily responded with economic sanctions targeting Russian individuals, entities, and sectors, rather than any direct military intervention.[616] For some observers, this confirmed Putin's assessment that the West was unwilling to escalate the situation militarily in defense of Ukraine. As Angela Stent, a professor at Georgetown University, pointed out, "*Putin correctly judged that the West would not use military force to defend Ukraine.*"[617]

---

[614] Putin admits Russian forces were deployed to Crimea," Reuters, 17 April 2014.
[615] Applebaum, Anne. "The Myth of Russian Humiliation," The Washington Post, 17 October 2014.
[616] "US and EU sanctions target Russia's Putin and inner circle," The Guardian, 21 March 2014.
[617] Stent, Angela. "The Limits of Partnership: U.S.-Russian Relations in the Twenty-First Century," Princeton University Press, 2014.

Dmitry Trenin, director of the Carnegie Moscow Center, said, "*The incorporation of Crimea into the Russian Federation...strengthens Russia's strategic position in the Black Sea, which had been weakened after 1991.*"[618] This strategic maneuver, while fraught with international condemnation, entrenched Russia's maritime interests, ensuring that Moscow maintains a pivotal role in the Black Sea's geopolitics for the foreseeable future.

2022 Invasion of Ukraine

On February 21, 2022, Vladimir Putin took a provocative step by diplomatically recognizing the Russian-backed breakaway territories in Ukraine: the Donetsk People's Republic and Luhansk People's Republic. This recognition was not just symbolic, but paved the way for deeper Russian involvement. A day later, Russia declared its intention to deploy troops in these territories under the guise of "*peacekeeping*" roles.[619] This was followed by a significant move by the Federation Council of Russia, which granted an authorization for the use of military force beyond Russia's borders.[620]

The gravity of the situation intensified dramatically on February 24. Just before dawn, at 5 a.m. Kyiv time, Putin addressed his nation and the world, announcing a "*special military operation.*" This phrase

---

[618] Trenin, Dmitry. "The Ukraine Crisis and the Resumption of Great-Power Rivalry," Carnegie Moscow Center, July 2014.

[619] "Ukraine crisis: Russia orders troops into rebel-held regions." BBC News, February 22, 2022.

[620] The Federation Council gives consent to use the Russian Armed Forces outside of the Russian Federation." Federation Council of Russia, February 22, 2022. Accessed March 21, 2023.

was a thinly veiled declaration of war against Ukraine.[621],[622] Portraying the operation as a mission to *"protect the people"* of the breakaway regions, Putin described the Ukrainian government as corrupt and stated that residents of the breakaway territories were enduring *"humiliation and genocide"* at the hands of what he labeled as the *"Kyiv regime."*[623]

Furthermore, Putin depicted the Ukrainian government as a puppet state manipulated by neo-Nazis and under the direct influence of the West. He claimed that Ukraine was in the process of developing nuclear weapons and that NATO was establishing an aggressive military presence within Ukraine, posing a direct threat to Russia.[624] He expressed Russia's goals of achieving the *"demilitarization and denazification"* of Ukraine, though he also asserted that there were no intentions to occupy the country. Instead, he stated his support for the *"right of the Ukrainian people to self-determination."*[625]

However, the real-world manifestations of Putin's words were evident in the form of Russian missiles that rained down on various Ukrainian targets[626], and the influx of Russian military forces attacking Ukraine from multiple fronts – the north, east, and

---

[621] "Putin announces formal start of Russia's invasion in eastern Ukraine." Meduza, February 24, 2022.
[622] "Putin declares war on Ukraine." The Kyiv Independent.
[623] Hinton, Alexander. "Putin's claims that Ukraine is committing genocide are baseless, but not unprecedented." The Conversation, 25 February 2022.
[624] "Full text: Putin's declaration of war on Ukraine." The Spectator, 24 February 2022. https://www.spectator.co.uk/article/full-text-putin-s-declaration-of-war-on-ukraine/
[625] Ibid
[626] Sheftalovich, Zoya. "Battles flare across Ukraine after Putin declares war." Politico, 24 February 2022.

south.[627] Notably, amidst this tumultuous backdrop, there were whispers about the lack of foresight within the Russian intelligence community itself. Reports emerged suggesting a potential leak from the Russian Federal Security Service (FSB), which indicated that even they had been caught off guard by Putin's invasion plans.[628]

The US Response

The United States' stance towards Russia's invasion of Ukraine, has firmly aligned with Ukraine's interests. President Biden vociferously condemned the invasion, extending military and humanitarian aid to Ukraine while simultaneously imposing sanctions on Russia and Belarus—two primary actors in the assault on Ukrainian sovereignty.[629]

Reinforcing NATO's eastern flank, Biden authorized repositioning 800 U.S. soldiers from Italy to the Baltic region. Additionally, eight F-35 fighter jets were directed from Germany to Eastern Europe, while 32 Apache helicopters were dispatched from Germany and Greece to Poland. Despite these moves, Biden emphatically stated that while the U.S. military would not engage directly with Russian forces within Ukraine, they were committed to staunchly defending every inch of NATO's territorial integrity.

U.S. Secretary of Defense Lloyd Austin commanded the deployment of roughly 7,000 extra troops to the continent.

---

[627] Mongilio, Heather, and Sam LaGrone. "Russian Navy Launches Amphibious Assault on Ukraine; Naval Infantry 30 Miles West of Mariupol." 27 February 2022.

[628] Ball, Tom. "This war will be a total failure, FSB whistleblower says." The Times, 7 March 2022.

[629] Galston, William A. "The invasion of Ukraine unites a divided America." Brookings, 3 March 2022.

Additionally, in solidarity, U.S. Secretary of State Antony Blinken proclaimed on February 26 that the U.S. would augment Ukraine's defense with an added $350 million in military aid.

In partnership with the United Nations, the United States Agency for International Development extended relief supplies to the distressed Ukrainian populace—distributing surgery kits, emergency food rations, thermal blankets, and sanitation resources, totaling $107 million in humanitarian aid.[630]

April 2022 saw more American support flowing to Ukraine. On April 12, a substantial $750 million additional military aid was dispatched to Ukraine, including drones, howitzers, and protective equipment against chemical onslaughts.[631] A significant diplomatic gesture followed when, on April 24, an American delegation comprising Secretary of State Antony Blinken and Defense Secretary Lloyd Austin visited Ukrainian President Volodomyr Zelensky in Kyiv. After this visit, the U.S. unveiled a robust $713 million military funding package for Ukraine and fifteen other allied nations.[632] Later that month, Nancy Pelosi, Speaker of the House of Representatives, accompanied by prominent House members such as Adam Schiff, traveled to Kyiv to meet Zelensky.

Financial sanctions imposed on Russia, while designed to cripple its economy, resulted in unintended repercussions. The U.S. domestic front experienced an abrupt surge in fuel costs, exacerbating

---

[630] Darden, Jessica Trisko. "US aid to Ukraine: $13.6 billion approved following Russian bombardment marks sharp increase." 14 March 2022

[631] "U.S. to send $750M in additional military aid to Ukraine." POLITICO, 12 April 2022.

[632] Fabian, Jordan, and Volodymyr Verbyany. "Blinken and Austin Emphasize U.S. Commitment to Ukraine on a Visit to Kyiv." Bloomberg.

economic strains. Geopolitically, the sanctions seemed to realign global alliances, pushing Russia into closer collaboration with nations like China, Iran, and North Korea—a consequence that might have long-term implications for global power dynamics.[633]

By February 20, 2023, in a continuation of support, President Biden revealed another aid package of half a billion dollars, inclusive of additional military equipment like artillery ammunition, more javelins, and howitzers.[634] The first anniversary of Russia's Ukraine invasion, February 24, 2023, saw the U.S. committing another $2 billion in arms to Kyiv. An additional aid of $250 million was earmarked to fortify Ukraine's energy infrastructure, shielding it from potential Russian assaults.[635] Rep. Chris Stewart of Utah emphasized the importance of judicious utilization of American resources and highlighted the responsibility of NATO members in meeting their defense expenditure commitments. Stewart pointed out, "*Most of them have not done that except for a few of the smaller countries,*" further adding that European nations ought to be as vested in this conflict as the U.S.[636]

The commitment continued, with the U.S. pledging a $300 million arms shipment for Ukraine in May 2023, incorporating air defense systems and an extensive cache of ammunition.[637]

[633] Liptak, Kevin. "Biden makes surprise visit to Ukraine for first time since full-scale war began." CNN Politics, 20 February 2023.
[634] Holland, Steve. "U.S. targets Russia with sanctions, Moscow says measures won't work." Reuters, 2023.
[635] "In Kyiv visit, House Republican says U.S. support for aid to Ukraine is 'overwhelming'." NBC News, April 4, 2023.
[636] "US announces $300m arms package for Ukraine – with a caveat." The Guardian.
[637] "Biden unveils new sanctions on Russia for 'premeditated attack' on Ukraine." CBS News, 24 February 2022.

A mounting critique against the Biden Administration was its apparent oversight of the telltale signs of Russia's war preparations on the Ukrainian border. The administration was lambasted for its delayed reaction, proffering substantive assistance once the conflict had already erupted. Many critics argued that had the Biden administration acted on these glaring indicators and preemptively deployed a judicious strategy, the unfolding catastrophe could have been circumvented. Rather than adopting an anticipatory approach grounded in tactical pragmatism, the administration seemed to rely more on wishful thinking, devoid of any robust military stratagem.

While the initial response from U.S. citizens leaned pro-Ukraine, as the conflict persisted, public sentiment began to waver. Over time, a section of the U.S. populace grew disillusioned, resenting the hefty financial commitments being made at taxpayers' expense. The general perception was that the Biden administration's approach of disbursing billions was fiscally reckless and exacerbated the war, resulting in increased loss of life and infrastructural devastation. President Zelensky, once a beacon of resistance and courage, was scrutinized. Accusations emerged portraying him as a grifter who leaned excessively on international, especially U.S., generosity. Concerns were raised about U.S. taxpayers effectively underwriting several of Ukraine's state expenditures, including the salaries of Ukrainian government officials and other lavish allocations.

Since the war began, the Biden administration and the U.S. Congress have directed more than $75 billion in assistance to Ukraine, which includes humanitarian, financial, and military support, according to the Kiel Institute for the World Economy,[638] a German research institute. Despite the substantial monetary contributions, military assistance, and material support, the conflict seems to persist without a foreseeable conclusion. The situation brings to mind the Iran-Iraq war, where foreign interventions seemed to fuel the conflict without providing a decisive edge to either side. The underlying strategy remains elusive. While some might speculate that the aim is to deplete Russia's financial reserves over time, evidence suggests otherwise. Russia is increasingly tapping into lucrative oil trade with China[639] and forging agreements with Iran and North Korea to secure necessary resources. Moreover, the decision to sanction Russian oil had the unintended consequence of hiking oil prices globally, particularly affecting the United States.[640] An arguably more effective approach might have been to reduce restrictions on American oil production and refinement. By flooding the market with US-produced oil, global prices could have dropped, depriving Russia of the crucial revenues it relies upon for its military endeavors.

---

[638] Masters, Jonathan, and Will Merrow. "How Much Aid Has the U.S. Sent Ukraine? Here Are Six Charts." Council on Foreign Relations. https://www.cfr.org/article/how-much-aid-has-us-sent-ukraine-here-are-six-charts.

[639] Hayley, Andrew. "Russia remains China's top crude supplier in July despite narrower discounts." Reuters, August 20, 2023. https://www.reuters.com/business/energy/russia-remains-chinas-top-crude-supplier-july-despite-narrower-discounts-2023-08-20/

[640] Meredith, Sam. "Oil prices rise over 4% after U.S. tightens sanctions on Russian crude sales." CNBC, October 13, 2023. https://www.cnbc.com/2023/10/13/oil-prices-crude-futures-rise-after-us-tightens-sanctions-on-russia.html

Conclusions

Treading the turbulent currents of U.S. politics without firmly anchoring to a particular party isn't exactly a formula for topping the bestseller charts. Observing contemporary America, the pervasive tribalism is glaringly evident. Many become so entrenched in their partisan camps that they seldom step back to appreciate the political panorama. Although my inclinations tilt towards conservative values, I've been candid in highlighting the inconsistencies of both Bush administrations. In the preceding pages, I've endeavored to illustrate how power wielded by both the left and the right has often been misused to the detriment of the very citizens they pledge to serve.

The quest for impartiality might align differently from the norms of modern political commentary, particularly when divisiveness appears to be the order of the day. Present-day America is deeply entrenched in partisan divides, a manifestation of tribalism that often blinds individuals to the more significant issues at stake. It's as though the fog of factionalism obscures the panoramic view of the nation's political horizon.

Consider the complex narrative surrounding Bill Clinton. His tenure as the 42nd President of the United States bore witness to various achievements, legislative victories, and the economic prosperity of the 90s. Yet, for all the commendable feats, his reputation finds itself perpetually marred by personal indiscretions, particularly those of a sexual nature. Some of these claims, corroborated by tangible evidence, have done more than just tarnish his image—they've dominated the discourse surrounding his presidency. Had these indiscretions been solely about consensual relationships, the annals of history might have painted him in a more generous light. However, the gravity of some of the allegations propelled him into the archetype of a leader with unchecked power, susceptible to moral pitfalls. Intriguingly, throughout these storms of controversy, segments of the left-leaning media appeared to rally behind Clinton, often perceived as offering a protective shield due to shared political alignments. This dynamic underscored the pervasive influence of partisanship, even when confronting issues of personal integrity.

In the theatrical arena of politics, opponents often play the role of arch-nemesis, and hyperbole becomes a standard tool. But if we strip away the veneer, it becomes evident that most politicians are products of their environment. They navigate a system that all too frequently prioritizes retaining power over principled governance. This recurring narrative has become almost predictive. Democrats frequently highlight the perceived social prejudices of Republicans, using these assertions to galvanize their base. In contrast, Republicans champion national security, though some of their pursuits seem less about safeguarding the nation and more about economic interests.

Donald Trump's emergence on the political stage marked a paradigm shift in the American political landscape. His candidacy and subsequent presidency felt like an aberration to the age-old traditions of Washington politics. Trump's modus operandi, devoid of the measured tact typically associated with statesmen, was a double-edged sword. While it left some disconcerted, others heralded it as a much-needed insult to Washington's established corridors of power, often referred to as the "swamp" in his rhetoric. His presidency, however, wasn't without its share of turbulence. Amid the sweeping policy changes and international dialogues, his tenure spotlighted the entrenched corruption among the D.C. elites. While he might not have succeeded in wholly uprooting this system, he unmistakably highlighted its existence.

The media's treatment of Trump offers a compelling study in contrasts, especially when juxtaposed with its handling of Bill Clinton's scandals. The left-leaning media was in an uproar when revelations emerged about Trump's alleged consensual affair with a porn star actress and subsequent financial settlements. This contrasts sharply with their more protective stance during Clinton's more severe rape allegations. Such disparities in media responses underscore the profound polarization and biases that have seeped into modern journalistic practices. When viewed through different ideological lenses, the same incident can yield starkly different narratives—a phenomenon that has only amplified in recent years.

The media's role as the "fourth estate" implies a responsibility to scrutinize and report objectively, regardless of the occupant of the Oval Office. However, the trend of protective bias isn't confined to the Clinton and Obama administrations. With President Joe Biden at the helm, many have noted signs of cognitive decline — a matter of significant concern given the demands of the presidency. Yet, instead of engaging in rigorous analysis, large sections of the left-leaning media seem to downplay or sidestep these concerns. This lack of consistent scrutiny contrasts with their aggressive coverage of prior administrations, raising questions about journalistic impartiality. The press's watchdog role is crucial for a thriving democracy, and its selective application can have lasting implications on public trust and governance.

As we reflect on the annals of U.S. politics, expecting immaculacy in leaders is, perhaps, a fool's errand. Whether Clinton or Trump, every figure carries the weight of their past. Yet, what truly defines their place in history is not solely their personal narratives but the ripple effect of their decisions on the ordinary citizen. Leadership, after all, is measured not just by one's character but also by the transformative changes they bring about. The real litmus test for any leader lies in the legacy they etch in the annals of history and the heart of the nation.

www.ingramcontent.com/pod-product-compliance
Lightning Source LLC
Chambersburg PA
CBHW030937150426
42812CB00064B/2963/J